Criminalising Medical Malpractice

The criminalisation of healthcare malpractice has become a highly topical and somewhat controversial question in recent years. Studies have demonstrated that in England and Wales, the trend towards holding healthcare professionals to account for malpractice is rapidly growing, abolishing the deference doctors enjoyed decades ago. The changing attitude of judges to claims for clinical negligence has been well documented. The role of the criminal process in England and Wales has been less fully analysed with the criminal law playing a very limited role until recently in the regulation of poor healthcare practice. In contrast, in France, the criminal process has for a long time been invoked more readily to respond to cases of healthcare malpractice, which involved even mere errors.

This book compares English and French criminal law responses to healthcare malpractice and considers what lessons the French model can provide for potential reform in England and elsewhere. The book takes the HIV-contaminated blood episode as a primary example of the different approaches France and England have in dealing with healthcare malpractice. Kazarian emphasises the impact of rules of substantive criminal law and criminal procedure on the way in which healthcare malpractice is criminalised in a given country.

This book explores the key lessons to be drawn on whether the criminal process is an appropriate means to respond to instances of healthcare malpractice. It proposes that features of French criminal law and criminal procedure might be useful to counteract healthcare malpractice.

Mélinée Kazarian is a lecturer in law at the University of Southampton. Mélinée's research interests are in medico-legal, criminal and comparative law issues, in particular the question of the criminalisation of negligence in the common law and civil law traditions. She has published widely on recent medico-legal debates, focusing on a comparative analysis of French and English criminal responses to healthcare scandals. She has been involved in different research projects which aimed to offer a comprehensive analysis of the role of the criminal justice system in regulating healthcare practice and ethics in the UK.

Criminalising Medical Malpractice

A Comparative Perspective

Mélinée Kazarian

Routledge
Taylor & Francis Group
LONDON AND NEW YORK

First published 2021
by Routledge
2 Park Square, Milton Park, Abingdon, Oxon OX14 4RN

and by Routledge
605 Third Avenue, New York, NY 10017

First issued in paperback 2022

Routledge is an imprint of the Taylor & Francis Group, an informa business

Publisher's Note
The publisher has gone to great lengths to ensure the quality of this reprint but points out that some imperfections in the original copies may be apparent.

British Library Cataloguing-in-Publication Data
A catalogue record for this book is available from the British Library

Library of Congress Cataloging-in-Publication Data
Names: Kazarian, Mélinée, author.
Title: Criminalising medical malpractice : a comparative perspective / Mélinée Kazarian.
Description: Abingdon, Oxon ; New York, NY : Routledge, 2020. | Based on author's thesis (doctoral – University of Manchester, 2013) issued under title: The role of the criminal law and the criminal process in healthcare malpractice in France and England. | Includes bibliographical references and index.
Identifiers: LCCN 2020005583 (print) | LCCN 2020005584 (ebook) | ISBN 9781138297562 (hardback) | ISBN 9781315099170 (ebook)
Subjects: LCSH: Medical personnel—Malpractice—England—Criminal provisions. | Medical personnel—Malpractice—France—Criminal provisions.
Classification: LCC KJC8410 .M39 2020 (print) | LCC KJC8410 (ebook) | DDC 345.41/025—dc23
LC record available at https://lccn.loc.gov/2020005583
LC ebook record available at https://lccn.loc.gov/2020005584

ISBN: 978-1-138-29756-2 (hbk)
ISBN: 978-0-367-50668-1 (pbk)
ISBN: 978-1-315-09917-0 (ebk)

DOI: 10.4324/9781315099170

To my son

Contents

Acknowledgements

I would like to thank my former supervisor and colleague Professor Margot Brazier for her continued support and for her insightful comments on earlier drafts of this book.

I would also like to extend my gratitude to my former supervisor and colleague Anne-Maree Farrell for her encouragement, and Professor Amel Alghrani for always believing in me.

Draft chapters of this book were also greatly improved thanks to the help, comments and feedback from Dr Alexandra Mullock, Dr Claire Lougarre, Dr Oche Onazi, Professor Hazel Biggs, Professor David Gurnham, Dr Harry Annison, Dr Jacob Eisler and Dr Alun Gibbs.

I am grateful to my colleagues at the University of Southampton, Dr Haris Psarras, Professor Adrien Viens, Dr Natasha Hammond-Browning, and members of HEAL and CLPS for their support and encouragement throughout this process.

Finally, I thank my caring and loving parents, partner, family and friends for their ongoing support with this project.

1 Introduction

'Responsable mais pas coupable'

Those were the words pronounced by Georgina Dufoix (then French Social Affairs Minister) on 4 November 1991, on a French national TV channel, when she was asked to explain her role in the 1980s contaminated blood scandal.[1] 'I feel deeply responsible', said Dufoix, 'however, I do not feel guilty, because really, at the time, we made decisions in a certain context, which were decisions that seemed right to us'.[2] The contaminated blood scandal had resulted in thousands of victims being infected with HIV and hepatitis C following the failure of health authorities to prevent the provision of tainted blood products to patients. In France, three sets of criminal proceedings saw prescribing doctors, blood centre officials and three ministers, including Dufoix, being prosecuted for various criminal offences such as deception and involuntary homicide. Dufoix, along with Laurent Fabius, then Prime Minister, was acquitted of the charges of involuntary homicide in 1999.[3] Out of over 30 health officials who were prosecuted for the failure to prevent the provision of contaminated blood products to patients, only two blood centre officials were jailed for deception.

Although a similar episode of the same scale occurred in the United Kingdom (UK), criminal charges were not brought. Nearly 40 years after the start of the contamination, in June 2017, a full public inquiry, the 'Infected Blood Inquiry', was ordered by the then UK Prime Minister Theresa May, to shed light on the failings which led to thousands of people being infected with HIV and the hepatitis C virus.[4] Following the contamination, victims were awarded *ex gratia*

1 In this book the 'contaminated blood scandal' is also referred to as the 'tainted blood scandal' or the 'infected blood scandal'.

2 J-A Heraud, F Kerr, T Burger-Helmchen, *Management créatif des systèmes complexes* (London: ISTE Editions 2019), 109.

3 E Favereau, 'Le procès du sang contaminé. Les trois accusés et l'avenir. Georgina Dufoix non coupable. Son action a été jugée positive', *Libération* (10 March 1999).

4 P Walker, A Topping, 'Theresa May Orders Contaminated Blood Scandal Inquiry', *The Guardian* (11 July 2017).

DOI: 10.4324/9781315099170-1

payments from various trusts and funds,[5] but the UK Government always denied liability.[6]

A crucial question in this book is to find out whether health authorities in both countries were merely *responsible* for the contamination, or whether they were *culpable* of causing the contamination and the death of thousands of patients. In this book, I do not address obviously blameworthy wrongdoing which *intentionally* aims to hurt others.[7] Instead, I discuss healthcare 'malpractice'[8] in the context of failure to provide the level of safe care expected from healthcare services and individual professionals. The causes of healthcare failure are diverse and may include mistakes that reasonable and competent professionals make in the course of their practice. Sometimes failure may be the result of behaviour that reveals a more culpable frame of mind, where an individual might disregard the life, and health and safety, of others. Negligent behaviour in everyday life can have serious consequences depending on the type of activity involved. Negligence in the healthcare context more particularly may lead to tragic consequences including life-threatening injury or death. Paradoxically, an activity which aims to heal may instead harm or kill. Victims or their families consequently ask for reparation and justice, and sometimes seek to attribute blame to an individual or an institution. This may result in recourse to legal proceedings.[9] Such legal proceedings may

5 Rt Hon Lord Archer, *Independent Public Inquiry Report on NHS-Supplied Contaminated Blood and Blood Products*, February 2009 (Archer Report), 73; Infected Blood Inquiry, Terms of Reference. www.infectedbloodinquiry.org.uk/sites/default/files/Terms-of-Reference-Infected-Blood-Inquiry.pdf; Additional payments to infected blood victims were made in 2017 in Scotland, Wales, Northern Ireland and England through infected blood support schemes: Scotland: https://nhsnss.org/services/practitioner/medical/scottish-infected-blood-support-scheme/;Wales:https://wibss.wales.nhs.uk/;Northern Ireland:www.hscbusiness.hscni.net/services/2876.htm; England: https://www.nhsbsa.nhs.uk/england-infected-blood-support-scheme.

6 UK Government, *Government Response to Lord Archer's Independent Inquiry Report on NHS-supplied Contaminated Blood and Blood Products*, 20 May 2009, 1–2.

7 In this book, I am concerned with healthcare malpractice in the sense of error and disregard for the life of others, but not intentional wrongdoing as was the case in the Shipman scandal in England, where Doctor Shipman was sentenced to life imprisonment for the murder of numerous patients; see http://webarchive.nationalarchives.gov.uk/20090808154959/www.the-shipman-inquiry.org.uk/backgroundinfo.asp, accessed 28 January 2020; 'Shipman Jailed for 15 Murders', *BBC News* (31 January 2000). Other examples of 'intentional' medical wrongdoing include the case of Dr Paterson, who was charged with 17 counts of wounding with intent, for performing unnecessary breast surgery on patients, or the case of Dr Bramhall, who was convicted of assault for branding his initials on patients' livers. See G James Rev'd (Chair), *Report of the Independent Inquiry into the Issues raised by Paterson*, February 2020; A Topping, 'Breast Surgeon Ian Paterson Jailed for 15 Years for Carrying Out Needless Operations', *The Guardian* (31 May 2017); '"Liver Branding" Surgeon Simon Bramhall Fined £10,000', *BBC News* (12 January 2018).

8 The terms 'medical malpractice' and 'healthcare malpractice' will be used interchangeably throughout this book as general terms for errors, negligence, and reckless or indifferent conduct endangering the life and health of patients which occur in the healthcare setting.

9 A Merry, W Brookbanks, *Merry and McCall Smith's Errors, Medicine and the Law* (2nd edn, Cambridge: Cambridge University Press 2017), 1.

take several forms. They may involve disciplinary proceedings against responsible professionals, claims for compensation for the harm caused, or criminal proceedings. This book focuses on the use of criminal proceedings in the healthcare malpractice context. It explores some of the key factors in the criminal justice system that contribute to explaining the differences between the approaches taken by France and by England and Wales on this matter, and considers whether lessons could be learnt from the French experience on the use of the criminal law in healthcare malpractice cases.

The over-criminalisation of healthcare malpractice?

In the past decade in England and Wales,[10] the medical profession has expressed growing concern that health professionals may unjustly face criminal prosecutions for gross negligence manslaughter (GNM) as a result of errors or negligence which caused the death of patients.[11] Instances of health professionals being prosecuted for and/or convicted of GNM are perceived to have risen in recent years, and have included health professionals who were characterised by their peers as both diligent and competent professionals.[12] Several other examples have included health professionals committing negligence in pressured and understaffed healthcare institutions. In November 2015, Dr Bawa-Garba and Nurse Amaro were both convicted of GNM for causing the death of Jack Adcock, a 6-year-old boy with Down syndrome, and were subsequently struck off the medical and nursing registers by the General Medical Council (GMC) and

10 This book compares the law in France and in England and Wales in relation to negligence committed within the healthcare setting. The law in other countries of the United Kingdom is not thoroughly discussed but may be mentioned where relevant.

11 Examples of 'medical manslaughter' convictions include the convictions of Dr Adomako, Drs Misra and Srivastava, Dr Garg, and more recently Dr Sellu and Dr Bawa-Garba. Dr Sellu was convicted and jailed for GNM, but his conviction was then quashed by appeal judges in 2016 as his conduct did not reach the criminal standard: C Dyer, 'Senior Surgeon's Conviction for Manslaughter Is Quashed', (2016) *British Medical Journal* 355; 'David Sellu Trial: Doctor's Conviction Over Patient's Death Quashed', *BBC News* (15 November 2016); see also *R v Adomako* [1994] 3 WLR 288; *R v Misra; R v Srivastava* [2004] EWCA Crim 2375; *R v Garg* (Sudhanshu) [2012] EWCA Crim 2520; *R v Bawa-Garba* [2016] EWCA Crim 1841; P Gooderham, B Toft, 'Involuntary Automacity: A Potential Legal Defence to an Allegation of Clinical Negligence?' (2009) 18(1) *Quality and Safety in Health Care* 69; M Brazier, A Alghrani, 'Fatal Medical Malpractice and Criminal Liability', (2009) 25(2) *Journal of Professional Negligence* 51.

12 C Dyer, 'Sellu Is Cleared of Medical Misconduct', (2018) *British Medical Journal* 360; S Boseley, 'Doctors Sign Letter Expressing Worry Over Criminalisation of Surgeon', *The Guardian* (6 August 2015). The use of the offence of GNM in the healthcare context has not been restricted to doctors: In July 2016, an optometrist, Mrs Honey Rose, was convicted of GNM, but the decision to convict her was quashed as the Court of Appeal decided that she could not have reasonably foreseen an obvious and serious risk of death. *R v Honey Maria Rose* [2017] EWCA Crim 1168; see also 'Vincent Barker Death: Optometrist Honey Rose Conviction Quashed', *BBC News* (31 July 2017). As will be explained in Chapter 2, the law on GNM was somewhat clarified in this case.

the Nursing and Midwifery Council respectively.[13] It appeared that 'a range of adverse systemic factors coalesced to form a catalogue of shortcomings that were cumulatively instrumental to the death of the patient'.[14] The decision was amply criticised by members of the medical profession, as well as academic commentators, who fear that 'simple errors could result in prosecution for gross negligence manslaughter, even if they [occurred] in the context of broader organization and system failings'.[15] Some medical professionals had even threatened to boycott their appraisals due to a fear that admitting medical mistakes could lead to legal action.[16] Dr Bawa-Garba was then able to return to work following a Court of Appeal judgement which reversed the decision to erase her from the medical register.[17] Following the judgement, however, Jack Adcock's mother expressed her anger as she was 'disgusted and 'devastated' by the decision.[18]

These episodes suggest that (over-)criminalisation of healthcare (gross) negligence could have a disastrous effect on patient safety as it may cause excessive defensive medicine, especially if systemic factors continue to be overlooked by courts, who generally focus on the culpability of one agent.[19] On the other hand, the Bawa-Garba criminal case demonstrates the victims' needs for retribution and explanations. Following the Bawa-Garba case, the GMC commissioned an independent review into GNM and culpable homicide. The review focused on how procedures and processes surrounding the criminal law can be improved to encourage a more just and fair culture in the Crown Prosecution Service (CPS) and court decisions.[20] The report suggested that 'greater transparency is needed to aid understanding about how decisions are made and improve confidence in

13 'Doctor and Nurse Given Suspended Jail Terms Over Boy's Negligence Death', *The Guardian* (14 December 2015). Following the Bawa-Garba case, Health and Social Care Secretary Jeremy Hunt ordered a review into manslaughter by gross negligence rulings in the National Health Service (NHS); see A Metthews-King, 'Bawa-Garba Latest: Jeremy Hunt Orders Review into Manslaughter by Gross Negligence Rulings in the NHS', *The Independent* (6 February 2018). The review was conducted by Professor Sir Norman Williams and will be discussed throughout this book; Department of Health, *Gross Negligence Manslaughter in Healthcare, The Report of a Rapid Policy Review*, June 2018 (Williams Review).

14 A Samanta, J Samanta, 'Gross Negligence Manslaughter and Doctors: Ethical Concerns Following the Case of Dr Bawa-Garba', (2018) 45(1) *Journal of Medical Ethics* 10.

15 Williams Review, above n13 at 7; H Agelholm, 'Dr Bawa-Garba: Doctors Threaten to Boycott Their Appraisals Over Treatment of Trainee Paediatrician', *The Independent* (1 February 2018); A Samanta, J Samanta, above n14 at 3–7; C Dyer, 'Society, Anger, Bewilderment: The Fallout from the Bawa-Garba Case', (2018) *British Medical Journal* 360.

16 H Agelholm, above n15; C Dyer, above n15.

17 *Bawa-Garba v GMC* [2018] EWCA Civ 1879.

18 'Struck Off Dr Hadiza Bawa-Garba Wins Appeal to Work Again', *BBC News* (13 August 2018).

19 O Quick, *Regulating Patient Safety: The End of Professional Dominance* (Cambridge: Cambridge University Press 2017), 108.

20 General Medical Council, *Independent Review of Gross Negligence Manslaughter and Culpable Homicide*, June 2019, 5 (Hamilton Review). www.gmc-uk.org/-/media/documents/independent-review-of-gross-negligence-manslaughter-and-culpable-homicide---final-report_pd-78716610.pdf, accessed 6 September 2019.

the integrity of key processes' both for the benefit of victims and families and for the benefit of the medical profession.[21] This book explores whether and how the criminal law could assist in contributing to more fairness and justice for both victims and defendants following healthcare errors.

Other episodes have involved healthcare institutions who had failed to deliver safe care to patients, causing multiple victims. What has been labelled the worst scandal in the history of the National Health Service (NHS), Mid Staffordshire ('Mid-Staffs'), featured appalling care provided by hospital staff at the Mid-Staffordshire NHS Foundation Trust which may have contributed to the deaths of between 400 and 1200 patients (although these numbers have never been confirmed by the inquiries conducted into Mid-Staffs).[22] Between 2005 and 2009, nursing staff and doctors routinely neglected patients, sometimes leaving patients in filthy beds or unfed for hours. There were also instances of bullying of patients by hospital staff.[23] In 2014 and 2015, the Trust was convicted of a criminal offence under the Health and Safety at Work Act 1974 (HSWA 1974) for the death of four patients.[24] Despite a three-year investigation, the police did not find sufficient evidence to charge a single individual for any criminal offence for what had happened at Stafford Hospital.[25]

Similarly, between 1989 and 2000, up to 650 elderly patients had died at Gosport War Memorial Hospital after being given unnecessary lethal doses of opiate drugs.[26] Following the scandal, again several police investigations were launched, but so far no prosecutions have ensued. The Gosport Independent Panel conducted an inquiry into the scandal and published its report in June 2018, finding evidence of 'a disregard for human life and a culture of shortening the lives of a large number of patients'.[27]

By contrast, in France, the criminal law has historically been used much more often in cases of healthcare negligence and failings, committed either by individual professionals or by health institutions. As mentioned above, the much-publicised contaminated blood episode culminated in three sets of criminal proceedings in France, and saw two blood centre officials sent to jail for deception. Although, as I will show in Chapter 4, British health officials' conduct was just as morally dubious as that of French officials, the criminal process was not used at the time in the UK.[28]

21 Hamilton Review, above n20 at 7.

22 R Francis, *Independent Inquiry into Care Provided by Mid Staffordshire NHS Foundation Trust January 2005–March 2009, Vol I* (2010), 352 (Francis Inquiry Vol I).

23 Ibid at 49, 52, 54.

24 P Sawer, L Donnelly, 'Stafford Hospital Trust Admits 'Significant' Health and Safety Breaches Related to Deaths of Four Patients', *The Telegraph* (4 November 2015).

25 'No One to Be Prosecuted' Over Mid-Staffs Scandal', *The Telegraph* (1 March 2016).

26 S Boseley, 'Gosport Hospital: More Than 450 Patients Died Due to Opioid Drugs Policy', *The Guardian* (20 June 2018).

27 *Gosport War Memorial Hospital: The Report of the Gosport Independent Panel*, 20 June 2018, 316, 322.

28 D Marchetti, 'La genèse médiatique du "scandale du sang contaminé"' in *Ethique, sida et société.* Rapport d'activité du Conseil national du sida (La Documentation Française, Janvier

As we will see in Chapter 2, French law allows for cases of healthcare negligence to reach the courts more easily than in England and Wales. However, whilst it is easier to seek individual prosecutions in the context of healthcare scandal in France, health officials are rarely convicted, and custodial sentences are rarely imposed against individual healthcare professionals. For instance, in what was named the 'human growth hormone scandal', seven medical doctors and scientists were cleared of charges of involuntary homicide and aggravated deception. Although they had been prosecuted for having knowingly provided growth hormone to child patients which caused them to contract Creutzfeldt-Jakob disease, no fault was found on the defendants' part as it could not be established that the defendants were aware of the risks of contamination in growth hormone provided to patients.[29] More recently, a criminal trial began in September 2019 against several individuals and corporations, including the Servier Laboratory and the *Agence Nationale de Sécurité du Medicament*,[30] for involuntary homicide and aggravated deception in the 'Mediator scandal'. The defendants are being accused of selling diabetic medicine to millions of patients which they knew would cause serious harm and/or death to patients.[31] The Mediator medicine was usually used to treat diabetes, but started to be used as an appetite-suppressant which was routinely prescribed by general practitioners from the 1970s. As early as September 1999, there was evidence that the drug could cause serious heart valve problems, but it was not banned until 10 years later.[32] The decision on the case is awaited at the time of writing.

Aims and methodology

This book analyses and assesses the role of the criminal process in healthcare malpractice. It does so with a number of key aims. In the first place it seeks to understand why in France the criminal process is more readily used to deal with healthcare malpractice than in England and Wales. Identifying some key differences in legal culture between France, on the one hand, and England and Wales, on the other, the book also explores more broadly how far the criminal process *should* be used as a regulatory mechanism in the healthcare context, and how critical reflection on the differences between the French and English responses to healthcare malpractice can help us answer this question. The book presents a comparative analysis of both the principles upon which criminal culpability is identified in the two systems and also the possible and potential effects of criminalisation. The comparison of two different approaches to the criminalisation of

1993); AM Farrell, M Kazarian, 'The Role of the Criminal Law in Healthcare Malpractice in France: Examining the HIV Blood Contamination Episode', in D Griffiths, A Sanders (eds), *Medicine, Crime and Society* (Cambridge: Cambridge University Press 2013), 265–279.

29 'Affaire de l'hormone de croissance: relaxe des deux derniers prévenus en vie', *Le Monde* (25 January 2016).

30 National Agency for the Safety of Medicines.

31 E Cazi, 'Le scandale du Mediator en procès', *Le Monde* (21 September 2019).

32 E Favereau, 'Laboratoires Servier: anatomie d'un système', *Libération* (20 September 2019).

healthcare malpractice offers useful opportunities to shed light on what should be the proper reach of the criminal law in addressing healthcare malpractice, to inform the debate about the relationship between criminal law and healthcare and to improve legal responses in this context.

The book argues that the criminal law can have a useful expressive[33] and retributive role in the healthcare context but only if it is used to penalise conduct which represents a disregard for the health and safety of patients, and if criminalisation is directed at people who actually have the power to make decisions which affect patients and to change practices within healthcare institutions. The book will further argue that corporate offences should have a more significant role to criminalise institutional fault than they currently do, and that alternative ways of control and regulation should be improved to ensure safety in the healthcare context. The book argues that victims of healthcare malpractice, or their families, should be given more opportunities to express their voice and obtain reparation following instances of healthcare failings which had caused them harm. The French compensation scheme ONIAM[34] is thus used as a model to suggest changes which can be made to achieve this.

To understand why France more readily uses the criminal process as a response to healthcare malpractice, the author has chosen to use the qualitative comparative method to analyse key factors in criminal law and procedure which influence differences and similarities between how the law of France and the law of England and Wales criminalise healthcare malpractice. The use of the qualitative method involves the choice of a limited number of country case studies and permits an in-depth analysis and understanding of the two systems and their responses to the same problem. It allows an investigation of how both countries have responded to the same problem, to analyse why they have chosen a different approach. Whilst one can only draw hypothetical conclusions from the country case studies, as acknowledged by Lijphart, 'scientific search should be aimed at probabilistic, not universal, generalizations'.[35] The benefit of employing the qualitative comparative method is that the results of this study can be very useful to both law and healthcare, both in France and in England and Wales as well as in other countries.[36] Indeed, 'partial generalizations may be useful as a first step and may be followed up by replications in different settings'.[37] These hypotheses will be 'generalisable to theoretical propositions' on whether the criminal

33 J Feinberg, 'The Expressive Function of Punishment', in J Feinberg (ed), *Doing and Deserving* (Princeton: Princeton University Press 1970), 96–97.

34 The *Office National d'Indemnisation des Accidents Médicaux, des Affections Iatrogènes et des Infections Nosocomiales* aims to award compensation to victims of medical accidents without the need to recourse to legal proceedings; see www.oniam.fr/indemnisation-accidents-medicaux, accessed 20 February 2019.

35 A Lijphart, 'Comparative Politics and the Comparative Method', (1971) 65(3) *American Political Science Review* 686.

36 G King, RO Keohane, S Verba, *Designing Social Inquiry* (Princeton: Princeton University Press 1994), 12–22.

37 A Lijphart, above n35 at 686.

process is a useful instrument to regulate healthcare malpractice as well as the testing of some of the assertions made out in earlier work, as is explained in the next section.[38]

A key part of this book is an analysis of the contaminated blood scandal: an example of a serious healthcare failure in response to which the criminal law was widely used in France, whilst in England and Wales, the criminal law was not used at all. This episode provides an opportunity to examine in detail how and why France and England and Wales have taken different approaches to using criminal proceedings in the context of healthcare failure. Data on the scandal include prosecution archives obtained from French courts and prosecution services that have investigated the role of individual directors and doctors in the blood supply organisation during the relevant period.[39] Data was also collected during semi-structured interviews conducted with a stakeholder in a famous healthcare scandal, and an expert on healthcare malpractice episodes.[40] This provided valuable information in support of this research on the proper reach of the criminal law following healthcare malpractice episodes and the views of both victims and defendants on the deterrent and retributive roles of the criminal law in these episodes.

Guiding the comparisons made in this book between the different applications of criminalisation in England and Wales and in France is a normative view of the appropriate *target* of criminal prosecutions. As is explained in more depth below, behaviours in a healthcare context in England and Wales that fall short of intentional or reckless wrongdoing can expect to attract the attentions of prosecutors only in the event that a person dies as a result, leading to a possible prosecution for GNM. Consequently, the involvement of criminal law in English healthcare contexts is for the most part confined to a comparatively narrow band of very serious cases. This book identifies in the French approach to criminalisation a principle of much broader application: targeting behaviours of various kinds that demonstrate culpable disregard for the life, health and safety of patients. A case is made in this book that this is a principle that provides a crucial first step in rethinking the scope, and possibilities, for using criminal sanctions in the healthcare context; in ways that respond more fairly, coherently and appropriately to wrongdoing that warrants the serious public censure represented by criminal

38 RK Yin, *Case Study Research Case Study Research: Design and Methods* (5th edn, Thousand Oaks, CA: Sage 2014), 13.

39 L Greilsamer, *Le procès du sang contaminé* (Paris: Le Monde Editions 1992); M Lucas, *Transfusion Sanguine et SIDA en 1985, Chronologie des faits et des décisions pour ce qui concerne les hémophiles*, Inspection Générale des Affaires Sociales, Septembre 1991; Commission d'instruction de la Cour de Justice de la République, Arrêt portant renvoi devant la Cour de Justice de la République, 17 juillet 1998, D6137; Tribunal de Grande Instance de Paris, Ordonnance de transmission du dossier et des pièces à conviction au procureur général et de non lieu partiel, D20917.

40 Interview with A (Cambridge, UK, 3 February 2011); Interview with B (Paris, France, 17 January 2011).

justice. It is for this reason that I suggest that although other comparators for assessing the role of criminalisation of healthcare in England and Wales may well yield useful conclusions in other respects, the comparison with France and the French experience is particularly apt. Although comparisons have been made on the role of the criminal law and medical errors between the approaches taken by England and Wales and other jurisdictions, such as New Zealand or France, they have so far not explored the role that the criminal law can play in systemic failure cases, in regulating wrongful decision-making, and in shedding light on events which led to the death or injury of patients, giving them, their families and the public a sense of closure.[41]

As we shall see in Chapters 2 and 3, understanding the differences between the French and English approaches to criminalising healthcare practices also means understanding factors such as the deeper legal histories and cultures of the two nations.[42] The English common law system, and its adversarial trial process, contrasts with the much more comprehensively codified French system, and its inquisitorial process. With this contrast in mind, the comparative *law* method is also used,[43] allowing me to isolate and to analyse these factors and their impact on the relationship between criminal law and healthcare.[44] Using the comparative law method helps to determine 'whether and how far it is reasonable to borrow' from each system. Where we seek to know what is the best way to proceed, the comparative law method assists in deciding 'whether it is possible to accept' the approach of either of the legal approaches examined 'with modification or without modification'.[45] It must be noted that this method has its limits, as the 'differences between legal systems and their historical, economic, social, geographical, political and cultural contexts are often too great to allow safe conclusions about the effect which certain rules will produce outside their native environment'.[46] But this kind of study can still 'produce more evidence . . . than an enquiry which limits itself to one legal system'.[47] Comparing the role of the criminal law in healthcare malpractice in

41 See, for instance, P Mistretta (ed), *French Law: From a Comparative Law Perspective: For an Overhaul of Medical Criminal Law?* (Institut Universitaire Varenne, Colloques et Essais 2017); A Merry, 'When Are Errors a Crime?-Lessons from New Zealand', in C Erin, S Ost (eds), *The Criminal Justice System and Heath Care* (Oxford: Oxford University Press 2007).

42 J Bell, *French Legal Culture* (Cambridge: Cambridge University Press 2008), 3; S Bernstein, *Les cultures politiques en France* (Paris: Seuil 1999), 10.

43 P De Cruz, *Comparative Law in a Changing World* (3rd edn, New York: Routledge-Cavendish 2007).

44 A Watson, *Legal Transplants. An Approach to Comparative Law* (2nd edn, Athens, GA: The University of Georgia Press 1993), 16; G Dannemann, 'Chapter 11: Comparative Law: Study of Similarities of Differences?' in M Reimann, R Zimmermann (eds), *The Oxford Handbook of Comparative Law* (Oxford: Oxford University Press 2006), 397.

45 A Watson, above n44 at 16; G Dannemann, above n44 at 410.

46 G Dannemann, above n44 at 398.

47 Ibid at 399.

France and in England and Wales as a case study aims at examining it 'in its real-world context'.[48]

Assessing the role of criminalisation in healthcare practice

The analysis of the relationship between the criminal process and healthcare requires an examination of various questions: is the criminal law an appropriate means to address healthcare malpractice? What level of conduct should be penalised (negligence, gross negligence or recklessness)? Should the outcome, or effect, of the conduct matter? Can and should the criminal process (effectively) ensure healthcare safety and provide accountability and justice to victims of healthcare malpractice? When should the criminal process be invoked in cases of healthcare malpractice?

Any such study must therefore note the more general question of the relationship between the criminal law and negligence, in particular between the law and healthcare negligence addressed by leading commentators who represent very different stances on the role of the criminal law in negligence. Put simply, the debate is this: should the criminal process play any role in the context of injury caused by negligence?

On the one hand, Hart has influentially argued that gross conduct should be included in the scope of criminal liability, where no 'exercise of reasonable care' has been carried out.[49] 'I just didn't think', argued Hart, 'is not an excuse'.[50] He explained that as long as an actor had the capacity to avert occurrence of a risk, that choice was a source of culpability.[51] Feinberg explained that criminalisation should instead focus on harmful conduct, as criminalising harmful conduct will prevent harm.[52] Emphasising the role of capacity, Duff stresses that 'we should be criminally responsible only for what lies within our control' and we could not be 'held responsible for risks of consequences that we could not have foreseen'.[53]

The debate also turns to what we want to achieve by criminalising unintentional conduct. In particular, Ashworth points out that 'crimes of negligence may exert a general deterrent effect, by alerting people to their duties and to the need to take special care in certain situations'. He defends 'negligence as a standard of liability for certain serious offences against the person'.[54] On the other hand,

48 RK Yin, 'The Case Study Crisis: Some Answers', (1981) 26(1), *Administrative Science Quarterly* 59; RK Yin, above n38 at 16.

49 HLA Hart, 'Negligence, Mens Rea, and Criminal Responsibility', in HLA Hart (ed), *Punishment and Responsibility: Essays in the Philosophy of Law* (Oxford: Oxford University Press 1968), 136.

50 Ibid.

51 Ibid.

52 J Feinberg, *Harm to Others* (New York, NY: Oxford University Press 1984), 26.

53 A Duff, *Answering for Crime: Responsibility and Liability in the Criminal Law* (Oxford: Hart Publishing 2009), 58, 73, 99.

54 J Horder, *Ashworth's Principles of Criminal Law* (9th edn, Oxford: Oxford University Press 2019), 207.

Williams has argued that negligence should not be punished as this would not achieve either retribution or deterrence.[55] Similarly, Hall argued that only morally wrongful (intentional or reckless) conduct should give rise to criminal responsibility.[56] Moore and Hurd affirm that 'negligence is a problematic basis for being morally blamed and punished for having caused some harm, because in such cases there is no choice to cause or allow – or risk causing or allowing – such harm to occur',[57] and that 'if defendants have *any* awareness of a risk, and yet choose to take it, they are not negligent but reckless'.[58]

In the specific context of healthcare provision, arguments made by academics on this debate have been dominated by the idea that the use of the criminal law to respond to healthcare malpractice is generally counterproductive and damaging to good healthcare practice and safety when there is no proof that the medical professional's conduct demonstrates subjective fault. They argue that the criminal law should be used with care in relation to healthcare negligence.[59] The criminal law does not achieve any useful function if the conduct of the alleged wrongdoer was not intentional. In healthcare practice, drawing from Merry and McCall Smith's work, Merry and Brookbanks explain that errors cannot be deterred, but 'violations', defined as actions which show deliberate risk-taking, *can* be deterred and therefore *should* be subject to criminal liability.[60] Brazier et al. agree, and stress that only 'disregard for the life of others should merit punishment'.[61] Quick argues further that 'there is no clear or strong case for additional specific offences beneath the level of recklessness'[62] and that there is a need to consider 'forms of organizational liability'.[63]

The analysis and comparison of the use of the criminal law in France and England and Wales is used to provide support for Merry and Brookbanks' claim that

55 G Williams, *Criminal Law: The General Part* (2nd edn, London: Stevens and Sons Ltd 1964), ch. III, 122–123.

56 J Hall, *General Principles of Criminal Law* (Clark, NJ: The Lawbook Exchange 2010), 366–367; J Hall, 'Negligence and the General Problem of Criminal Responsibility', (1972) 81(949) *Yale Law Journal* 962.

57 MS Moore, HM Hurd, 'Punishing the Awkward, the Stupid, the Weak, and the Selfish: The Culpability of Negligence', (2011) 5(2) *Criminal Law and Philosophy* 147.

58 Ibid at 150.

59 O Quick, 'Medicines, Mistakes and Manslaughter: A Criminal Combination?' (2010) 69(1) *Cambridge Law Journal* 186, 199–201; O Quick, 'Medical Killing: Need for a Specific Offence?' in CMV Clarkson, S Cunningham (eds), *Criminal Liability for Non-Aggressive Death* (Ashgate 2008), 175; O Quick, 'Medical Manslaughter: The Rise (and Replacement) of a Contested Crime?' in C Erin, S Ost (eds), above n41 at 47; D Griffiths, A Sanders, above n28; O Quick, above n19; M Brazier, A Alghrani, above n11 at 51.

60 A Merry, W Brookbanks, above n9 at 4–5.

61 M Brazier, N Allen, 'Criminalizing Medical Malpractice', in C Erin, S Ost (eds), above n41 at 27; M Kazarian, D Griffiths, M Brazier, 'Criminal Responsibility for Medical Malpractice in France', (2011) 27(4) *Journal of Professional Negligence* 188, 199.

62 O Quick (2008), above n59 at 175.

63 O Quick, 'Medical Manslaughter: The Rise (and Replacement) of a Contested Crime?' in C Erin, S Ost (eds), above n41 at 47; see also O Quick (2010), above n59 at 199–201.

the role of the criminal law should be limited and that it should normally be used to punish morally wrongful conduct, in the form of 'violations', or what I define in this book as conduct which shows disregard for the health and safety of others. Furthermore, the criminal law should only be used as last resort when other means of prevention have been exhausted. As Husak argues, 'If non-criminal means to prevent the conduct in question succeed as well or better, the criminal sanction should not be employed'.[64] In this book, it is argued that a critical comparison of the role of criminal law in healthcare malpractice in France and England and Wales grants support to the argument that the criminal process is not an appropriate means to respond to many instances of healthcare malpractice, where medical professionals have made mistakes or errors. But the criminal process should have a role to play where the conduct of the professional, or decision-maker, has shown no regard for the safety of patients, and/or when s/he has knowingly put patients at risk. Contrary to what some previous studies have tended to argue, this book does not dismiss the useful role that the criminal law can play in relation to what should be seen as wrongful conduct in the healthcare context, and the role it can play in giving victims some answers, in particular when other means of regulation or liability have not been effective in doing so.

The criminal process and healthcare in England and Wales

The relationship between criminal law and healthcare malpractice has not always been as fully debated as it has come to be in the latter part of the 20th century and the start of the 21st.[65] A distinguishing feature of the English and Welsh approach to applying criminal sanctions to the healthcare context is its emphasis on 'medical manslaughter', targeting individual healthcare professionals, with the consequence that other potential applications of criminal law have not been so well developed. In 2006, a claim was made that there was an unjustified rise of criminal prosecutions against medical practitioners for this offence in England and Wales.[66] The study was based on a search in newspapers from 1795 to 2005. The results of this study suggested that the threshold to prosecute doctors for GNM had become lower. A study conducted by Griffiths and Sanders analysing

64 D Husak, 'The Criminal Law as Last Resort', (2004) 24(2) *Oxford Journal of Legal Studies* 217.

65 There is an extensive body of literature addressing this question. Some good starting places for considering the literature on this are: C Erin, S Ost (eds), above n41; D Griffiths, A Sanders (eds), above n28; O Quick, above n19; D Griffiths, O Quick, 'Managing Medical Manslaughter Cases: Improving Efficiency and Transparency?' Law Research Paper Series, May 2019, Paper No 007 2019, University of Bristol. www.bristol.ac.uk/media-library/sites/law/documents/BLRP%20No.%207%202019%20Quick%20et%20al%20-%20merged.pdf; P Mistretta (ed), above n41.

66 RE Ferner, SE McDowell, 'Doctors Charged with Manslaughter in the Course of Medical Practice, 1795–2005: A Literature Review', (2006) 99 *Journal of the Royal Society of Medicine* 309.

75 prosecution case files on 'medical' manslaughter showed instead that the CPS demonstrated rather a reluctance to prosecute doctors.[67] Griffiths and Quick more recently found that 'the vast majority of cases which are referred to the CPS are not prosecuted'.[68]

Several studies demonstrate that healthcare professionals do not enjoy the deference that the courts once showed them, and recent medical manslaughter cases have reinforced the perception that healthcare professionals are becoming more vulnerable to criminal liability for harm caused by gross negligence or recklessness.[69] However, the 2018 Williams Review on GNM in healthcare, which looked 'at prosecutions of health care professionals for gross negligence manslaughter since the *Adomako*[70] case in 1994', found that during that time, the deaths of 38 patients have led to GNM prosecutions of 47 healthcare professionals (37 doctors, nine nurses and one optometrist). Twenty-three of these healthcare professionals were convicted, with four prosecutions subsequently overturned on appeal.[71]

The review further found that

> the most recent cases have seen a marked decline in conviction rates. Since 2013, 15 healthcare professionals have been prosecuted for gross negligence manslaughter in relation to the death of nine patients. These resulted in just six convictions, relating to five of those patients, two of which were subsequently overturned on appeal.[72]

Thus, although in England and Wales evidence shows that there has been an increase in investigations by coroners and the police against health professionals,[73] prosecutions of healthcare professionals for GNM remain very rare, and a small number of prosecutions actually result in convictions.

In England and Wales, prosecutions of medical professionals have so far been limited to manslaughter prosecutions, via the use of the GNM offence, and applying the *Adomako* (objective) test: whether the defendant's conduct 'should

67 D Griffiths, A Sanders, 'The Road to the Dock: Prosecution Decision-Making in Medical Manslaughter Cases', in D Griffiths, A Sanders (eds), above n28 at 117.

68 D Griffiths, O Quick, above n65 at 25.

69 Ibid at 7; Hamilton Review, above n20 at 7. However, as will be explained in Chapter 2, two recent Court of Appeal decisions seem to have raised the threshold in some instances; see *R v Rudling* [2016] EWCA Crim 741 and *R v Rose* [2017] EWCA Crim 1168.

70 Dr Adomako was a locum anaesthetist who was convicted of GNM for failing to notice that a tube which carried oxygen to the patient had become disconnected during a minor eye operation. *R v Adomako* [1994] 3 WLR 288.

71 Williams Review, above n13 at 12.

72 Ibid.

73 D Griffiths, A Sanders, 'The Road to the Dock: Prosecution Decision-making in Medical Manslaughter Cases', in D Griffiths, A Sanders (eds), above n28 at 117; J Vaughan, O Quick, D Griffiths, 'Medical Manslaughter: Where Next?' (2018) 100(6) *The Royal College of Surgeon Bulletin* 251.

be characterized as gross negligence and therefore a crime; . . . whether, having regard to the risk of death involved, the defendant's conduct was so bad in all the circumstances as to amount to a criminal act or omission'.[74] Following the aforementioned Mid-Staffs scandal and Robert Francis QC's recommendations on improving healthcare safety in the NHS, in his review on the scandal, the Government established an independent review chaired by Professor Don Berwick which concluded that 'the Government should create a new offence of willful neglect or reckless neglect or mistreatment applicable both to organisations and individuals'.[75] The offences of wilful neglect and ill-treatment by care professionals, so far only used in relation to patients lacking capacity, were thus extended to cover all patients in receipt of care, by the Criminal Justice and Courts Act 2015. However, it must be noted that the level of culpability required by the offences is higher than for GNM – although the *Adomako* test remains unclear on what threshold of grossness is actually required for a GNM conviction.[76] It will be argued in Chapter 5 that this reform could indicate a trend towards criminalising a wider range of conduct which leads to injury rather than death, focuses on culpability more than outcome, and mirrors the French model of criminal liability in this area. However, it remains to be seen how these new offences will be used and interpreted by the CPS and subsequently the courts.

Criminalising healthcare malpractice in France: a product of legal tradition

In France, fatal and non-fatal offences have long been used in the context of healthcare malpractice. This book proposes that substantive criminal law is one of the main factors which impact on the way healthcare malpractice is criminalised in France. As will be explained more fully in Chapter 2, the way in which French legal tradition defines 'criminal' negligence means that it has a broader scope than in the English common law. This is because it includes the penalisation of 'simple' negligence, or mere errors, and negligence resulting in injury. In contrast, until 2015, only gross negligence resulting in death was criminalised in the context of healthcare malpractice in England and Wales. Given the historical role assigned to the criminal process in France, arguments that healthcare practitioners and officials should be treated differently and protected against criminal proceedings become harder.

The differences between a civil and a common law system also have an impact on the way criminal law is used in the context of healthcare malpractice in both countries. French laws, including criminal law, are written and codified, in codes enacted by the Parliament, whereas much of English law relating to homicide

74 *R v Adomako* [1994] 3 WLR 288.
75 D Berwick, *Improving the Safety of Patients in England, a Promise to Learn-A Commitment to Act*, National Advisory Group on the Safety of Patients in England, August 2013, 34.
76 Ss. 20–21 Criminal Justice and Courts Act 2015.

and offences against the person is based on common law, on judicial precedent, although there has been a trend to create statutory offences in the past decades.[77] In England and Wales, the most relevant part of criminal law can be found in a range of sources including statutes, case law, the common law, administrative guidelines and directions (e.g. CPS practice and policy).[78]

In contrast, the bases of the French law of negligence are set out in articles 1382 and 1383 of the *Code Civil* (Civil Code), which provide tort liability for intentional acts as well as for negligence, and article 121-3 of the *Code Pénal* (Penal Code), which gives the general conditions for criminal liability for negligence.[79] The French legal system tends to generalise and provide abstract definitions, whereas the English system is built on individual cases.[80] As a consequence, criminalising negligent behaviour is generally set out by the French Parliament in the *Code Pénal.* On the contrary, the evolution of GNM in England and Wales has been case driven. English criminal law does not contain a general criminal sanction for negligent conduct. Some offences penalise particular cases of negligence, for example road traffic offences, safety at work offences, or the recent offences of wilful neglect and ill-treatment by care workers, but there is no general criminalisation of negligence applicable in any context.[81]

It is worth noting that in France, both the Civil Code and the Penal Code were products of the *Ancien Régime*, the French Revolution and the Napoleonic regime.[82] French laws result from a socialist background influenced by the 1789 Revolution, the importance of the '*Service Public*', and the emphasis in the law, and the Constitution, on the interest of society, or *Intérêt Général.* The French state is represented by a strong executive.[83] A consequence of this is the recourse to court proceedings (*judiciarisation*) to judge actions committed by officials or politicians, as a way of regulating public life, which we see in criminal proceedings arising out of several healthcare scandals described above.[84] As public activities may be subject to criminal liability, public bodies and their employees, such as hospitals and healthcare professionals, are more vulnerable to criminal liability in France than in England and Wales.

77 The Offences Against the Person Act 1861 forms the basis of the law on non-fatal offences against the person, but the development of the law depends largely on subsequent cases; K Zweigert, H Kotz, *An Introduction to Comparative Law* (3rd edn, Oxford: Oxford University Press 1998), 69; see, for instance, the Criminal Justice and Courts Act 2015.

78 C Van Den Wyngaert, *Criminal Procedure Systems in The European Community* (London: Butterworths 1993).

79 Article 1382 *Code Civil* (CC); Article 1383 CC; Article 121-3 *Code Pénal* (CP).

80 K Zweigert, H Kotz, above n77; J Bell, above n42 at vi; B Nicholas, *The French Law of Contract* (2nd edn, Oxford: Oxford University Press 1992), 5.

81 JR Spencer, MA Brajeux, 'Criminal Liability for Negligence—A Lesson from Across the Channel?' (2010) 59 *International and Comparative Law Quarterly* 18.

82 K Zweigert, H Kotz, above n76 at 83, 86.

83 H Machin, 'Retooling the State Machine', in A Guyomarch, H Machin, PA Hall, J Hayward (eds), *Developments in French Politics 2* (Basingstoke: Palgrave 2001), 139.

84 Ibid at 147; J Bell above n42 at 107.

French criminal law distinguishes between three levels of severity of criminal offences: *contraventions*, *délits* and *crimes*. *Crimes* are the most serious offences and may be punished with between 10 years and life imprisonment with a possible fine.[85] They are dealt with by the *Cour d'Assises*, the highest criminal court. *Délits* are major offences and may be punished with up to 10 years imprisonment with a possible fine. They are dealt with by the *Tribunal correctionnel*, a lower criminal tribunal.[86] *Contraventions* are the least serious offences and are only subject to a fine, dealt with by the *Tribunal de Police*, the lowest criminal tribunal.[87] What is most relevant to our discussion is that offences which penalise negligent conduct are listed in the Penal Code as either *délits* or *contraventions*, which are not the most serious criminal offences and are only punished by maximum 5 years imprisonment. On the other hand, in England and Wales, GNM might be seen as the third most serious charge in the 'criminal hierarchy' after treason and murder and can (in theory) attract a life sentence. Therefore, a prosecution for GNM in England and Wales is much more serious than a prosecution for involuntary homicide in France. I argue that the very high level at which English criminal law sets liability for (gross) negligence makes it paradoxically harder to use criminal law to prosecute for GNM. A criminal prosecution or conviction for GNM in England and Wales involves a greater degree of stigma than a prosecution or conviction for negligence offences in France, which are considered relatively minor offences.

It will also be shown in Chapter 3 that crucial differences in French and English criminal procedures go a long way in explaining the divergence between how healthcare malpractice has been criminalised in the two countries. Legal tradition has had a crucial influence on the evolution of criminal procedure in France and in England and Wales. Roman law influenced the French legal system up until the 18th century, and this led to the adoption of an inquisitorial system of criminal procedure.[88] The inquisitorial procedure is mainly characterised by a strong involvement of state bodies especially during the pre-trial phase of the criminal proceedings.[89] It provides for a wide set of powers to be given to the *Ministère Public* (Public Prosecution Service) and the *juge d'instruction* (investigative judge).[90] Importantly, it is characterised by a greater involvement and participation of victims in the criminal process, who can join civil claims for compensation to criminal complaints and thus 'ask' for the launching of a criminal prosecution.[91] They are then called *parties civiles*.[92] On the contrary, the criminal procedure in England and Wales is based on an adversarial type of procedure, which implies the confrontation of two equal parties (the Crown and the accused) arbitrated by judges. The

85 Article 131-1 CP.
86 Article 131-2 CP.
87 Article 131-13 CP.
88 C Elliott, *French Criminal Law* (Cullompton: Willan 2001), 2–3.
89 J Bell, above n42 at 147.
90 Ibid.
91 Article 2-3 *Code de Procédure Pénale* (CPP); B Bouloc, H Matsopoulou, *Droit pénal général et procédure pénale* (21e edn, Paris: Sirey 2018), 179, 197.
92 Article 2-3 CPP; B Bouloc, H Matsopoulou, above n91.

English adversarial procedure also involves a jury, who decides on guilt, whereas in France, juries are not involved in criminal proceedings for offences penalising negligent conduct, and as will be shown in Chapter 3, juries tend to be more reluctant to convict than magistrates in medical manslaughter cases.

The most prominent differences between the French inquisitorial system and the English adversarial system are that a greater emphasis is put on pre-trial investigations in the French system.[93] Thorough investigations are conducted by a single *juge d'instruction* who has wide coercive powers of investigation. In England and Wales, no *juges d'instruction* or *parties civiles* are involved in criminal proceedings. Criminal investigations are conducted by the police with the help of the CPS, which (as we shall see) are in comparison more reluctant to prosecute health professionals for GNM. Victims cannot easily influence and push for a criminal prosecution as French victims may do.

Notwithstanding those differences, the general aims of English and French criminal law are much the same: to punish the offender to achieve deterrence, incapacitation, retribution, rehabilitation and restoration.[94] Criminal law also aims to protect victims and society from antisocial conduct and to protect the offender from himself/herself and from others, for instance the victims or their relatives who seek restorative justice.[95] In the words of Ashworth, 'the chief concern of the criminal law is to prohibit behaviour that represents a serious wrong against an individual or against some fundamental social value or institution'.[96] One question that is much debated in England and Wales, and is a central question in this book, is whether deterrence and retribution can be achieved in relation to any conduct short of recklessness.[97]

In France, criminal law is seen as a regulatory tool to restore social order and protect society from antisocial behaviour and wrongdoing, as well as to fulfil the need of victims for retribution and compensation.[98] This can be seen in several healthcare scandals, including the contaminated blood scandal and the human growth hormone scandal, which have led to criminal proceedings involving healthcare

93 J Bell, above n42 at 147.

94 SR Kyd, T Elliott, MA Walters, *Clarkson and Keating: Criminal law* (9th edn, London: Sweet and Maxwell 2017), 23–55; P Poncela, *Droit de la peine* (2e edn, Paris: Presses Universitaires de France 2001), 59–73; M Cusson, *La criminologie* (7e edn, Paris: Hachette 2017), 128–133.

95 D Lanham, BF Bartal, RG Evans, 'The Purposes of Criminal Law', in D Lanham, BF Bartal, RG Evans, D Wood (eds), *Criminal Laws in Australia* (Alexandria: The Federation Press 2006), 1–9.

96 A Ashworth, J Horder, *Principles of Criminal Law* (7th edn, Oxford: Oxford University Press 2013), 1.

97 A Merry, W Brookbanks, above n9 at 4–5; M Brazier, N Allen, above n61 at 27; M Kazarian, D Griffiths, M Brazier, above n61 at 199; MS Moore, HM Hurd, above n57 at 148; D Husak, above n64 at 217; N Lacey, 'Responsibility Without Consciousness', (2016) 36(2) *Oxford Journal of Legal Studies*, 219.

98 V Wester-Ouisse, 'Dépénalisation du droit médical', (2008) *Hors Série juillet Revue générale de droit medical* 245; V Turcey, 'Le point de vue du magistrat', in D Dreyfuss, F Lemaire, H Outin (eds), *La judiciarisation de la médecine* (Paris: Médecine-Sciences Flammarion 2004), 4.

professionals and officials being prosecuted for various criminal offences. The criminal law is characterised as just another instrument to claim for justice and compensation, one amongst other instruments, i.e. civil and administrative claims.[99]

French criminal law is viewed as a

> system based on the notion that, where anything bad has happened, somebody must be singled out for public blame and punishment; a bonanza for the criminal law bar and a joy for the editors of tabloid newspapers, but for the proponents of a civilised criminal justice system, a cause of misery and depression.[100]

The HIV-contaminated blood episode, as will be seen in Chapter 4, illustrates this, and it is used to explore the questions exposed above and shed light on the overall aim of the book, which is to assess what the role of the criminal law should be in the healthcare malpractice context and in particular in relation to healthcare decision-makers and officials. Although the book does not argue that individuals should be 'singled out' following healthcare failure episodes, there is a pressing need to rethink ways in which decision-makers can be included in the scope of criminal liability when they have disregarded the life and health of patients.

Rethinking criminal liability for healthcare malpractice

One of the reasons for bringing the English and Welsh approach to the criminalisation of healthcare malpractice into conversation with the French is to consider opportunities for rethinking the former, and for the potential for a change of direction in policy in England and Wales in particular, but this study's findings aim to inform changes in this context in other jurisdictions also.

Criminal responses to healthcare malpractice in England and Wales have been considered unsatisfactory in many respects. The GNM offence has for some time been said to be ill-defined and unclear, and to have applied unfairly in healthcare malpractice cases, leaving too much discretion to the CPS and experts.[101] The aforementioned Williams Review has, for instance, recommended that a 'working group . . . be set up to set out a clear explanatory statement of the law on gross negligence manslaughter', and that proper guidance should be given on how the offence should apply.[102] The review also found that there is a need to improve consistency in the use of experts in GNM cases.[103] Griffiths and Quick found that 'the refusal of the common law to be drawn into greater specificity has, somewhat

99 V Turcey, above n98 at 3.

100 JR Spencer, MA Brajeux, above n81.

101 See, for instance, O Quick (2010) above n58 at 199–201; Williams Review, above n13 at 19.

102 Williams Review, above n13 at 47.

103 Ibid at 20.

predictably, placed pressure on the CPS to provide the missing detail from the leading authorities'.[104]

The shortcomings of the GNM offence are discussed in Chapter 2, and I will show that negligence offences used in France in the healthcare malpractice context are more clearly defined than the GNM offence, leaving less discretion to prosecution services and experts. As explained above, they are minor offences, which means that prosecution services and judges might be more willing to use them and hold healthcare professionals to account, but as will be seen, healthcare professionals who are convicted of negligence offences in France often receive suspended sentences. French criminal law contains offences which encompass different situations in which healthcare professionals could be held to account, providing insight into how offences could be constructed to address gaps in English criminal law. The way the French courts interpret causation rules also ensures accountability of people in managerial positions. Both individuals and corporations can be held to account for the same offences in France. This provides coherence and clarity in the law, and it will be argued that this should be a lesson for English law in the context of healthcare failures.

The new offences of wilful neglect and ill-treatment by care workers and providers in England and Wales help to address the previous gap in criminal law which meant that healthcare professionals would escape liability if their wilful neglect or ill-treatment had not resulted in the death of a patient. I argue throughout this book that the new offences which capture all care workers and providers (including decision-makers and healthcare institutions) have the potential to include a large range of actors who may have caused injury to patients. These lesser offences are likely to be regarded by prosecutors as more circumstantially appropriate than GNM.

It will be shown that specific features of the French criminal process could also inform responses to healthcare malpractice in England and Wales. Victims of crimes, when they become *parties civiles* in France, are more involved in criminal proceedings. This feature of the French criminal process goes some way in providing victims closure and explanation of what went wrong and makes the criminal process more accessible. In Chapter 3, I highlight the importance of in-depth investigations in healthcare malpractice cases, examining the role of prosecutors and investigative judges in criminal proceedings involving healthcare professionals or officials. In particular, the book will suggest that lessons could be learnt from *pôles de santé publique*.[105] These bodies were created specifically to treat cases of healthcare accidents and environmental disasters which involve either systemic error or corporate failure and a great number of victims, such as exposure to

104 D Griffiths, O Quick, above n65 at 22.

105 *Pôles de santé publique* are authorities within criminal courts which are in charge of investigating cases of dangerous health products, foods or substances which have caused multiple victims; 706-2 CPP; M Obadia, 'L'expérience d'un pôle de santé publique', (2008) *Revue de droit sanitaire et social* 44; MO Bertella Geffroy, 'Justice Pénale, Santé Individuelle et Santé Publique', (2008) (2) *Droit de la Santé*, Nos 282 à 283 at 14.

asbestos, or the contamination of the human growth hormone with vCJD (variant Creutzfeldt-Jakob disease).[106]

It must be noted, however, that the criminal process is not the only solution and certainly not the most effective one in addressing many instances of healthcare malpractice. Even in France, where the criminal law is often invoked as a response to healthcare malpractice, there seems to have been, in the past two decades, a partial withdrawal from criminal law in the context of negligence generally and thus healthcare malpractice. Two reforms undertaken in 2000 and 2002 have aimed to limit the impact of the criminalisation of negligent wrongdoing in France.

The first reform was the *Loi Fauchon* in 2000, which aimed to 'restore a balance between punishment and reparation'.[107] Prior to the *Loi Fauchon*, any negligent conduct resulting in death or injury could be the subject of a criminal prosecution in France. The *Loi Fauchon* was enacted to prevent over-criminalisation of decision-makers who were remotely connected to the harm caused by negligence.[108] The reform imposed a requirement of proving at least *faute caractérisée* (gross negligence) when the causal link between conduct and harm was only 'indirect'.[109] The effect of this reform is that to successfully prosecute a decision-maker (e.g. a mayor), prosecutors would have to prove that the individual decision-maker had caused harm by being at least grossly negligent in the making of decisions leading to the harm. An example of this would be a mayor failing to prohibit cycling in dangerous areas, which would lead cyclists to potentially suffer injuries following accidents. Proof of gross negligence would have to be shown on the part of the official for a criminal prosecution to be successful.

The second reform was the creation of ONIAM, a no-fault compensation scheme set up in 2002 and aimed at limiting the scope of healthcare malpractice litigation by awarding compensation to harmed patients without the need for recourse to court proceedings.[110] Although a direct correlation cannot be established, it is interesting to note that there has been a significant drop in criminal

106 'Scandale de l'amiante: 705 nouveaux dossiers de victimes', *Le Point*, 4 April 2012; MO Bertella-Geffroy, above n105 at 1.

107 Assemblée Nationale, *Rapport No* 2266 fait au nom de la commission des lois constitutionnelles, de la législation et de l'administration générale de la République sur la proposition de loi, adoptée par le Sénat, tendant à préciser la définition des délits non intentionnels, par M René Dosière, 22 mars 2000, 48.

108 B Bouloc, H Matsopoulou, above n91 at 105; Sénat, Session ordinaire de 1995–1996, Annexe au procès-verbal de la séance du 18 octobre 1995, N° 32, Proposition de loi relative à la responsabilité pénale des élus locaux pour des faits d'imprudence ou de négligence commis dans l'exercice des fonctions, Rapport.

109 See Chapter 2 for a more in-depth exploration of causation rules in French criminal law.

110 Loi n° 2002-303 du 4 mars 2002 relative aux droits des malades et à la qualité du système de santé; S Taylor, 'Providing Redress for Medical Accidents in France: Conflicting Aims, Effective Solutions?' (2011) 2(1) *Journal of European Tort Law* 61; S Taylor, *Medical Accident Liability and Redress in English and French Law* (Cambridge: Cambridge University Press 2015), 56–57.

complaints against healthcare professionals since ONIAM was established[111] with one academic commentator noting that the scheme appears to have had a 'calming' effect on the rate of civil litigation against healthcare professionals.[112] I argue in Chapter 6 that a no-fault compensation scheme for victims of serious medical accidents should be considered in England and Wales to provide the same easy access to compensation for victims of medical accidents.

The structure of this book

Chapter 2 explains the differences in French and English substantive criminal law when used in relation to death or injury caused by medical negligence. The chapter shows that fundamental differences in the framing of principles in criminal law play a major role in explaining different responses in France and England and Wales to healthcare malpractice. The chapter compares the rules on the criminal liability of individuals and corporations in the context of medical negligence in France and England and Wales, including causation principles, and suggests that French prosecution services and courts generally have a more victim-friendly approach than their English counterpart in their interpretation of these rules on liability for criminal negligence.

Chapter 3 will explore the vastly different procedural issues between the French inquisitorial system and the adversarial system in England and Wales, particularly how these differences impact on the initiation and success of prosecutions of health professionals and officials for criminal malpractice. The comparison suggests that an inquisitorial type of procedure, and especially the advantages that the inquisitorial system offers to victims, explains a wider recourse to criminal law where there have been allegations of medical malpractice. The chapter argues that in-depth investigations conducted by an investigative judge with a wide range of powers, and the active involvement and role of victims in criminal proceedings in France, help to explain the wider recourse to criminal proceedings in this context.

Chapter 4 offers a comprehensive analysis of the legal responses given to the contaminated blood scandal in France and England and Wales, highlighting differences in approach and a readiness to use the criminal law in France to hold doctors, health officials and ministers to account. Building on the insights of Chapters 2 and 3, this chapter examines the very different responses to the scandals in the respective countries in light of considerations about the proper reach and breadth of application of criminal sanctions. Noting the much more limited recourse to criminal prosecution in England and Wales, the chapter argues

111 For instance there was a decrease in criminal complaints against doctors by patients alleging bodily injury from 8% to 3% in the period 2005–2016. This is based on a percentage of the total of all lawsuits filed against doctors, including civil, administrative and criminal lawsuits; see MACSF, Rapport Annuel 2016 Sur La Sinistralité, Synthèse Des Chiffres Clés. www.mafexerciceprofessionnel.fr/Rapport-annuel-sur-le-risque-medical/A-la-une, accessed 30 March 2020.

112 S Taylor (2015), above n110 at 86.

that a broader application is arguably more justifiable. Although some failures were mere mistakes (and hence beyond the proper reach of criminal law), others reflected a disregard for the health and life of patients – the benchmark that, drawing from the French experience, I argue is appropriate for invoking criminal punishment. The findings on the contaminated blood episode are also contextualised in light of more recent healthcare scandals in France and England and Wales. Themes approached in this chapter include more general questions such as whether the law can ever adequately address victims' demands in this context, and the suitability of criminal offences as a response to healthcare systemic failings. Overall, the chapter evaluates how the criminal may address the need for greater accountability when prosecuting authorities are faced with multi-level failings in healthcare systems in England and Wales.

A move towards wider criminalisation of individual health professionals can be observed in England and Wales, as is discussed in Chapter 5. The French example is therefore informative on how cases of medical malpractice in England and Wales could be addressed by the CPS and courts in the next 10 to 15 years. This chapter contemplates the likely impact the new offences of wilful neglect and ill-treatment will have on the criminalisation of healthcare malpractice in England and Wales, and assesses how far they contribute to offering effective and fair responses to cases of healthcare malpractice. The chapter also points to the deference the law affords to decision-makers, who effectively escape all types of legal repercussions following instances of healthcare failings. Drawing from the French and English experiences in several healthcare cases, I argue that resort to the criminal law should be constrained to decision-making which deliberately fails to consider the safety of patients within a health institution. I suggest that a reckless homicide offence should replace the current notoriously unclear and ill-defined GNM offence. This new offence will ensure more coherence and consistency with the level of culpability required for cases of wilful neglect and ill-treatment currently defined in the Criminal Justice and Courts Act 2015. There is little empirical evidence that the criminal process effectively deters health professionals from committing negligence (as shown, for instance, in the blood episode), and the criminalisation of healthcare malpractice should therefore be limited to conduct that clearly disregards the safety of patients.

Drawing lessons from my analysis of the contaminated blood episode and other healthcare failure cases, Chapter 6 discusses whether, in cases of systemic failings, corporate criminal liability is useful to prevent harm to patients. The chapter argues that corporate liability should be used when there is no proof of individual culpability. The chapter explains that offences which penalise involuntary corporate fault – namely corporate manslaughter, health and safety offences, and wilful neglect and ill-treatment when committed by care providers – are underused in this context and should be used more often. The proper use of these offences has the potential to more readily achieve the various aims of criminal law, including deterrence, rehabilitation and prevention of healthcare disasters. The chapter, however, highlights some inadequacies of the corporate manslaughter offence in England and Wales in the context of healthcare malpractice and suggests ways in which we can address these shortcomings. Whilst this author is hopeful, the chapter also recognises that there are limits to what the criminal law can achieve when responding to institutional healthcare failings. Other mechanisms must therefore be used, alongside the criminal process. In particular, the chapter argues that no-fault compensation schemes and transparency mechanisms should be used alongside the criminal law to help ensure reparation to victims, as well as to restore public confidence in the healthcare system.

Chapter 7 summarises the main themes and arguments of the monograph and concludes that the criminal law should have only a limited role in healthcare malpractice, namely when there is evidence of disregard for the life and safety of patients. The chapter contends that there is a pressing need to improve preventive mechanisms, to ensure that healthcare failure does not recur in the future and to provide reparation to victims outside the use of the criminal process.

2 Healthcare negligence in French and English criminal law

Introduction

For a long time, in France and England and Wales, the medical profession enjoyed a certain status of deference.[1] The deference attached to doctors resulted in few civil claims or criminal prosecutions against them. Although no formal immunity existed,[2] 'it may sometimes have appeared that doctors enjoyed a special status close to immunity from the usual rigours of the law'.[3] Patients had an absolute trust in their doctors, and any unexpected damage caused to their body as a result of medical treatment was seen as a consequence of fate, not a result of the doctor's negligence.[4] In the past three to four decades, there has been a growing number of civil claims for clinical negligence in France and England and Wales, and the culture of deference is on the decline; although some argue that deference has not been completely eradicated.[5]

This chapter explains that differences in substantive criminal law play a significant role in the criminalisation of healthcare negligence in France and England and Wales. The range of conduct which can give rise to criminal charges in France in the healthcare context is much broader than in England and Wales, where, so far, only gross negligence causing death could be subject to criminal prosecutions. By contrast, in France, mere negligence causing death or injury is criminalised. In France, both individual health professionals and health institutions can be subject to the same criminal charges, whereas in England and Wales,

1 C Sureau, 'L'erreur, la faute, l'aléa, sanction ou prévention?' in C Sureau, D Lecourt, G David, *L'erreur médicale* (Sem.) (Paris: Presses Universitaires de France 2006), 23; M Brazier, N Allen, 'Criminalizing Medical Malpractice', in C Erin, S Ost (eds), *The Criminal Justice System and Health Care* (Oxford: Oxford University Press 2007), 15.

2 C Sureau, above n1 at 23; M Brazier, E Cave, *Medicine, Patients and the Law* (6th edn, Manchester: Manchester University Press 2016), 193; M Brazier, N Allen, above n1 at 15.

3 M Brazier, N Allen, above n1 at 15.

4 C Sureau, above n1 at 23.

5 Lord Woolf, 'Are the Courts Excessively Deferential to the Medical Profession?' (2001) 9 *Medical Law Review* 1–3; C Sureau, above n1 at 23–41; M Brazier, E Cave, above n2 at 193; S Devaney, S Holm, 'The Transmutation of Deference in Medicine: An Ethico-Legal Perspective', (2018) 26(2) *Medical Law Review* 202.

DOI: 10.4324/9781315099170-2

it has been very difficult to prosecute and convict healthcare institutions for failings which have caused death. French criminal courts' interpretation of causation rules also means that health professionals are more easily convicted, even for conduct which only indirectly caused a patient to die or be injured. The chapter illustrates and compares these differences using examples of cases of healthcare negligence which were subject to criminal prosecutions and/or convictions in both France and England and Wales. In later chapters, this comparative analysis will then be used to argue that lessons can be learnt from the French approach to criminalising healthcare negligence.

Data on criminal prosecutions involving healthcare professionals

It has been suggested that the past 10 to 20 years have seen an increase in the use of the criminal law against healthcare professionals in France and England and Wales; although there are no official statistics in either country to confirm the number of professionals prosecuted, or convicted, for charges relating to professional errors committed in the course of their employment.[6] The 2018 Williams Review remarks that in England,

> prosecutions for gross negligence manslaughter occur infrequently. Data on gross negligence manslaughter cases is not routinely collected and it has not been possible for the Crown Prosecution Service (CPS) to identify an accurate number of such cases referred to them, though they estimate that they receive about 200 referrals a year nationally. These are referrals for all categories of gross negligence manslaughter, not just those involving healthcare professionals.[7]

The rate of criminal prosecutions against healthcare professionals in France since 2014 seems stable, although slightly on the decline, with 28 prosecutions in 2014 compared to 12 in 2017. However, the rate of successful prosecutions (i.e. prosecutions leading to convictions) seems to have increased since 2014 (60% of prosecutions resulted in convictions in 2014, whilst 67% of prosecutions

6 S Ost, C Erin, 'An Ill-Suited and Inappropriate Union? Exploring the Relationship Between the Criminal Justice System and Health Care', in C Erin, S Ost (eds), above n1 at 2; D Griffiths, A Sanders, 'The Road to the Dock: Prosecution Decision-making in Medical Manslaughter Cases', in D Griffiths, A Sanders (eds), *Medicine, Crime and Society* (Cambridge: Cambridge University Press 2013), 117–158; RE Ferner, SE McDowell, 'Doctors Charged with Manslaughter in the Course of Medical Practice, 1795–2005: A Literature Review', (2006) 99 *Journal of the Royal Society of Medicine* 309; Interview with A (Paris, France, 18 January 2011), 15.

7 Department of Health, *Gross Negligence Manslaughter in Healthcare, the Report of a Rapid Policy Review*, June 2018, 12 (Williams Review).

resulted in convictions in 2017).[8] These numbers are not limited to prosecutions for negligent conduct, and may include prosecutions and convictions of healthcare professionals for intentional conduct. It is not currently possible to obtain statistics on the number of prosecutions and convictions of medical professionals for non-intentional offences only, given the lack of a systematic approach to data collection on the issue.[9] What data are available show that approximately 23% of cases involving substandard care, which has resulted in bodily injury or death by medical professionals that are investigated, lead to criminal prosecutions in France.[10] Of those that are prosecuted, approximately 52% of cases brought to trial result in criminal convictions against the medical professionals in question.[11] In the event of a conviction, however, it would be rare for a medical professional to receive a custodial sentence, with a judicial preference for awarding fines and/ or suspended sentences in such cases.[12] Of course, there have been notable exceptions to this approach, but they usually arise in high profile cases such as the HIV blood contamination and human growth hormone scandals.[13]

A wider use of the criminal law in France

As explained in Chapter 1, in France, there is wider recourse to the criminal law for medical malpractice, whether intentional, reckless, or negligent. In England and Wales, prosecutions of medical professionals have so far been limited to manslaughter prosecutions, via the use of the gross negligence manslaughter (GNM) offence. They have also featured intentional offences, as seen in the case of Dr Ian Paterson, convicted of 17 counts of wounding with intent for performing unnecessary breast operations on patients, and Dr Simon Bramhall, who was charged with assault by beating for branding his initials on patients' livers.[14]

In the UK, prosecutions of healthcare professionals for GNM remain very rare, and a small number of prosecutions actually result in convictions. Nevertheless,

8 MACSF, Rapport Annuel 2018 Sur La Sinistralité, Synthèse Des Chiffres Clés.

9 M Kazarian, *The Role of the Criminal Law and the Criminal Process in Healthcare Malpractice in France and England* (PhD thesis, University of Manchester 2013), 37.

10 MO Bertella-Geffroy, 'Justice Pénale, Santé Individuelle et Santé Publique', (2008) (2) *Droit de la Santé*, Nos 282 à 283 at 9.

11 MACSF, Rapport Annuel 2016 Sur La Sinistralité, Synthèse Des Chiffres Clés. www.mafexerciceprofessionnel.fr/Rapport-annuel-sur-le-risque-medical/A-la-une, accessed 30 March 2020.

12 JR Spencer, MA Brajeux, 'Criminal Liability for Negligence-A Lesson from Across the Channel?' (2010) 59 *International and Comparative Law Quarterly* 22–23; M Kazarian, above n9 at 82.

13 A Jouan, MA Lombard, 'La Chronologie de l'Affaire', *Le Nouvel Observateur* (15 January 2009); 'PIP: Les Trois Clés d'une Enquête Complexe', *Le Figaro* (27 January 2012); 'Breast Implants: PIP's Jean-Claude Mas Gets Jail Sentence', *BBC News* (10 December 2013).

14 'Ian Paterson: 'Sheer Volume' of Victims Delays Breast Surgeon Report', *BBC News* (5 April 2019); '"Liver Branding" Surgeon Simon Bramhall Fined £10,000', *BBC News* (12 January 2018).

the offences of wilful neglect/ill-treatment by care professionals, which so far only applied to specific categories of patients (such as patients lacking capacity), were extended in 2015 to all patients receiving care, in a move to criminalise a wider (albeit reckless and/or deliberate) range of conduct in this context, following the outcry over the Mid-Staffordshire scandal. These offences will be referred to here as 'conduct offences', as they do not require any harm to ensue from the conduct, unlike GNM, which I will refer to as a 'result offence'. One aim of the 2015 reform was to allow the prosecutions of care professionals for 'wrongful' conduct without having to prove that harm had resulted from the neglect or ill-treatment of the patient.[15] The new offences can now be used to penalise conduct which may or may not cause death, without necessarily having to prove intentional conduct. One aspect of the offences, which is welcome, is that unlike GNM (which requires 'gross' negligence) wilful neglect and ill-treatment encompass deliberate and reckless conduct, therefore limiting the scope of criminal liability for wilful neglect/ill-treatment to misconduct which is more serious than gross negligence.[16] As will be explained in this chapter, one problem with GNM is that a wide range of conduct may come under the definition of 'gross negligence', thereby making negligent medical professionals potentially more vulnerable to criminal charges, and this adds to the sense of uncertainty about what gross negligent conduct actually is, and results in variations in criminal decision-making.

Across the Channel, offences penalising negligent conduct resulting in injury, or requiring no proof of harm, have long been used in the medical context. Recourse to the criminal law for medical negligence in France is common, the criminal law being seen as just another way to provide patients with compensation.[17] Yet, as mentioned in Chapter 1, in the past two decades in France, the trend has been to limit the criminalisation of negligence, including medical negligence, after the 2000 (the *Loi Fauchon*) and 2002 (the creation of the ONIAM) reforms.

Despite the *Loi Fauchon*, the criminalisation of negligence in French law encompasses a broader range of conduct than in English law. The French *Code Pénal* allows a more generalised criminalisation of negligent conduct than English law. In France, 'simple'[18] negligence is criminalised. Furthermore, French criminal law provides for a broad range of offences used in the context of

15 K Laird, 'Filling a Lacuna: The Care Worker and Care Provider Offences in The Criminal Justice and Courts Act 2015', (2016) 37(1) *Statute Law Review* 6.

16 Ibid at 9.

17 As will be more thoroughly explored in the following chapter, the criminal law and process are seen as attractive tools for victims of medical negligence in France, who can become parties to the civil action in the criminal proceedings (*parties civiles*) and receive civil compensation should the court decide in their favour. The amount of compensation is calculated on the basis of the harm suffered, in the same way as it would be in civil proceedings. See Article 418 Code de Procédure Pénale (CPP).

18 'Simple' negligence is to be understood here as mere negligence or mistake, which does not demonstrate any culpability on the part of the defendant.

healthcare malpractice (see Table 2.1). By comparison, in England and Wales, only three criminal offences can now be used in the medical negligence context: GNM and wilful neglect/ill-treatment (see Table 2.1).

When is negligence a crime in France and England and Wales?

French and English criminal laws take a different view to negligence, which explains the greater scope for criminalisation of healthcare malpractice in France. The starting point in both French and English criminal law is that a criminal offence normally requires *mens rea* (a guilty mind). The French Penal Code states

Table 2.1 Comparative table of French and English criminal offences against the person

	France	*England and Wales*
Fatal offences	***Homicide involontaire***	**Gross negligence manslaughter**
▪ Degree of fault	▪ Negligence	▪ Gross negligence
▪ Maximum sentence	▪ 5 years imprisonment + fine (€75,000)	▪ Life imprisonment + fine
▪ Court	▪ *Tribunal correctionnel*	▪ Indictable only: Crown Court
Non-fatal offences	***Blessures involontaires***	**S. 20 Offences Against the Person Act 1861, Inflicting Grievous bodily harm**
▪ Degree of fault	▪ Negligence	▪ Recklessness
▪ Maximum sentence	▪ 3 years imprisonment + fine (€45,000)	▪ 5 years imprisonment and/or a fine
▪ Court	▪ *Tribunal correctionnel*	▪ Triable either way: Crown or Magistrates' Court
Conduct offences		**S. 20, 21 Criminal Justice and Courts Act 2015**
	Mise en danger délibérée	**Ill-treatment**
▪ Degree of fault	▪ Recklessness	▪ Recklessness
▪ Maximum sentence	▪ 1 year imprisonment + fine (€15,000)	▪ 5 years imprisonment and/or a fine
▪ Court	▪ *Tribunal correctionnel*	▪ Triable either way: Crown Court or Magistrates' Court
	Non-assistance à personne en danger	**Wilful neglect**
	▪ Wilfulness	▪ Wilfulness
	▪ 5 years imprisonment + fine (€75,000); 7 years imprisonment + fine (€100,000) if committed on a minor aged 15 years or less	▪ 5 years imprisonment and/or a fine
	▪ *Tribunal correctionnel*	▪ Triable either way: Crown Court or Magistrates' Court

that 'there is no felony or misdemeanour in the absence of intent to commit it',[19] meaning that all criminal offences in French law should usually require intention. However, negligent conduct – where no intention to harm has been shown – is an exception to this requirement, justified by the importance of protecting human life and the bodily integrity of a person.[20] To that effect, article 121-3 of the French Penal Code states that a criminal offence[21] exists

> where the law so provides, in cases of recklessness, negligence, or failure to observe an obligation of due care or precaution imposed by any statute or regulation, where it is established that the offender has failed to show normal diligence, taking into consideration where appropriate the nature of his role or functions, of his capacities and powers and of the means then available to him.[22]

In France, therefore, any individual, including healthcare professionals and officials,[23] may be criminally liable for conduct which did not show intention to cause harm, including mere negligence, recklessness or failure to observe an obligation of security or care. Article 121-3 of the French Penal Code provides the basis of liability for all *fautes* (wrongful conduct) which are considered to be criminal offences in French law.[24] This article applies to various types of situations where negligence may cause serious damage, including road traffic, work accidents and the delivery of healthcare.[25]

In English and Welsh law, there is no general principle for criminalising negligence. The most 'general' common law offence of negligence is GNM, which evolved through the cases since the 19th century.[26] As previously explained, until 2015, the only criminal offence used in the context of medical negligence was GNM; as although non-fatal offences against the person exist in English criminal law,[27] these were never used by the CPS to prosecute negligent doctors for negligent wrongdoing. This gap in prosecutorial policy was criticised in the academic literature; as prosecutions of medical professionals for criminal negligence

19 Article 121-3 Code Pénal (CP).

20 JR Spencer, MA Brajeux, above n12 at 16.

21 The article refers to a *délit*, the second category of criminal offences in French criminal law (see Chapter 1).

22 Article 121-3 al 3 CP.

23 This will be illustrated in Chapter 4 in the analysis of the HIV-contaminated blood episode, where both medical professionals and health officials were prosecuted for negligence offences in France.

24 Y Mayaud, *Violences involontaires et responsabilité pénale* (Paris: Dalloz Référence 2003), 5.

25 Assemblée Nationale, *Rapport No 2266 fait au nom de la commission des lois constitutionnelles, de la législation et de l'administration générale de la République sur la proposition de loi, adoptée par le Sénat, tendant à préciser la définition des délits non intentionnels*, par M René Dosière, 22 mars 2000, 12.

26 F Stark, 'Reckless Manslaughter', (2017) 10 *Criminal Law Review* 771–772.

27 See s. 20 Offences Against the Person Act 1861 (OAPA 1861).

relied too heavily on the harm caused (death) because only medical professionals who were 'unlucky enough' to cause the death of a patient could be prosecuted, whereas a medical professional who had recklessly caused injury short of death would in fact escape criminal liability.[28] Neglect or ill-treatment of a patient would not have led to criminal prosecution if it had not caused the death of the patient, unless the patient lacked capacity or was receiving care under the Mental Health Act 1983 (MHA 1983), in which case the criminalisation of such conduct was provided for at s. 127 of the MHA 1983 and s. 44 of the Mental Capacity Act 2005 (MCA 2005).[29] These offences had been limited to charges for abusive conduct by staff or managers working in care homes for the elderly or learning disabled.[30] However, many other (vulnerable) patients were not protected by these provisions.

The new offences of wilful neglect and ill-treatment at s. 20 of the Criminal Justice and Courts Act 2015 (hereafter s. 20 CJCA 2015) may be committed by either an individual care worker or a care provider (body corporate or individual).[31] The offences do not require any harm to result from the behaviour, but the neglect must have reached a higher threshold of culpability than mere negligence, or even gross negligence. Contrary to the gross negligence test, s. 20 offences aim to penalise individuals who have 'deliberately or recklessly [failed] to carry out an action'[32] which they knew they were under a duty to perform, or individuals who have engaged in deliberate mistreatment.

The maximum penalty is 5 years imprisonment for an individual when convicted of the care worker offence(s). The explanatory notes to the Act provide that 'care worker' includes care professionals who are providing care to patients, i.e. 'front-line' staff, but also individuals 'who [are] paid specifically to supervise or manage individuals providing such care', and 'director[s] or equivalent of an organisation providing such care'.[33] It is further explained that 'the intention [was] to ensure that the individual offence [could] apply to any individual perpetrator, not just those on the "front line" of care provision'.[34] The offences may therefore be used to prosecute supervisors and directors if they have themselves ill-treated or wilfully neglected a patient. Supervisors and directors will however not be liable for the failure to prevent neglect or ill-treatment committed by individual care workers they supervise or manage under the care worker offence,

28 M Brazier, A Alghrani, 'Fatal Medical Malpractice and Criminal Liability', (2007) *Professional Negligence* 57.

29 It is worth noting here that children have so far been protected from neglect by s. 1 Children and Young Persons Act 1933; s. 44 MCA 2005; s. 127 MHA 1983; N Allen, 'Psychiatric Care and Criminal Prosecution', in D Griffiths, A Sanders (eds), above n6 at 159.

30 Ibid at 160.

31 Ss. 20–23 CJCA 2015.

32 J Bibby, C Tomkins, 'Would Criminalising Healthcare Professionals for Wilful Neglect Improve Patient Care?' (2014) 348 *British Medical Journal* 1.

33 S. 20(3) CJCA 2015.

34 CJCA 2015 Explanatory Notes, 215.

although they may be liable under the care provider offence (s. 21 CJCA 2015).[35] The acts or omissions of a supervisor which could have led a care professional to ill-treat a patient are excluded from the scope of s. 20 CJCA 2015. It has been argued, however, that 'although the explanatory notes are undoubtedly correct that a supervisor cannot be *vicariously* liable for the ill-treatment or wilful neglect of "front line" staff, it is submitted that they will be liable if they aid and abet it, or assist or encourage it'.[36] Under s. 21 CJCA 2015, an individual 'care provider' may be liable for the offences. Thus the director of a care institution will be included in that scope.[37] One consequence, however, would be that directors of small corporations are more likely to be subject to prosecutions than directors of large healthcare corporations, which would usually have more than one director. Unfortunately, the Act is not very clear on how this section is to be interpreted in relation to individual care providers. In France, as will be shown below, a hospital manager or supervisor can be criminally liable for the failure to prevent ill-treatment committed by an individual medical professional s/he supervises, and this is made clear in the *Code Pénal*.

It is worth noting here that, as explained in Chapter 1, offences punishing negligent conduct in France are classified as minor offences, and therefore are not punishable by life imprisonment as may be the case in England and Wales for GNM. This has had an impact on the use of criminal law in healthcare malpractice, at least until the enactment of the CJCA 2015, because French courts have shown more willingness to convict medical professionals for less serious offences as there is less stigma attached to a conviction for a more minor offence than a conviction for a serious offence. A conviction for GNM would necessarily have a more devastating effect than a conviction for *homicide involontaire* (involuntary manslaughter) on a medical professional's career. Furthermore, in practice French courts elect to give suspended prison sentences for offences which punish negligent conduct, and those who are convicted of negligence offences in France rarely go to jail.[38] As Spencer and Brajeux have explained, 'in France, it seems to be accepted that a proper judicial reaction to a negligent homicide or wounding is a fine, plus the stigma of a conviction and a "virtual"[39] prison sentence'.[40]

Individual criminal offences

In both countries, a fatal error could result in prosecutions for involuntary homicide. In France, this will be for *homicide involontaire*, the closest equivalent to GNM. In addition, French criminal law contains wide-ranging fatal and non-fatal

35 Ibid.

36 K Laird, above n15 at 3.

37 Ibid at 13.

38 JR Spencer, MA Brajeux, above n12 at 22; Sénat, *Les délits non intentionnels-La Loi Fauchon: 5 ans après*, Actes du colloque, 1er mars 2006, Palais du Luxembourg, 48.

39 'Virtual' is used here as a synonym of 'suspended'.

40 JR Spencer, MA Brajeux, above n12 at 22.

criminal offences which may be used in the context of medical negligence. It is worth noting here that for all 'negligence' offences in the French Penal Code, various degrees of culpability are criminalised. Three types of *fautes* are penalised under French criminal law: *faute simple* (mere negligence), *faute caractérisée* (gross negligence) and *faute délibérée* (reckless and/or wilful conduct). Offences in the French Penal Code have been used widely in relation to medical negligence, including in cases of negligent diagnosis, negligent delivery of care, negligent surgery, negligent supervision of junior doctors or negligent organisation of a medical service.

A *faute simple* in French law includes conduct of 'ineptitude, carelessness, inattention, negligence or a breach of an obligation of security or of care imposed by legislation or regulation'.[41] Hence, an obstetrician was found criminally liable for using forceps on a patient where the evidence showed that the use of forceps was not necessary in the circumstances. In another case, a surgeon was found criminally liable for removing the wrong kidney.[42] In England and Wales, two doctors were cleared of manslaughter even though they had removed the wrong kidney from a patient because it could not be proved that the error had led to the death.[43]

Faute caractérisée is broadly the equivalent of the English recklessness, although in various cases, it seems to have been interpreted more broadly, and therefore contains aspect of gross negligence.[44] It is defined as 'exposing another person to a particularly serious risk of which they ought to have been aware'.[45] One commits *faute caractérisée* when s/he does not seek to cause damage but is indifferent to the damage. One also commits *faute caractérisée* when his/her conduct amounts to gross carelessness or negligence that a sensible professional would not commit,[46] or 'a series of negligent and careless conducts which, each, has a certain causal link with the damage, and that the accumulation permits to establish the negligence . . . of particular gravity of which consequences could not have been ignored'.[47] As explained earlier, since 2000, *faute caractérisée* is required when the (negligent) conduct has indirectly caused the harm.[48] To establish that a medical professional had knowledge of a risk of harm, for his/her behaviour to constitute *faute caractérisée*, French courts will aim to determine whether the professional had considered the foreseeable risks of injury or death[49] or will sometimes simply presume that

41 Article 221-6 CP.

42 M Daury-Fauveau, *La responsabilité pénale du médecin* (Bordeaux: Les études hospitalières 2003), 26–27.

43 R Alleyne, 'Surgeons Who Removed the Wrong Kidney Are Cleared', *The Telegraph* (26 June 2002).

44 Although the definitions of *faute caractérisée* and gross negligence are somewhat different.

45 Article 121-3 al 4 CP.

46 VD Commaret, *La Loi Fauchon, 5 ans après* (2006) Chron. N7, spec. N18 *Droit Pénal*.

47 Cass Crim 10/01/2006 n° 04-86.428; B Cotte et D Guihal, *La Loi Fauchon, 5 ans de mise en oeuvre jurisprudentielle* (2006) chron. N6, et spéc. N44 *Droit Pénal*; B Bouloc, H Matsopoulou, *Droit pénal général et procédure pénale* (21e edn, Paris: Sirey 2018), 105–106.

48 Article 121-3 CP.

49 Cass Crim 18/06/2002 Bull Crim no 138.

the defendant was aware of the risks.[50] For instance, an anaesthetist was convicted of *homicide involontaire* with *faute caractérisée* when he had not given sufficient instructions to nurses with regard to monitoring the condition of a child who was bleeding profusely following a tonsillectomy. He was considered to have underestimated the haemorrhage and had contributed to the death of the patient, who died of a cardiac arrest during the anaesthesia and further treatment.[51] *Faute délibérée*, on the other hand, requires a higher level of culpability than *faute caractérisée.* It is defined in the *Code Pénal* as deliberate risk-taking. It can be used as either an aggravating circumstance of negligence offences or a free-standing criminal offence.[52] *Faute délibérée* is committed when one has 'broken a duty of care or precaution laid down by statute or regulation in a manifestly deliberate manner'.[53]

Homicide

Contrary to how French *fautes* have been defined, defining gross negligence in English criminal law has proved difficult. Until the *R v Adomako* case[54] in 1995, English courts admitted involuntary manslaughter by gross negligence and by recklessness. Courts used two types of recklessness: *Cunningham*[55] recklessness and *Caldwell*[56] recklessness (which has since been rejected).[57] According to *Cunningham*, a person was reckless if s/he knew that there was a risk that harm might occur but nevertheless took that risk. *Caldwell* went further in the sense that a defendant was reckless if 'he [did] an act which . . . [created] an obvious risk', and 'he either [had] not given any thought to the possibility of there being any such risk or [had] recognised that there was some risk involved and [had] nonetheless gone on to do it'.[58] Since 1995, gross negligence alone would be enough to establish culpability for involuntary manslaughter.

However, the definition of what makes negligence 'gross', as defined in the *Adomako* case, has so far been unclear, leaving room for prosecutorial, expert and jury discretion.[59] Dr Adomako was a locum anaesthetist who, during

50 Cass Crim 24/09/2003 no 02-81.820.
51 Cass Crim 13/02/2007 no 06-82.202 Bull Crim 2007 n° 44, 261.
52 Article 223-1 CP.
53 Ibid.
54 [1994] 3 WLR 288. But from 1986, it was thought that GNM had been 'absorbed into and replaced by reckless manslaughter'; J Horder, *Ashworth's Principles of Criminal Law* (9th edn, Oxford: Oxford University Press 2019), 301.
55 *R v Cunningham* [1957] 2 QB 396.
56 *R v Caldwell* [1982] AC 341 (HL).
57 J Herring, *Criminal Law: Text, Cases and Materials* (8th edn, Oxford: Oxford University Press 2018), 137.
58 [1982] AC 341 (HL).
59 O Quick, 'Medicine, Mistakes and Manslaughter: A Criminal Combination?' (2010) 69(1) *Cambridge Law Journal* 186, 193; O Quick, 'Prosecuting "Gross" Medical Negligence: Manslaughter, Discretion and the Crown Prosecution Service', (2006) 33(3) *Journal of Law and Society* 421–450; O Quick, 'Expert Evidence and Medical Manslaughter: Vagueness in Action', (2011) 38(4) *Journal of Law and Society* 496–518.

a minor eye operation, had failed to notice that a tube from the ventilator which carried oxygen to the patient had become disconnected, even though the patient had ceased to breathe. This caused the patient to die from cardiac arrest.[60] Dr Adomako was convicted of GNM at first instance, and appealed the decision. His appeal was heard together with the appeal of two junior doctors, Dr Prentice and Dr Sullman, in the Court of Appeal. Dr Prentice, a pre-registration house officer, was under the supervision of Dr Sullman, a house officer, when he injected vincristine, a cytotoxic drug, into a 16-year-old leukaemia patient's spine, instead of intravenously. The patient died 2 weeks later. It appeared that neither defendant had previously had significant experience with cytotoxic drugs. The two doctors were initially convicted of GNM.[61] Prentice and Sullman's appeals succeeded as the Court of Appeal considered that the jury had been misdirected by the trial judge. Adomako's appeal failed. The Court found that 'the standard of care that the patient [had] received was abysmal'.[62] Evidence was brought to the court that the defendant had shown 'gross dereliction of care'.[63]

The Court of Appeal held that three matters needed to be proved in order to convict an individual of GNM: '(1) the existence of the duty; (2) a breach of the duty causing death; (3) gross negligence which the jury considered justified a criminal conviction'.[64] It is this last condition that has proved problematic. Adomako then appealed to the House of Lords, but his appeal was dismissed.[65] The House of Lords held that

> [w]hether the defendant's breach of duty amounted to gross negligence depended on the seriousness of the breach of duty committed by the defendant in all the circumstances in which he was placed when it occurred and whether, having regard to the risk of death involved, the conduct of the defendant was so bad in all the circumstances as to amount in the jury's judgment to a criminal act or omission.[66]

For a conviction of GNM to succeed, at least one of the following criteria would need to be fulfilled:

(1) indifference to an obvious risk of injury to health;
(2) actual foresight of the risk coupled with the determination nevertheless to run it;

60 [1994] 3 WLR 288.
61 *R v Prentice and another; R v Adomako; R v Holloway* [1993] 4 All ER 935.
62 Ibid a4t 952.
63 Ibid at 936.
64 Ibid.
65 [1994] 3 WLR 288 at 298.
66 Ibid. The impact of the jury on criminal proceedings involving healthcare professionals prosecuted for GNM is analysed in Chapter 3.

(3) an appreciation of the risk coupled with the intention to avoid it but with such a high degree of negligence in the attempted avoidance that the jury considered it justified conviction;
(4) inattention or failure to advert to a serious risk which went beyond 'mere inadvertence' in respect of an obvious and important matter which the defendant's duty demanded the jury should address.[67]

Hypothetically, if this case had occurred in France, Drs Prentice and Sullman could have been convicted of ***homicide involontaire*** as there was evidence of a *faute simple*, which had directly caused the death of the patient. The outcome of the *Prentice and Sullman* case could be explained by the fact that they were junior doctors, and they 'could have been helped more than [they] were helped', the sentencing judge telling them that they were 'far from being bad men'.[68] Junior doctors[69] have, however, not escaped criminal liability for GNM in England following *Prentice and Sullman*; as can be shown in *R v Misra & Srivastava*[70] or the more recent case of Dr Bawa-Garba.[71]

Drs Misra and Srivastava were two junior doctors who worked at Southampton General Hospital and had failed to diagnose a post-operative infection on a patient who had undergone surgery to treat his patella tendon. The infection was left untreated for two days as the two doctors 'entirely disregarded' the results of blood tests which could have given indications of the infection, even though the patient showed obvious signs of infection.[72] The patient died of toxic shock.[73] By comparison to Dr Prentice and Sullman's mistake, it appeared that the quality of the care provided by the doctors 'did not even begin to approach the standard to be expected of them'.[74] Drs Misra and Srivastava were convicted of GNM and received an 18 months suspended sentence. The two doctors then appealed the decision on the grounds that the test on gross negligence was circular and consequently involved uncertainty, contrary to article 7 of the European Convention of Human Rights. The Court of Appeal ruled that the *Adomako* test on gross negligence involved 'no uncertainty' and did not violate the convention. Drs Misra and Srivastava's appeal was dismissed.[75]

It must be noted furthermore that recently there has been an interesting development in the case law on GNM in relation to medical professionals. The Court

67 [1994] 3 WLR 288 at 292.
68 [1994] QB 302.
69 Junior doctors are qualified doctors in clinical training. They have up to 8 years' experience working as a hospital doctor, or up to 3 years in general practice. They must work under the supervision of a senior doctor; British Medical Association, *Doctors' Titles: Explained*, 2017, 4.
70 *R v Misra; R v Srivastava* [2004] EWCA Crim 2375.
71 *R v Bawa-Garba* [2016] EWCA Crim 1841.
72 [2004] EWCA Crim 2375 at [18].
73 Ibid.
74 Ibid.
75 Ibid.

of Appeal in two decisions has attempted to provide more clarity to the GNM test. *R v Rudling*[76] concerned the death of 12-year-old patient Ryan, who had died from Addison's disease on 8 December 2012. On Thursday, 6 December 2012, Ryan's mother had called the surgery and spoken to the defendant doctor (D), explaining her child's symptoms. The doctor told her that she needed to ring the surgery again on Monday. Ryan's condition deteriorated, and he sadly died of Addison's disease on Saturday the 8th of December, one week short of his 13th birthday. D was initially charged with GNM as the CPS considered that the 'failure to appreciate Ryan's symptoms were serious and dangerous and to see him in person, or send him to hospital constituted gross negligence'.[77] At trial in Cardiff Crown Court, Nicola Davies J dismissed the jury and decided that there was no case to answer. The decision was appealed as the CPS insisted that D's failure constituted GNM. The Court of Appeal, however, held that 'a recognizable risk of something serious is not the same as a recognizable risk of death',[78] and the risk known to D was not an obvious and serious risk of death. The defendant was acquitted.

Similarly, Honey Rose, an optometrist, was convicted of GNM for having failed to examine the back of a patient's eyes, in accordance with her statutory duty, which led to the patient's death.[79] Her conviction was quashed on appeal as the Court of Appeal considered that Rose's failure did not amount to gross negligence. The Court stated that 'in assessing reasonable foreseeability of serious and obvious risk of death in cases of gross negligence manslaughter, it was not appropriate to take into account what the defendant would have known *but for* his breach of duty'.[80] The Court further held that

> the potentially life-threatening seriousness of the deceased's condition, as manifested by visible swelling of the optic nerve (papilloedema) would not have been apparent to the defendant unless and until she had carried out a proper examination of the back of the deceased's eyes with particular equipment.[81]

In other words, the defendant could not have committed GNM if she had merely breached her statutory duty of care, as GNM would have been committed *only* if she had been aware of a serious and obvious risk of death, which could only have occurred if she had conducted a proper examination of the patient's eyes. The Court of Appeal further held that the judge 'should not have directed the jury that, when considering whether there had been a "serious and obvious risk

76 [2016] 151 BMLR 79.

77 A Mullock, 'Gross Negligence (Medical) Manslaughter and the Puzzling Implications of Negligent Ignorance, *Rose v R* [2017] EWCA crim 1168', (2018) 26(2) *Medical Law Review* 350.

78 [2016] 151 BMLR 79 at 80.

79 *R v Rose* [2017] EWCA Crim 1168.

80 Ibid at [77], [78], [94].

81 Ibid [83], [86].

of death", they had to consider whether the risk would have been obvious to a reasonable competent optometrist with the knowledge that the defendant would have had if she had not acted in breach of her duty'.[82] The Court explained that

> the judge appeared to have confused or elided two separate matters: a) the actual knowledge of R at the time of the breach; and b) the putative knowledge of the reasonably prudent optometrist in the position of R at the time. The two were quite different concepts: the former was subjective; the latter was objective.[83]

The patient (V) had died of acute hydrocephalus, and it was found that 'early surgical intervention to drain the fluid would have saved V's life'.[84]

Whilst the attempts by the Court of Appeal to clarify the law were laudable, the decision can be criticised on several grounds. The *Rose* case can be criticised for its lack of consistency with what criminalisation under GNM aims to achieve. As Laird argues,

> [t]he Court of Appeal seems to have underappreciated the fact that the practical impact of its judgment is that the more egregious the breach of the duty of care, the less likely it is that the defendant will be found guilty. This is because the defendant may have been so negligent that he or she was not in a position to appreciate the risk of death.[85]

Comments have also highlighted the confusion that this decision created, with Laird arguing that

> [t]he court's caveat in the instant case and the outcome of *Rudling* beg the question of how severe V's symptoms must be, and how clearly they must be communicated, before the risk of death becomes clear and unambiguous, even though the breach of the duty of care precluded D from knowing for sure that such a risk existed.[86]

Contrary to GNM, French offences against the person as written in the *Code Pénal* provide more clarity and precision to courts. *Homicide involontaire* requires only proof of simple negligence when the causal link between conduct and harm is direct. *Homicide involontaire* is defined as 'the fact of causing, in the conditions and according to the distinctions laid down by article 121-3, by ineptitude,

82 Ibid [83], [85], [86], [93].
83 Ibid [84].
84 K Laird, 'Manslaughter: R v Rose (Honey Maria) Court of Appeal (Criminal Division), Sir Brian Leveson PQBD, Haddon-Cave J and HH Judge Inman QC: 31 July 2017; [2017] EWCA Crim 1168', (2018) 1 *Criminal Law Review* 76.
85 Ibid at 79.
86 Ibid at 80.

carelessness, inattention, negligence or a breach of an obligation of security or of care imposed by legislation or regulation, the death of another'.[87] Thus, any individual, including medical professionals, may therefore be prosecuted and/or convicted of *homicide involontaire*, sentenced to up to 3 years in prison and fined €45,000. A medical professional could therefore be convicted of *homicide involontaire* if s/he committed a *faute simple* and directly caused a patient's death, or if s/he committed a *faute caractérisée*, or *délibérée*, and indirectly caused the death of a patient. For example, a surgeon was convicted of *homicide involontaire* with *faute caractérisée*, and sentenced to 2 years suspended, for causing the death of a patient. Following surgery, the surgeon had failed to conduct a clinical examination of the patient even after the patient had complained of abdominal pain. The patient had actually developed severe sepsis, for which antibiotic treatment was required but was never administered. Even after the doctor was informed of the patient's state, she had failed to attend to the patient and had turned off her phone. The patient died of septic shock. The court found that septic shock could have been avoided if the patient had been properly attended by the doctor and had been administered the proper antibiotics.[88]

Unlike French offences, which are more clearly defined in the French Penal Code, GNM leaves room for interpretation to prosecutors and the courts. In all the cases described above, the same offence was used against several defendants who had shown very different levels of culpability.[89] Drs Prentice and Sullman had made a mistake – albeit fatal – whilst Dr Adomako's standard of care was said to be appalling and would be seen as a *faute caractérisée* in France, and Drs Misra and Srivastava were consistently 'grossly' negligent over a long period of time, which would seem to constitute *faute délibérée*.

The use of GNM in relation to healthcare negligence has been widely criticised by scholars, who have advocated for a change in the law.[90] For instance, Quick has consistently argued that there should be a 'stiffer test of subjective recklessness' and has suggested that the gross negligence test be abolished because 'the idea that the offence ingredients involve no uncertainty is at best unrealistic and at worst disingenuous'.[91] In Chapter 5, I propose that the gross negligence test be changed, mirroring the French *faute caractérisée*.

87 Article 221-6 CP.

88 Cass Crim 19/04/2017 no 16-83640.

89 V Tadros, 'The Limits of Manslaughter', in CMV Clarkson, S Cunningham (eds), *Criminal Liability for Non-Aggressive Death* (Aldershot: Ashgate 2008), 42.

90 M Kazarian, D Griffiths, M Brazier, 'Criminal Responsibility for Medical Malpractice in France', (2011) 27 (4) *Journal of Professional Negligence* 196; D Griffiths, A Sanders, above n6 at 153; O Quick (2010), above n60 199; V Tadros, above n90 at 49; CMV Clarkson, 'General Endangerment Offences: The Way Forward?' (2005) 32 *University of Western Australian Law Review* 131.
D Griffiths, A Sanders, above n6 at 153.

91 O Quick, 'Medical Manslaughter and Expert Evidence: The Role of Context and Character', in D Griffiths, A Sanders (eds), above n6 at 109; O Quick, 'Medical Killing: Need for a

Non-fatal offences against the person

Blessures involontaires (involuntary wounding) appears to have no direct equivalent in English criminal law[92] but is a criminal offence under the French *Code Pénal*.[93] It is defined as

> the fact of causing, in the conditions and according to the distinctions laid down by article 121-3, by ineptitude, carelessness, inattention, negligence or a breach of an obligation of security or of care imposed by legislation or regulation, a total incapacity to work in excess of three months to another person.[94]

The closest equivalent found in English criminal law is 'unlawfully or maliciously wounding or causing grievous bodily harm' under s. 20 of the Offences Against the Person Act 1861 (OAPA 1861).[95] Intent to harm is not required to be proved by s. 20 of the OAPA as only recklessness may be sufficient.[96] S. 20 has been used sparingly in England and Wales in the context of healthcare malpractice and only when the medical professional had committed intentional conduct.

On the contrary, in France *blessures involontaires* is an offence used in that context to criminalise *negligent* conduct. For instance, an anaesthetist and director of a private clinic was convicted of *blessures involontaires* and received a 6 months suspended sentence for causing severe brain injury to a patient. The patient had been hospitalised in that private clinic to receive several medical procedures, including surgery under general anaesthetic, an endometrial biopsy and a laparoscopy. During the surgery, a tube which was providing oxygen to the patient became disconnected, and the patient suffered bronchospasm, which caused her heart to stop for a few minutes, but was reanimated, put in an induced coma and transferred to the nearest hospital centre. The patient, however, suffered irreversible brain injury. The court found that the doctor had committed *faute caractérisée*, as it was found that she had left the patient for a few minutes to attend

Specific Offence?' in CMV Clarkson, S Cunningham (eds), above n90 at 160–161; O Quick (2011), above n60 at 496, 500.

92 M Brazier, A Alghrani, 'Fatal Medical Malpractice and Criminal Liability', (2009) 25(2) *Journal of Professional Negligence* 51–67.

93 Article 121-3 CP; S18 and S20 Offences Against the Persons Act 1861.

94 Article 222-19 al 1 CP; Article R625-2 CP. In the case of *blessures involontaires*, the sentence will depend on how long the victim was unable to work after s/he was injured. The term used in the CP is *incapacité totale de travail* (literally, 'incapacity to work'). When the *incapacité totale de travail* (ITT) lasts longer than 3 months, *blessures involontaires* are considered a *délit* and may be punished by up to 2 years in prison and a fine of €30,000. When the ITT is less than 3 months, the offence of *blessures involontaires* is considered a *contravention* and is punished only by a fine.

95 S. 20 OAPA 1861.

96 *R v Mowatt* [1968] 1 QB 421; *R v Savage and Parmenter* [1992] AC 699 (HL); J Horder, above n54 at 321.

to an emergency without asking any other doctor to attend to the patient, and this had been the sole cause of the damage suffered. It is worth noting here that the patient, who was also *partie civile* to the criminal action, received over a million Euros in civil compensation.[97] In England and Wales, the victim of a crime may receive compensation for an injury sustained under the Criminal Injuries Compensation Scheme, but the maximum award which may be made under this scheme is £500,000. The role of *parties civiles* in proceedings involving healthcare professionals is further explored in the next chapter.

A third offence which has been used against negligent medical professionals and officials in France is *non-assistance à personne en danger* (failure to assist a person in danger or the failure to rescue – also known as the 'Good Samaritan Law').[98] It may be committed by

> anyone who, being able to prevent by immediate action a *crime* or a *délit* against the bodily integrity of a person, without risk to himself or to third parties, wilfully abstains from doing so . . . The same penalties apply to anyone who wilfully fails to offer assistance to a person in danger which he could himself provide without risk to himself or to third parties, or by initiating rescue operations.[99]

A breach of the Good Samaritan Law is subject to a maximum sentence of 5 years imprisonment and a fine of €75,000, which, we may note, is higher than for *homicide involontaire* (3 years). *Non-assistance à personne en danger* has been used in France in the healthcare context.[100] English criminal law does not recognise the failure to rescue as a criminal offence unless a duty of care is recognised (e.g. parent to child or medical professional to patient), but this offence's definition is very close to that of wilful neglect at s. 20 CJCA 2015 in the sense that one commits the offence if s/he has wilfully failed to protect a person from physical harm, similarly to wilful neglect. The *mens rea* of the two offences is therefore the same (wilfulness), and so is the maximum punishment. One particular feature of *non-assistance à personne en danger* is that if the offence is committed on a minor of maximum 15 years of age, the maximum sentence increases to 7 years imprisonment and a fine of €100,000.[101] As will be explained in Chapter 4, the offence penalising the failure to rescue was used in the HIV-contaminated blood scandal against officials and ministers involved in the blood supply organisation, who had failed to protect patients from contamination. At the time no offence of wilful neglect or ill-treatment of patients existed in English law.

97 Cass Crim 15/01/2019 no 17-86461.

98 M Daury-Fauveau, above n42 at 26–27.

99 Article 223-6 CP.

100 P Mistretta, Cass.crim.7 mars 2017, no 16-80.754: omission de porter secours: le medecin urgentiste, le malade en fin de vie et les querelles de famille.

101 This change was made to the law in August 2018; see Loi n°2018-703 du 3 août 2018 - art. 5.

Mise en danger délibérée d'autrui (deliberately putting someone in danger) is another offence used in the context of healthcare malpractice in France. Article 223-1 of the French Penal Code provides that

> [t]he direct exposure of another person to an immediate risk of death or injury likely to cause mutilation or permanent disability by the manifestly deliberate violation of a specific obligation of safety or prudence imposed by any statute or regulation is punished by one year's imprisonment and a fine of €15,000.[102]

This offence will only be used when the defendant has deliberately exposed the patient to a risk of serious injury when the defendant had a specific obligation of safety. It is thus very close to what Merry and Brookbanks have labelled 'violations' (actions which reflect deliberate risk-taking) in the medical context.[103] *Mise en danger délibérée* may be used as a free-standing criminal offence or as an aggravating circumstance of other criminal offences. For instance, a defendant may be convicted of *homicide involontaire* aggravated with *mise en danger délibérée* if it is shown that s/he has deliberately put the victim at immediate risk of death or injury. The maximum punishment for this offence increases from 3 to 5 years imprisonment.[104] The intention behind the creation of this offence was to penalise conduct which showed disregard for another.[105] As an offence on its own, it can be used whether or not any harm was actually caused by the deliberate risk-taking.[106] It is the only offence in French criminal law punishable by imprisonment that does not need to result in harm.

Prosecutions for *mise en danger délibérée* on its own are rarely recorded, but it is said to be widely used in the field of healthcare malpractice as an aggravated circumstance of *homicide involontaire* and *blessures involontaires*.[107] For example, an anaesthetist was convicted of *blessures involontaires* aggravated with *faute délibérée*, for having caused six patients various injuries as a result of injecting them with propofol, a strong sedative, prior to performing endoscopy, using only two different syringes, and by failing to examine the patients following the surgery. Standard medical practice would require the doctor to use one syringe for each patient to avoid the risk of infection. But as a result of the doctor's reckless wrongdoing, the product became infected with bacteria, which caused the patients to suffer various medical conditions for which they had to be admitted to the emergency service.[108] The doctor's behaviour did not constitute mere

102 Article 223-1 CP.

103 A Merry, W Brookbanks, *Merry and McCall Smith's Errors, Medicine and the Law* (2nd edn, Cambridge: Cambridge University Press 2017), 4–5.

104 Article 221-6 CP.

105 M Daury-Fauveau, above n42 at 26–27.

106 Sénat, above n38 at 8.

107 M Daury-Fauveau, above n42 at 29.

108 Cass Crim 11/09/2001 Bull N°176.

negligence or carelessness. It was considered to be obvious selfishness and deliberate risk-taking.[109] The closest English equivalent to *mise en danger délibérée* seems to be found in the offences of wilful neglect/ill-treatment provided for at s. 20 and s. 21 of the CJCA 2015. Like *mise en danger délibérée*, wilful neglect/ill-treatment are conduct offences and do not require proof of any harm, but unlike *mise en danger délibérée*, only individuals who are paid to provide health or social care may be liable for wilful neglect or ill-treatment of patients. In France, *mise en danger délibérée* can be committed by any individual, and thus the offence has a much broader scope.

A category of offences that might be considered close to negligence *délits* are health and safety offences in England provided by the Health and Safety at Work Act 1974 (HSWA 1974). Under this Act, the Health and Safety Executive (HSE) may prosecute individual healthcare practitioners, but it has not at present done so. An employee at work who fails 'to take reasonable care for the health and safety of himself and of other persons who may be affected by his acts or omissions at work' is criminally liable under s. 7 of the HSWA 1974.[110] However, the HSE does not prosecute matters relating to quality of care or clinical judgement, which excludes a great number of cases of healthcare malpractice from criminalisation under the Act.[111]

Corporate criminal offences

Healthcare errors may be the result of individual healthcare negligence, but very often they are the result of various types of systemic issues within healthcare services which threaten patient safety.[112] In the past two decades, cases of 'medical manslaughter' in England and Wales have shown that medical professionals working either in the National Health Service (NHS) or in private practice are working in unsafe environments, and are therefore more likely to commit fatal or non-fatal errors for which they may be held to account.[113] As we will see in this section, cases of systemic failings are also recorded in France, and are often subject to criminal liability.

109 Ibid.

110 S. 7(a) and s. 33(1)(a).

111 See www.hse.gov.uk/healthservices/arrangements.htm.

112 L Kohn, J Corrigan, M Donaldson (eds), *To Err Is Human: Building a Safer Health System* (Washington DC: National Academy Press 1999); Department of Health, *An Organisation with a Memory: Report of an Expert Group on Learning from Adverse Events in the NHS Chaired by the Chief Medical Officer* (London: HMSO 2000); O Quick, 'Medical Manslaughter: The Rise (and Replacement) of a Contested Crime?' in C Erin, S Ost (eds), above n1 at 35–36; N Allen, 'Medical or Managerial Manslaughter', in C Erin, S Ost (eds), above n1 at 49.

113 M Kazarian, 'Who Should We Blame for Healthcare Failings? Lessons from the French Tainted Blood Scandal', (2019) 27(3) *Medical Law Review* 390–391.

In England and Wales, Wayne Jowett, a patient diagnosed with leukaemia, was prepared to receive an injection of vincristine as part of his treatment.[114] A senior house officer injected the drug intrathecally instead of intravenously, and this was fatal for the patient.[115] The doctor pleaded guilty and was sentenced to 8 months in prison.[116] An inquiry was conducted and found that 'the adverse incident that led to Mr Jowett's death was not caused by one or even several human errors but by a far more complex amalgam of human, organisational, technical and social interactions'.[117] It is worth noting that this case and many others happened following, and despite, the *Prentice and Sullman* case, which was highly publicised at the time. This has led Merry and Brookbanks to note that the *Prentice and Sullman* case 'appears to have had little if any benefit in avoiding recurrences of the same mistake or of errors in drug administration in general'.[118]

In both France and England and Wales, corporations may be criminalised for negligence, but again, French criminal law offers a wider range of corporate offences than English criminal law. Since 1994, the French *Code Pénal* provides that corporations, apart from the state, can be criminally liable in the conditions set out in the Code for individuals.[119] Hence, in France, a hospital may be prosecuted for any of the criminal offences which apply to individuals, i.e. *blessures involontaires*, *homicide involontaire*, *non-assistance à personne en danger* or *mise en danger délibérée*, in addition to possible convictions of individual health professionals in relation to the same harm.[120] Even if the directing body or member of the organisation is not found guilty, the corporation may still be convicted.[121]

In 2003, the *Tribunal correctionnel* of Paris convicted a hospital of *homicide involontaire* and *mise en danger délibérée d'autrui* for failings in the service which caused the death of a child.[122] The child was presented at the emergency room of the hospital with severe gastroenteritis and vomiting. He could not be admitted to the gastroenterology service as no beds were available. He was admitted to the pneumology service instead. One trainee doctor and two nurses looked after the child in the two days following his arrival at the hospital. On the second day, one of the nurses noticed that the drip providing fluids had stopped working and informed the nurse on duty, who subsequently asked the trainee doctor for instructions. The trainee doctor ordered the drip to be removed but failed to check on the child and left the service without giving any other recommendations to the other nurses. The mother of the child later noticed that the child

114 B Toft, *External Inquiry into the Adverse Incident That Occurred at Queen's Medical Centre, Nottingham* (Department of Health, 4 January 2001), 9.

115 Ibid.

116 'Anger as Fatal Jab Doctor Freed', *BBC News* (23 September 2003).

117 B Toft, above n115 at 40.

118 A Merry, W Brookbanks, above n104 at 24.

119 Article 121-2 CP.

120 Ibid.

121 CA Grenoble, 12/06/1998, affaire du Drac.

122 TGI de Paris, 16e Chambre, jugement du 3 septembre 2003, affaire n° 9926423046.

was shaking and his stools were abundant. The child was eventually transferred to intensive care the next morning and died a few days later. Nurses, doctors and the director of the hospital were all convicted of *homicide involontaire* and *mise en danger délibérée* through breach of an obligation of security or care, particularly the breach of a regulation[123] which required the nursing staff and hospital directors to make sure that tasks were shared by nurses and nursing auxiliaries; as well as a circular[124] which provided that hospital staff could not expose very young patients to an immediate risk of death or serious wounding.[125]

In England, before the Corporate Manslaughter and Corporate Homicide Act 2007 (CMCHA 2007) came into force in 2008, corporations could be criminally liable for manslaughter using either direct corporate liability; vicarious liability, which applied in several contexts including health and safety at work;[126] or the identification doctrine.[127] According to the doctrine of vicarious liability, senior managers were criminally liable only for certain offences for the acts of their employees.[128] The identification principle required that when the directing mind of the corporation was culpable, then the corporation itself would be culpable, which was very difficult to prove.[129] Since 2008, English criminal law includes the criminalisation of corporations for manslaughter under the CMCHA 2007. The Act provides that a corporation is criminally liable 'if the way in which its activities are managed or organised (a) causes a person's death and (b) amounts to a gross breach of a relevant duty of care owed by the organisation to the deceased'.[130] In convicting an organisation of corporate manslaughter, the jury must consider, for instance, 'attitudes, policies, [and] systems of accepted practice within the organisation that were likely to have encouraged any such failure'.[131] The criminalisation under the CMCHA 2007 affects health institutions but also admits a large range of exceptions in the healthcare context (as will be demonstrated in Chapter 6).

Although the CMCHA 2007 has been in force for over 10 years, only one NHS Trust has so far been prosecuted for corporate manslaughter – albeit unsuccessfully – for the death of a patient, as a result of negligent medical treatment by healthcare professionals.[132] The Maidstone and Tunbridge Wells Trust was prosecuted for corporate manslaughter for the death of Mrs Frances

123 Décret n° 93-345 du 15 mars 1993 relatif aux actes professionnels et à l'exercice de la profession d'infirmier, JORF n° 63 du 15 mars 1993, 4098.

124 Circulaire DGS/PS3/DH/PH1 N° 9631 du 19 janvier 1996 relative au rôle et aux missions des aides-soignants et des auxiliaires de puériculture dans les établissements hospitaliers.

125 TGI de Paris, above n123.

126 S. 3 HSWA 1974.

127 N Allen, above n113 at 60–62; CMV Clarkson, HM Keating, SR Cunningham, *Criminal Law* (7th edn, London: Thompson Sweet and Maxwell 2010), 243–247; *Tesco Supermarket Ltd v Nattrass* [1972] AC 153.

128 J Gobert, 'Corporate Criminality: Four Model of Fault', (1994) 14(3) *Legal Studies* 393, 396.

129 N Allen, above n113 at 56.

130 S. 1(1) CMCHA 2007.

131 S. 8 CMCHA 2007.

132 *R v Errol Cornish and Maidstone and Tunbridge Wells NHS Trust* [2015] EWHC 2967 (QB).

Cappuccini, who had died on 9 October 2012 at Penbury Hospital in Tunbridge Wells. Following the delivery of her baby by caesarean section, she had 'suffered extensive bleeding and was transferred to theatre for an examination under anaesthetic'.[133] Two anaesthetists, Dr Azeez and Dr Cornish, who were involved in Mrs Cappuccini's care, had committed failures which had ultimately caused the death of Mrs Cappuccini. Dr Azeez had returned to his native Pakistan during the investigation into Mrs Cappuccini's death and could not be charged, but Dr Cornish was charged with GNM.[134] Maidstone and Tunbridge Wells Trust were also charged for having breached their duty of care by failing to 'take reasonable care to ensure that the anaesthetists involved in the care of Mrs Cappuccini held the appropriate qualifications and training for their role' and 'to ensure that there was the appropriate level of supervision for the anaesthetic treatment of Mrs Cappuccini'.[135] Both the Trust and Dr Cornish were acquitted of the charges in the High Court, as the court found that there was no evidence of a gross breach.[136]

The offence has been criticised for its inability to relate to healthcare institutions, which explains the low rate of prosecutions and convictions of healthcare institutions and corporations more generally for corporate manslaughter.[137] On commentator notes that

> [w]here companies have complex management structures, the difficulties encountered by the prosecuting authorities attempting to establish senior management failure have persisted and much criticism has in fact targeted the persistent invulnerability of larger organisations to prosecution.[138]

It is also argued that the CMCHA 2007 is 'complex and the offence definition itself is full of ambiguities and interpretive uncertainty'.[139]

As explained above, care providers may also be liable for the offences of ill-treatment or wilful neglect, which also apply to individual 'care workers' under s. 21 CJCA 2015. The care provider will be liable under this section if 'an individual who has the care of another individual, by virtue of being part of the care provider's arrangements ill-treats or wilfully neglects that individual'. Similarly to corporate manslaughter, and as emphasised in the explanatory notes to the Act, liability under s. 21 of the CJCA 2015 mirrors liability under the CMCHA 2007 as it must be proved that the way in which the care provider's activities are managed or organised 'amounts to a gross breach of a relevant duty of care owed by

133 Ibid [1].
134 Ibid [2], [21].
135 Ibid [3].
136 Ibid.
137 S Field, 'Ten Years on: The Corporate Manslaughter and Corporate Homicide Act 2007: Plus ca Change?' (2018) *International Company and Commercial Law Review* 512.
138 Ibid.
139 C Wells, 'Medical Manslaughter: Organisational Liability', in D Griffiths, A Sanders (eds), above n6 at 200.

the care provider to the individual who is ill-treated or neglected', and that 'in the absence of the breach, the ill-treatment or wilful neglect would not have occurred or would have been less likely to occur'.[140]

Healthcare services, including primary care trusts, hospital trusts, mental care services and ambulance service trusts, may also be criminally liable under the HSWA 1974 for exposing their employees or other persons (i.e. patients and members of the public) to 'risks to their health or safety'.[141] For example, an NHS Trust was fined £100,000 by the HSE for failing to monitor doctors properly and spot mistakes.[142] Similarly, the Southampton University Hospital Trust was fined £100,000 following the conviction of Drs Misra and Srivastava for gross negligence.[143] However, current HSE policy does not admit the application of the HSWA 1974 to cases of clinical judgement or quality of care. In England and Wales, the HSWA 1974 seems to be used more often than corporate manslaughter even in the context of healthcare malpractice.[144] However, currently, 'prosecutions against health care providers for breaches under [section 3(1) of the HSWA 1974] are very unusual, and certainly less prevalent than manslaughter prosecutions against individual practitioners'.[145] In Chapter 6 I will explore what these three groups of offences can achieve in cases of healthcare systemic failings.

A victim-oriented approach to causation?

Another crucial feature in the way France and England and Wales take a different view on the criminalisation of healthcare malpractice is causation. Even after the *Loi Fauchon* reform, French criminal courts demonstrate an extensive approach to causation in the context of healthcare negligence. French courts apply the *théorie de la causalité adéquate*, which takes into account the conduct which has the strongest causal link with the damage.[146] Causation will be proved if the negligence has *directly* or *indirectly* caused the damage. A direct causal link will be proved if the defendant has himself/herself, through his/her negligence, caused the harm. An indirect causal link will be proved if the defendant has created or has contributed to creating a situation which allowed the damage to occur, or when the defendant has failed to take the measures necessary to prevent the damage from occurring.[147] As explained previously, someone who has indirectly caused damage may be criminally liable only if s/he has committed a *faute caractérisée* or

140 S. 21 CJCA 2015; CJCA 2015, Explanatory Notes, 232.

141 Ss. 2–3 HSWA 1974; C Wells, above n144 at 202.

142 See www.healthandsafetyatwork.com/hsw/content/nhs-trust-fined-%C2%A3100,000-for-poor-supervision.

143 *R v Southampton University Hospital NHS Trust* [2006] EWCA Crim 2971; 'Hospital Trust Fined for Knee op Death', *The Guardian* (11 April 2006).

144 O Quick, above n113 at 40.

145 Ibid.

146 Assemblée Nationale, above n25 at 18; JR Spencer, MA Brajeux, above n12 at 12.

147 Cass Crim 15/01/2019 no 17-86461.

délibérée.[148] In other words, a defendant who has only contributed to the damage, or has failed to prevent damage caused by another individual, for instance, would have to show gross or reckless conduct to be held criminally liable.

This reform has therefore limited the scope for criminalisation of negligence. The *Loi Fauchon* seems to be contextualised in terms of a move away from criminalisation.[149] With this law, the French Parliament intended to restrict the courts' capacity to hold criminally liable people remotely related to negligent conduct in cases of *homicide involontaire* and *blessures involontaires*, particularly decision-makers.[150] In the context of healthcare negligence, a house officer could be criminally liable for injecting the wrong drug into a patient's artery (direct negligence). The senior doctor who fails, by either gross negligence or recklessness, to check that the injection was properly done by the house officer would be indirectly liable for the death or injury of the patient.[151] It therefore follows that the senior doctor in *Prentice and Sullman* in charge of supervising them could have been prosecuted and/or convicted in France for the failure to prevent the junior doctors' negligence if it was shown that he had committed *faute caractérisée*. Before the *Loi Fauchon* came into force, simple negligence would have been enough to convict him/her.

However, has the *Loi Fauchon* actually limited the scope for criminalisation of negligence in practice? Spencer and Brajeux argue that the *Loi Fauchon* has not greatly affected the criminalisation of healthcare malpractice as French courts still seem to interpret causation in an extensive way.[152] French courts are ready to find a direct causal link even where an analysis of the link seems to suggest it is indirect, or if they cannot prove a direct causal link, they are ready to find that a defendant medical professional has committed *faute caractérisée*, to allow a successful conviction.[153] The following example illustrates this. A court of appeal had acquitted a senior doctor of *homicide involontaire* for the death of a patient following surgery performed by a trainee doctor. The defendant senior doctor was supervising the trainee doctor, who had performed a surgical cut which then caused the patient to suffer a haemorrhage. The court of appeal had found that the senior doctor had not committed *faute caractérisée*, which had to be proved when the negligence had only indirectly caused the harm. The *parties civiles* appealed the decision. The *Cour de Cassation* quashed the appeal judgement, finding that there was a direct causal link between the doctor's failure and the

148 Article 121-3 CP.

149 Sénat, above n38 at 7.

150 B Bouloc, H Matsopoulou, above n47 at 105; Sénat, Session ordinaire de 1995–1996, Annexe au procès-verbal de la séance du 18 octobre 1995, N° 32, Proposition de loi relative à la responsabilité pénale des élus locaux pour des faits d'imprudence ou de négligence commis dans l'exercice des fonctions, Rapport.

151 M Daury-Fauveau, above n42 at 26–27.

152 JR Spencer, MA Brajeux, above n12 at 16.

153 See Cass Crim 10/02/2009 n° 08-80.679 Bull crim 2009, n° 33; Cass Crim 11/09/2012 n° 11-88.269.

harm caused, and therefore there was no need to prove that the doctor had committed *faute caractérisée*. The *Cour de Cassation* had found that the doctor had failed to properly supervise the trainee doctor, and had failed to diagnose the haemorrhage early enough; therefore, the death of the patient was the 'exclusive, certain, and direct consequence of successive failings which had occurred during the surgery' which the senior doctor was supervising. The *Cour de Cassation*, without providing much justification for its decision – which is very typical of its judgements[154] – held that there was a direct causal link between the doctor's failings and the death of the patient, because the patient would not have died if surgery had not been performed negligently.[155]

One further example illustrates the point that even though French criminal law requires proof of 'gross' negligence when the causal link is indirect, the criminalisation of healthcare malpractice still has a large scope either by the court managing to find a direct link or by a readiness to find *faute caractérisée*. A doctor was found guilty of *blessures involontaires* for failing to proceed to a scan on a pregnant woman during the last prenatal examination, even though he was aware of the risks of a 'big' baby, notably: an obese mother, the position of the baby in the uterus and the fact that it was her second baby. The baby was born with a paralysed right arm because of a difficult delivery. The appeal court considered that there was a causal link between the doctor's intervention and the harm caused to the baby. The causal link was, however, indirect because the aforesaid doctor was not the one who had attended the woman during labour; he was the one who was in charge of prenatal examinations. The harm caused during labour/delivery was thus an indirect consequence of a failure committed during the prenatal examination. The court held that the doctor had committed *faute caractérisée* which had indirectly caused the damage.[156]

It is also worth noting here that contrary to individual negligence offences, the new rules on causation contained in the *Loi Fauchon* do not apply to corporations. If the causal link between the corporation's negligence and the damage is indirect, it does not have to be a *faute caractérisée* to constitute a criminal offence.[157] Thus, the provision of the *Code Pénal* for negligence committed by corporations provides for an even wider scope for the criminalisation of healthcare malpractice.

On the contrary, English criminal law always requires at least gross negligence that leads to death for criminal liability. And as we will see in the next chapter, the CPS tends to interpret that standard in a restrictive way, which narrows the scope of criminalisation of negligence even more.[158] In English criminal law,

154 J Bell, *French Legal Cultures* (Cambridge: Cambridge University Press 2008), x.

155 Cass Crim 10/02/2009 n° 08-80.679 Bull crim 2009, n° 33.

156 CA Nancy, 29/03/2001. Even though the decision was quashed by the *Cour de Cassation*, this may indicate that lower courts are also ready to admit a large scope in relation to causation; Cass Crim 26/03/2002 mars 2002 no 01-83.416.

157 Assemblée Nationale, above n25 at 37; Y Mayaud, above n24 at 206.

158 See chapter 3.

causation will be proved if *but for* the defendant's conduct, the result would not have happened, and the cause must be more than minimal.[159] Although, in theory, causation in French and English criminal law seems to rely on the same general principles, in practice, English courts have a more restrictive approach with regard to causation than French courts, as, generally, a *but for* cause will not be sufficient, and a significant cause will need to be proved.[160] In the healthcare context, only a breach of duty that 'caused or significantly contributed to the death' would be criminalised, which would be the equivalent of a direct causal link in French criminal law. However, in England and Wales, that breach of duty would require proof of gross negligence to be criminalised. Similarly, under the CMCHA 2007, a corporation can be liable for manslaughter only if 'the way in which its activities are managed or organised by its senior management is a *substantial element* in the breach' (emphasis added).[161]

While French courts interpret causation in a broad sense, English prosecution authorities are restrictive in their interpretation of a causal link in healthcare negligence cases. For instance, a surgeon who had proceeded to a non-essential operation on a patient who was at serious pre-operative risk escaped prosecution, even though the patient suffered a cardiac arrest during the surgery.[162] Similarly, a midwife had committed serious omissions in the management of pre-labour and labour, notably the lack of treatment of worsening symptoms of the mother for two days, which caused the baby's death. In both cases, prosecution was not considered feasible because experts could not establish causation.[163] Both cases would have led to criminal proceedings in France, with the courts finding an indirect causal link and *faute caractérisée* on the part of the defendants.

Conclusion

French criminal law, based on the civil law tradition of codes, provides for a wider criminalisation of negligent conduct than does English criminal law, based on common law precedents and scattered statutory offences. This chapter has shown that this has an impact on how healthcare professionals and institutions are criminalised for negligent wrongdoing. French criminal offences penalise a wider range of conduct, including simple mistakes which English law does not penalise. It also encompasses various wrongdoings which have so far not given rise to prosecutions in England and Wales in the medical context. Until very recently, medical professionals would only be subject to criminal prosecutions under the offence of GNM, whilst medical professionals who had caused injury

159 *R v Cato* (1976) 62 Cr App R 41, 45.
160 *R v Kennedy (No 2)* [2008] UKHL 1 AC 269, at 274.
161 S. 1 (3) CMCHA 2007.
162 D Griffiths, A Sanders, above n6 at 141.
163 Ibid.

to patients would be absolved of criminal liability. The extension of the offences of wilful neglect/ill-treatment to all patients in receipt of medical care means that medical professionals and providers can now be prosecuted for conduct which did not result in death, mirroring the French model; although these offences require a higher threshold for culpability than gross negligence. The rules on causation in French criminal law and their interpretation by the courts also create a greater scope for criminalising health professionals and institutions who have indirectly contributed to the damage, with examples showing that senior doctors may be vicariously (criminally) liable for the fault of junior doctors. In England and Wales, there is no record of successful prosecutions of senior doctors being charged for the fault of a junior or trainee doctor. The harm would have to have been caused by their own wrongdoing. The following chapter will discuss the differences in criminal procedure in France and England and Wales to demonstrate that features of the French inquisitorial process and features of the English adversarial process have a significant influence on how cases of healthcare malpractice are decided in both countries.

3 Criminal proceedings for healthcare negligence in France and England and Wales

Introduction

Whilst key differences in substantive criminal law help to explain the French and English approaches to the criminalisation of healthcare negligence, this chapter demonstrates that key differences in criminal procedure are factors which influence the use of the criminal law in relation to healthcare negligence even more than substantive criminal law. As explained in Chapter 1, fundamental differences in the legal traditions of the two systems (inquisitorial and adversarial) play a crucial role in the criminalisation of healthcare negligence. The French inquisitorial system is characterised by an emphasis on the pre-trial phase of the procedure and pre-trial investigations conducted by a *juge d'instruction* (JI), an investigative judge who has wide coercive powers to conduct investigations, as well as a strong involvement of victims in the pre-trial stage of the proceedings. In France, victims can join civil claims for compensation to criminal complaints and consequently take an active part in the launching of criminal prosecutions; they are then called *parties civiles* (civil parties). The English adversarial system, on the contrary, is more focused on the trial phase, characterised by the confrontation of two equal parties, with a jury deciding on the verdict, and where victims cannot have such an influential role in launching criminal prosecutions, or benefit from the evidence collected by a JI.

In this chapter, I argue that the involvement of victims at an early stage of the proceedings, the role of JIs and the absence of juries in criminal proceedings for offences which penalise negligent conduct are factors which have a substantial role in explaining the greater number of prosecutions leading to convictions of medical professionals and health officials in France. It is shown, however, that on the whole, both types of procedure also bear some similarities. For instance, the role of prosecutors in both jurisdictions is much the same. The role of the Crown Prosecution Service (CPS) in England and Wales can be compared to the role of the *Ministère Public*[1] (MP) in France and shares similar aspects with the French JI. The police and experts have the same role in both types of procedure. But

1 The public prosecution service may be called *Ministère Public* or *Parquet* in French.

DOI: 10.4324/9781315099170-3

Table 3.1 Comparative table of decision-making bodies involved in criminal proceedings for non-intentional offences against the person in France and England and Wales

	France	*England and Wales*
Prosecution	▪ *Parties civiles* ▪ *Ministère Public*	▪ Victims: private prosecution (much rarer); or ▪ Prosecuting authority (e.g. Crown Prosecution Service or Health and Safety Executive)
Pre-trial investigations	▪ Police + *juge d'instruction*	▪ Police + prosecuting authority (e.g. Crown Prosecution Service or Health and Safety Executive)
Trial	▪ Magistrates	▪ Magistrates ▪ Jury

as is explained in this chapter, the willingness to investigate and prosecute cases of healthcare negligence is much stronger in France, and this has to do with the selected features mentioned above, as well as the legal culture of the jurisdiction. The above table sets out the differences and similarities between the two procedures at each stage of the proceedings.

The role of victims

Constitution de partie civile[2]

The French and English criminal procedures are based on two distinct systems. For comparative lawyers, France is the archetype of an inquisitorial procedure, and the system used in England and Wales was once a pure representation of an adversarial criminal procedure.[3] The inquisitorial model (from Latin *inquisitio*, meaning 'search') is founded on the intervention and supervision of an authority in the criminal proceedings, which are directed to 'searching for the truth',[4] which 'will be as nearly objective as possible', while the adversarial model is underpinned by a confrontation between two parties 'before a passive

2 *Constitutions de partie civile* are civil claims for compensation brought in criminal courts in French criminal proceedings. Victims who join *constitutions de partie civile* are called *parties civiles* because they are parties to the civil action in the criminal proceedings. Article 2-3 Code de Procédure Pénale (CPP); B Bouloc, H Matsopoulou, *Droit pénal général et procédure pénal* (21e edn, Paris: Sirey 2018), 179, 197.

3 J Hodgson, 'The Police, the Prosecutor and the Juge d'Instruction', (2001) 41(2) *The British Journal of Criminology* 344; F Pakes, *Comparative Criminal Justice* (4th edn, London: Routledge 2019), 86–90.

4 *Recherche de la vérité* (search for the truth) is a basic notion in French criminal law. It implies that the MP and the JI work on finding the true facts of the case, by not being influenced by anyone's testimony; R Van Ruymbeke, *Le juge d'instruction* (Paris: Presses Universitaires de

and impartial judge [and] a jury . . . pronouncing one version of events to be the truth'.[5] The French inquisitorial criminal process is focused on the pre-trial phase of the procedure, which aims at 'discovering the truth',[6] involving 'one central (judicial) figure representing the public interest . . . which might inculpate or exculpate any named suspect',[7] whereas the English adversarial system puts more emphasis on the trial phase of the proceedings.[8] Even though both systems aim to protect society and punish wrongful conduct, French criminal procedure reflects a victim-oriented approach.[9] This is evidenced by the fact that victims of criminal offences in France have the right to join *constitutions de parties civiles* to criminal complaints. As a consequence they can take part in the launching of the *action publique* (public prosecution) and are parties to the civil action in the proceedings. In England and Wales, 'the police and the CPS do not prosecute for the victim. They prosecute for the state. Offences are offences against society (not against the victim) and the consequences of conviction is punishment not compensation (although the reality is not this straightforward)'.[10]

Although victims have been given a more active role in criminal proceedings in the English model in recent years, features of the French model still account for the greater number of prosecutions for healthcare malpractice in France. On the contrary, criminal prosecutions for medical manslaughter are lower in number in England and Wales, as victims cannot themselves 'launch' criminal prosecutions.[11] At most, they can be involved in the investigations, but they do not influence the process until sentencing.[12]

However, both systems have acquired features of one another. For instance, in France, there have been reforms to reinforce the rights of the suspect during custody, which is usually a feature of the adversarial type of procedure.[13] Since the creation of the CPS in 1986, English criminal procedure may have moved a little

---

France 2016), 36–37; J Bell, *French Legal Cultures* (Cambridge: Cambridge University Press 2008), 111.

5 N Jorg, S Field, C Brants, 'Are Inquisitorial and Adversarial Systems Converging?' in C Harding et al. (eds), *Criminal Justice in Europe: A Comparative Study* (Oxford: Oxford University Press 1995), 42–43.

6 However, we will see that trials in the *Tribunal correctionnel* involve adversarial elements.

7 J Hodgson, 'Hierarchy, Bureaucracy, and Ideology in French Criminal Justice: Some Empirical Observations', (2002) 29(2) *Journal of Law and Society* 227, 230.

8 N Jorg, S Field, C Brants, above n5 at 52.

9 Sénat, *Les délits non intentionnels-La Loi Fauchon: 5 ans après* (Actes du colloque, 1er mars 2006, Palais du Luxembourg), 58.

10 A Sanders, 'Victims' Voices, Victims' Interests and Criminal Justice in the Healthcare Setting', in D Griffiths, A Sanders (eds), *Medicine, Crime and Society* (Cambridge: Cambridge University Press 2013), 83.

11 Ibid.

12 Ibid.

13 Loi n° 2000-516 du 15 juin 2000 renforçant la protection de la présomption d'innocence et les droits des victimes.

closer to the French system, although it remains mostly adversarial.[14] Furthermore, although the introduction of features of the French model of *partie civile* may find resistance in England and Wales,[15] it is interesting to note here that the involvement of victims in criminal proceedings originally came from England and Wales and travelled across the Channel, as 'the inquisitorial tradition originally meant a powerful prosecutor, whose legal muscle represented the power in criminal justice of an autocratic king'.[16]

In France, an alleged victim of healthcare negligence can choose to either sue for compensation in civil or administrative courts (depending on whether the defendant worked in private or public practice) or lodge a criminal complaint with or without *constitution de partie civile*. If the victim chooses to join a *constitution de partie civile* to a criminal complaint, the *action publique* will be launched if the MP is in favour of prosecution.[17] To bring a civil claim for compensation before a criminal court, the victim has to demonstrate that the offence is punishable by criminal law and that it attacked a public interest, and s/he has to show that s/he suffered a personal harm in direct relation to the offence.[18] It is argued that notably in cases of healthcare malpractice, *constitutions de partie civile* usually occur after the MP has informed the victims that they will not pursue the case as they do not consider it serious enough to merit punishment.[19] Then, the MP decides whether the case should be brought before a court or be resolved in an alternative way such as offender-victim mediation.[20] In serious and complex cases (which generally include cases of healthcare negligence), the MP will decide to order an investigation by the JI.[21]

In England and Wales, a victim cannot join a civil claim for damages to a prosecution even in the case of a private prosecution, which is a rare and expensive process[22] as the victim will have to bear the cost of the proceedings 'out of his own pocket'.[23] In England and Wales, therefore, 'the police will be alerted

14 What is interesting to note, however, is that the creation of the CPS was a demonstration of a move towards a more centralised justice system, which used to characterise the inquisitorial system; see N Jorg, S Field, C Brants, above n5 at 46; J Hodgson, above n7 at 227.

15 See, for instance, JR Spencer, 'The Victims and the Prosecutor', in A Bottoms, J Roberts (eds), *Hearing the Victims: Adversarial Justice, Crime Victims and the State* (Cullompton: Willan Publishing 2010), 153.

16 Ibid at 157.

17 Article 3 CPP; B Bouloc, *Procédure Pénale* (27e edn, Paris: Dalloz 2019), 579.

18 C Elliott, *French Criminal Law* (Cullompton: Willan 2001), 33.

19 J Guigue, 'Les inconvénients de la pénalisation du droit de la santé', (2008) *Revue de droit sanitaire et social* 36; B Bouloc, above n17 at 579.

20 F Pakes, above n3 at 80. As mentioned in Chapter 1, there is since 2002 an alternative way to claim compensation for healthcare accidents in France via the ONIAM scheme, which will be discussed in Chapter 6.

21 P Verrest, 'The French Public Prosecution Service', (2000) 8(3) *European Journal of Crime, Criminal Law and Criminal Justice* 210, 213.

22 A Sanders, above n10 at 83; C Van Den Wyngaert, *Criminal Procedure Systems in the European Community* (London: Butterworths 1993), 96–97; JR Spencer, above n15 at 145.

23 J Spencer, above n15 at 145.

to a suspected case of gross negligence manslaughter involving a health care professional from one or more of a number of sources – these include coroners, Clinical Commissioning Groups, the Care Quality Commission, NHS England, families of the deceased patient or possibly journalists'.[24]

Victims and their family may only get a criminal investigation if the police listen or the coroner 'pushes' the case, but the police do not have to investigate no matter how much victims want to prosecute.[25] In England and Wales, 'there is no requirement that the prosecution take any particular heed of the wishes or interests of victims, receive information from victims, or provide information to victims'.[26] However, it is acknowledged that 'the families of victims seem to be increasingly engaged in inquests and in the work of coroners. Coroners and the police feel increasingly obliged to respond positively to the concerns of families'.[27] Victims are, for instance, informed of the progress of their cases via Victim Liaison Units.[28] Nevertheless, victims do not usually influence investigations conducted by the police in the same manner as do *parties civiles* in France in the healthcare negligence context.

If an alleged victim of healthcare negligence in France decides to bring a claim for compensation before a civil court, s/he will not be able to bring a civil action before a criminal court according to the maxim *electa una via, non datur recursus ad alteram*, which literally means that once someone has chosen one way, s/he cannot choose the other.[29] This provides an important explanation for the victims' choice to use the criminal process in cases of medical negligence, as joining civil claims for compensation to criminal complaints may offer victims advantages over suing a medical professional in a civil court. Notably, if an alleged victim of medical negligence brings a legal action before a civil court and his/her action is not successful, s/he would have lost the opportunity to use the criminal process. There will of course be cases where a criminal complaint will be dismissed, if, for instance, the causal link between the offence and the harm cannot be proved, or if bringing a prosecution is not in the public interest (e.g. there is insufficient evidence that a criminal offence was committed).

Advantages for victims of medical negligence

In France, from the point of view of victims, the criminal process offers many advantages over civil or administrative procedures where victims would only

24 Department of Health, *Gross Negligence Manslaughter in Healthcare, The Report of a Rapid Policy Review* (Department of Health, June 2018) (Williams Review), 19.

25 A Sanders, above n10 at 83.

26 Ibid.

27 Ibid at 89.

28 A Sanders, 'The CPS-30 Years on', (2016) 2 *Criminal Law Review* 90.

29 R Van Ruymbeke, above n4 at 18; F Vignaud, 'La judiciarisation de la médecine, comparaison entre droit français et droit américain', in D Dreyfuss, F Lemaire, H Outin (eds), *La judiciarisation de la médecine* (Paris: Médecine-Sciences Flammarion 2004), 7.

receive financial compensation, should their action be successful. In the criminal court, however, if a healthcare professional is convicted of a criminal offence, the victim will receive some degree of retribution, as well as civil compensation. In the French criminal process, compensation is awarded on the same basis as in civil proceedings, and the standard of proof for the civil claim in the criminal court is the same as in civil courts.[30] Thus, the amount of civil damages awarded in criminal proceedings is equivalent to what would be awarded in civil proceedings for the same injury.[31] *Dommages-intérêts* (civil damages) take into account bodily, material and moral damages caused by the defendant to the victim and his/her close relatives.[32] Since 2000, civil compensation can still be awarded to victims by civil courts, even if the defendant was acquitted by criminal courts, if civil liability is found on the part of the defendant.[33] The *Loi Fauchon*[34] tried to ensure that victims are compensated for the harm caused even when no criminal fault is found on the part of the defendant.[35]

However, access to compensation may not be the principal factor motivating *parties civiles*. There is evidence that victims of medical negligence who choose to use the criminal process do not usually want to get financial compensation. In France, alleged victims of medical negligence choose the criminal process for several reasons. Criminal proceedings are mostly free of charge, whereas other proceedings entail expert costs.[36] Expert-related expenses and criminal evidence-related expenses are provided by the justice system.[37] Hiring a lawyer is optional but strongly recommended to facilitate proceedings for victims. In a civil or administrative proceeding, the victim would have to provide evidence and hire experts to support his/her claim. And criminal proceedings are said to be quicker than civil or administrative proceedings.[38] This also allows victims with no financial means to fund their claim and access justice. In the English system, since the enactment of the Legal Aid, Sentencing and Punishment of Offenders Act 2012, it is no longer possible to get legal aid for clinical negligence claims except

30 JR Spencer, MA Brajeux, 'Criminal Liability for Negligence-A Lesson from Across the Channel?' (2010) 59(1) *International and Comparative Law Quarterly* 1, 10; D Thouvenin, *La responsabilité médicale, Analyse des données statistiques disponibles et des arrêts rendus par la cour de cassation et le conseil d'état de 1984 à 1992* (Paris: Médecine-Sciences Flammarion 1999), 12.

31 JR Spencer, MA Brajeux, above n30 at 30.

32 D Thouvenin, above n30 at 12, 48.

33 Article 4-1 CPP.

34 See Chapters 1 and 2.

35 M Tapia, 'Décadence et fin éventuelle du principe d'identité des fautes pénales et civiles', (2003) 67 *Gazette du Palais* 2.

36 Ibid; Sénat, above n9 at 58.

37 M Daury-Fauveau, *La responsabilité pénale du médecin* (Bordeaux: Les études hospitalières 2003), 45; Sénat, above n9 at 58.

38 Assemblée Nationale, *Rapport n° 2266 fait au nom de la commission des lois constitutionnelles, de la législation et de l'administration générale de la République sur la proposition de loi, adoptée par le Sénat, tendant à préciser la définition des délits non intentionnels*, par M René Dosière, 22 mars 2000, 5.

where the negligence would have caused 'a neurological injury to an individual' which would have resulted in the individual being disabled, but only in his/her mother's womb, during his/her birth or during his/her first 8 weeks of life.[39] Children and adults who have been injured outside of these strict categories are therefore left in a difficult situation where obtaining compensation may prove to be a very costly process.

Griffiths and Sanders' research found that in England and Wales, victims often want to use the criminal process because there is a lack of other means of accountability.[40] Victims usually want explanations, rather than retribution, and the investigation itself often offers them the level of closure they need. Similarly, the main motivation of victims of healthcare negligence to use the criminal process in France is that it offers them transparency on what happened thanks to investigations conducted by the JI, who 'searches for the truth', and victims argue that they use the criminal process so that similar negligence does not occur in the future.[41]

As will be more fully discussed below, means of investigation are greater in criminal proceedings than in civil or administrative proceedings in France; so victims have more opportunities to understand what went wrong in the healthcare setting if they engage in criminal proceedings.[42] In French criminal procedure, victims' and defendants' advocates can obtain the investigative/prosecution file after their first hearing.[43] On the contrary, in England and Wales, victims have no access to the police and prosecution files.[44]

Scholars agree that victims choose to use the criminal process for the reasons stated above.[45] But one commentator argues that the only reason why victims in France choose to use the criminal process over other procedures is for pure vengeance.[46] He claims that the great powers of investigation of the JI and the 'easiness' of the procedure in terms of evidence and burden of proof are not factors that influence the preference of the victims for the criminal law because civil procedure provides similar advantages in terms of *recherche de la vérité*.[47] However, an investigating judge who had worked on medical negligence cases disagrees, arguing that victims choose the criminal process mostly because it gives

39 Sch 1 para 23 Legal Aid, Sentencing and Punishment of Offenders Act 2012.

40 D Griffiths, A Sanders, 'The Road to the Dock: Prosecution Decision-making in Medical Manslaughter Cases', in D Griffiths, A Sanders (eds), above n10 at 154–155.

41 M-O Bertella Geffroy, 'L'évolution des rapport justice-santé', (2004) 4(5) *Les Tribunes de la santé* 28.

42 Assemblée Nationale, above n38 at 36.

43 Article 114 al 4 CPP.

44 A Sanders, above n10 at 145–146.

45 A Laude, B Mathieu, D Tabuteau, *Droit de la santé* (3e edn, Paris: Presses Universitaires de France 2012), 480; M Daury-Fauveau, above n37 at 45; N Carrère, 'Le juge pénal et les professionnels de santé', (2008) 283 *Gazette du Palais* 23.

46 G Memeteau, *Traité de la responsabilité médicale* (Bordeaux: Les études hospitalières 1996), 168.

47 Ibid.

them the 'truth', which they cannot obtain from using civil or administrative procedures, or in adversarial proceedings.[48] The judge affirms that JIs conduct an in-depth investigation, which gives victims the transparency they need, whereas in civil or administrative proceedings, they must rely on each party's documents, which do not necessarily analyse the case in-depth.[49] Victims, though they do not necessarily admit it, do use the criminal process for vengeance and retribution sometimes in healthcare negligence cases, although it is not their primary goal.[50] There is evidence that victims may sometimes want to see someone being held accountable, especially when something seriously wrong has occurred, and this explains their preference for the criminal process in France.[51] Moreover, victims also want proceedings to be 'public' and 'mediatised'.[52] French civil and administrative proceedings only offer a mostly 'written' procedure and short pleadings with no witnesses.[53] Criminal proceedings are more likely to be subject to media coverage.[54]

It is argued that in England and Wales too, there is increasing 'public pressure, particularly from victims, to invoke the criminal process' in the healthcare context.[55] This may result in 'more police investigations and protracted inquests'.[56] However, the number of prosecutions still seems 'lower than expected'.[57] It is therefore submitted that if victims in England and Wales had the right to join civil claims for compensation in criminal courts as do French victims, the use of the criminal process would be greater, even though there are other factors at play in healthcare negligence cases which have been explained in the previous chapter (notably, the difficulty of establishing causation and the uncertainty of the gross negligence test in English law).[58]

The role of prosecutors

The decision to prosecute healthcare professionals, officials or institutions for 'negligence' offences rests on the MP in France and the CPS in England and Wales. The Health and Safety Executive (HSE) has a role in investigating and prosecuting offences under the Health and Safety at Work Act 1974

48 M-O Bertella-Geffroy, above n41.
49 Ibid.
50 Interview with A (Cambridge, 3 February 2011), 15.
51 See, for instance, criminal proceedings arising out of the HIV-contaminated blood scandal, discussed in chapter 4. Sénat, above n9 at 57; Assemblée Nationale, above n38 at 5; A Keller, 'We Just Wanted the Law to Recognise Our Mum Had Been Killed', *Lichfield Mercury* (12 February 2009).
52 Sénat, above n9 at 57.
53 Ibid.
54 Assemblée Nationale, above n38 at 21.
55 D Griffiths, A Sanders, above n40 at 146.
56 Ibid.
57 Ibid.
58 Ibid at 140–144.

(HSWA 1974) but at present does not prosecute individuals in the healthcare context.

The MP and the CPS have a similar role in cases of healthcare negligence in France and England and Wales. In France, the MP, when deciding whether or not to prosecute, will look at whether the offender breached the law (committed an offence) and if a prosecution is in the public interest.[59] In England and Wales, the CPS will also look at the appropriateness of the prosecution. The CPS decides whether to prosecute a case by raising two questions: the sufficiency of the evidence and the 'public interest' criterion, comparably to the French MP.[60] The requirement of sufficiency of the evidence is fulfilled when it seems that it is more likely than not that the defendant will be convicted and the evidence is admissible and reliable.[61] Then the case has to pass the public interest stage. Usually a case will pass this stage when it is of such character that a prosecution is required in the public interest.[62] Usually in England and Wales, the CPS considers that a case should be prosecuted only when there is evidence of blameworthiness.[63]

In France, the MP is generally very reluctant to prosecute, and JIs have a great role in 'pushing' cases of healthcare negligence to court.[64] In England and Wales, it has also been found that the CPS is cautious in its decision to prosecute medical professionals for gross negligence manslaughter (GNM) and there are no equivalents to the JIs to encourage prosecutors to prosecute.[65] Griffiths and Sanders have found that 'prosecutors seem to be searching for something beyond what we might term "threshold gross negligence" in order to prosecute', including the fact that they do not see any reasonable prospect of conviction by a jury.[66] This occurs 'because of the vagueness and circularity of the "gross negligence" test'.[67] As will be explained below, no juries are present at criminal trials for alleged medical negligence in France, and the central role of judges explains the higher rate of convictions for negligence offences.

As highlighted in the previous chapter, the scope of a criminal prosecution for negligence in France is much broader than in England and Wales, as the MP can prosecute a defendant for committing simple negligence (when there is a direct causal link between negligence and harm), whereas in England and

59 Article 40-1 CPP; B Bouloc, above n17 at 580–582; V Dervieux, 'The French System', in M Delmas-Marty, JR Spencer (eds), *European Criminal Procedures* (Cambridge: Cambridge University Press 2002), 232.

60 Director of Public Prosecution, Code for Crown Prosecutors, 26 October 2018.

61 N Padfield, J Bild, *Text and Materials on the Criminal Justice Process* (5th edn, London: Routledge 2015), 186; Director of Public Prosecution, above n60.

62 Director of Public Prosecution, above n60.

63 D Griffiths, A Sanders, above n40 at 126.

64 D Cartron, 'Quelle place pour la victime d'un accident médical devant le juge pénal?' (2013) 5(27) *Responsabilité civile et assurance* 4–5.

65 D Griffiths, A Sanders, above n40.

66 Ibid at 145.

67 Ibid.

Wales, the CPS could only prosecute gross negligence (that resulted in death) until April 2015, when the offences of wilful neglect and ill-treatment were extended to all care professionals.[68] It has been argued that 'the definition of [GNM] depends on the use of discretion by prosecutors'.[69] On the contrary, in France, if the investigations conducted by the JI showed evidence that the conduct matched any of the negligence offences in the *Code Pénal*, and if the JI has suggested charges, prosecutors might have less freedom in the interpretation of the offence.[70] According to Griffiths and Sanders' empirical research, which reviewed 75 files referred to the Special Crime and Counter Terrorism Division[71] (SCCTD) for medical manslaughter in England and Wales, only four cases were prosecuted, resulting in two convictions. Their research showed that the CPS is reluctant to prosecute medical manslaughter unless there is strong evidence of subjective recklessness in healthcare negligence cases.[72] Moreover, CPS prosecution files often contain the likely views of the jury on the case, because of the 'awareness that judges and juries do not like having these cases (particularly involving doctors) in front of them' in courts.[73] So the CPS will prosecute only when it is likely that the jury will find the defendant guilty, which is a rare occurrence. In France, approximately 33% of investigated cases of healthcare malpractice are prosecuted, whereas in England and Wales only 5% proceed to prosecution. Griffiths and Sanders' research has also shown that the CPS considered that in 27% of cases (20 cases) there was no breach of duty, 13 cases involved negligence but failed to reach the 'gross' threshold, and 33 cases lacked a sufficient causal link or expert evidence was not strong enough.[74] The reluctance of the CPS to prosecute means that the difference in practice in the use of criminal law in cases of healthcare negligence in France and England and Wales is even greater. As Sanders argues, 'the CPS is not, and is structurally incapable of being, a neutral arbiter between defendant and police. It was never given the type of power or constitutional position enjoyed by prosecutors in inquisitorial systems'.[75]

68 M Brazier, A Alghrani, 'Fatal Medical Malpractice and Criminal Liability', (2009) 25(2) *Journal of Professional Negligence* 51.

69 O Quick, 'Prosecuting 'Gross' Medical Negligence: Manslaughter, Discretion and the Crown Prosecution Service', (2006) 33(3) *Journal of Law and Society* 421, 429.

70 D Griffiths, A Sanders, above n40; O Quick, 'Medical Killing: Need for a Specific Offence?' in CMV Clarkson, S Cunningham (eds), *Criminal Liability for Non-Aggressive Death* (Aldershot: Ashgate 2008), 161.

71 This section of the CPS is in charge of special crimes including gross negligence 'medical manslaughter' cases in England and Wales, assisted suicide and corporate manslaughter. See www.cps.gov.uk/special-crime-and-counter-terrorism-division-scctd, accessed 20 January 2020.

72 D Griffiths, A Sanders, above n40 at 143.

73 Ibid at 135.

74 D Griffiths, A Sanders, above n40 at 138–139, 142.

75 A Sanders, above n28 at 96.

Reinforcing the difficulty of the CPS to interpret the gross negligence test, resulting in few cases being prosecuted in this area, Sanders argues that

> the evidential test is never precise, and in gross negligence manslaughter cases it is very far from precise. In fact, the concept of 'gross negligence' is so vague (and potentially over-inclusive) that, as Quick observes, the courts have endorsed CPS judgements that the presence or absence of subjective recklessness can help to determine whether or not there is gross negligence.[76]

Furthermore, as explained in Chapter 2, the interpretation of rules on causation by French courts has influenced the number of cases of medical negligence which will lead to successful convictions. Interpretation of rules on causation also has a role in the pre-trial stage of the procedure, because French JIs and prosecution services may find causation more readily than the CPS. Griffiths and Sanders found that in England and Wales, 44% of cases of medical manslaughter which they had reviewed had failed on causation.

In order to provide a fuller picture of prosecutions in the context of healthcare negligence, it is worth looking briefly at the role of the HSE in that context. The CPS and the HSE work together in cases of work-related deaths in particular when there is evidence that a serious criminal offence or a health and safety offence has been committed. According to their protocol for liaison in work-related deaths, they have to work together to investigate thoroughly, and to prosecute appropriately, those responsible for work-related deaths in England and Wales.[77] It is suggested that the HSE only prosecute the worst cases, and thus the conviction rate is high.[78] In 2018/19, the HSE prosecuted 400 cases (including non-medical cases), of which 364 resulted in a conviction; this is a high conviction rate of approximately 91% (which is much higher than the usual rate of conviction in this type of cases when prosecuted by the CPS).[79] In practice, the HSE do not usually get involved in healthcare cases because of a lack of resources, although in theory they could. So, many cases which should be investigated are not.

The role of investigators

The role of investigators also has an influence on the number of prosecutions for medical negligence, as well as on how many cases go to trial. In France,

76 A Sanders, above n10 at 90.

77 Health and Safety Executive, *Work-related Deaths, a Protocol for Liaison (England and Wales)*, February 2016, 5.

78 C Wells, 'Medical Manslaughter: Organisational Liability', in D Griffiths, A Sanders (eds), above n10, 197.

79 Health and Safety Executive, *Health and Safety at Work, Summary Statistics for Great Britain 2019*, October 2019, 11.

although preliminary investigations may be undertaken by the police in most cases, it appears that in the context of healthcare negligence, the police have a limited role and investigations are usually conducted by one JI on his/her own (although several JIs might be in charge of the same investigation successively).[80] The *instruction* (criminal investigation conducted by the JI) aims to discover the 'truth' and to determine whether the case should go to court. Investigations conducted by the JI start following either a demand from the MP or a *constitution de partie civile*.[81] The JI *may* (i.e. is not obliged to) choose to investigate in cases of *délits*, which include all criminal offences used in the context of healthcare negligence.[82] The *parties civiles* and the MP can appeal his/her decision not to investigate.[83] In most cases of healthcare negligence, the JI *will* investigate following prosecution by the MP, especially if the case requires expert evidence.[84]

This part of French criminal procedure has been subject to debate in the past two decades, and reforms have been suggested in order to restrict the powers of JIs.[85] Until 2007, all *constitutions de partie civile* were received by the JI. Since 2007, the JI has to send the *constitutions de partie civile* to the MP so that they can either order an investigation or close the case, hence giving more decision-making power to the MP.[86] It is claimed that this has reduced the number of prosecutions of healthcare professionals for negligence because the MP, much like the CPS, is generally more reluctant to prosecute cases of healthcare malpractice than JIs are.[87] This was part of a reform that aimed to limit the role and powers of the JI and give the MP a stronger role.[88]

JIs are considered to have wide coercive powers.[89] According to the *Code de Procédure Pénale*, a JI can carry out *any* 'acts of procedure' allowed by law, which may be useful for establishing the truth.[90] A JI may, for instance, visit the scene of a crime, search, collect objects or documents, hear evidence from witnesses and interrogate the victim(s) and suspect(s).[91] JIs can also order the arrest of the

80 Investigations are conducted by one JI, but s/he may ask for help from the police or experts; V Dervieux, above n59 at 234; I Jamin, 'La responsabilité pénale en milieu de soin: une préoccupation réelle, une menace relative?' (2009) *Actualité Juridique Pénal* 340.

81 Article 51 CPP.

82 Article 79 CPP.

83 B Bouloc, above n17 at 613.

84 M-O Bertella-Geffroy, above n41 at 28.

85 G Gaetner, 'Les juges d'instruction sont les mal aimés du système pénal français', *L'Express* (8 January 2009).

86 Article 86 al 1 CPP.

87 Article 85 CPP; 86 CPP; M-O Bertella-Geffroy, above n41 at 23.

88 Commission Justice pénale et Droits de l'homme, *La mise en état des affaires pénales*, Rapport final (Paris: La Documentation française 1991), 126–136.

89 R Van Ruymbeke, above n4 at 48; J Hodgson, above n7.

90 Article 81 CPP.

91 Article 92 CPP; Article 97 CPP; Article 101 CPP; Article 114 al 1 CPP.

suspect(s)[92] and use the police or experts to conduct the investigations and gather evidence through *commission rogatoire*.[93,94]

After analysing the evidence gathered during the investigations, the JI can then ask for the suspect to be prosecuted through an act called *mise en examen*[95] and request charges to be used against the defendant if the JI considers that there is sufficient evidence that an offence has been committed. Once the JI has decided whether the case should be sent to court, or the charges dropped, the case goes to the MP. The MP may then decide whether to prosecute the defendant. The conclusion of the JI on the case may greatly affect the decision of the MP, as charges suggested by the JI may be followed by the MP, who then may rely on the information collected by the JI during the investigations to decide on prosecution.[96]

The impact of the JI on criminal proceedings involving allegedly negligent healthcare professionals is largely due to his/her power to search and collect documents.[97] This is particularly true in complex cases where the error or negligence was the result of a chain of events and decisions. The JI may analyse in detail all the factors which led to the 'incident' and cast light on who was responsible. The JI may also choose to proceed to a *mise en examen* for other healthcare professionals who were involved in the chain of events, thus making the scope of criminal prosecution very broad.[98]

In England and Wales, criminal investigations are not conducted by a single judge with wide coercive powers. Rather, when a healthcare related death occurs, investigations may be conducted by coroners and the police.[99] When the police begin an investigation, 'they either refer the case to the CPS for advice or investigate fully and then refer the case to the CPS'.[100] It has been found that

> criminal investigations into medical deaths have three main sources: relatives making complaints to the police directly, a hospital contacting the police or a coroner becoming concerned that there is something unnatural or suspicious about a death and referring it to Criminal Investigation Department (CID).[101]

The role of the police in England and Wales is comparable to the role of the police in France. They may arrest or question the defendant, or conduct searches,

92 Article 122 CPP. However, there is no evidence that this may happen in healthcare negligence cases.
93 This is a document through which the JI delegates certain acts of investigating to police officers; Article 81 al 4 CPP.
94 Article 14 al 2 CPP; Article 151 CPP.
95 '*Mise en examen*' is an act of the JI by which s/he requests that the case be pursued as there is enough evidence of criminal wrongdoing on the part of the defendant. Article 80-1 al 1 CPP.
96 M-O Bertella-Geffroy, above n41.
97 Ibid.
98 Ibid.
99 D Griffiths, A Sanders, above n40 at 118.
100 Ibid.
101 Ibid.

but they may not decide on the prosecution of offenders or request charges like JIs in France.[102]

In the past two decades in England and Wales, the police have been more pressured to investigate deaths, notably resulting from an obligation stemming from Article 2 of the European Convention of Human Rights, 'which states that everyone has a 'right to life', and which

> has been interpreted to mean that states have a duty to investigate deaths that are unnatural, unexpected or suspicious, as well as to protect life. It follows that public bodies (such as coroners, the police and the CPS) are obliged to conduct extensive investigations to establish who may have been responsible for any deaths.[103]

'"Right to life" obligations and associated coronial investigations' may lead to many cases being 'investigated more thoroughly than would appear necessary'.[104] Sanders suggests that

> even without the pressures on the police created by Article 2 the expectations of victims would pressure the police into more extensive investigations than would otherwise have happened. Either way, the end result is a significant effort put into inquiries that rarely lead to a tangible result. These are resources that could be used in arguably more productive ways.[105]

Sanders further explains that 'many victims (that is, the bereaved families) understandably want to know if a person or organisation is to blame for a death, and a coronial investigation, for example, is in principle a good way of discovering this'.[106] Coroners have an important function in improving patient safety, and in providing justice to families and the public.[107] However, contrary to JIs in France, 'in practice, coroners have very limited resources',[108] and there is a 'lack of consistency about which cases coroners report to the police'.[109] Although victims in the English criminal process cannot be civil parties to a criminal prosecution, in recent years, coroners and the police have felt 'progressively more obliged to respond positively to the concerns of families',[110] and some cases are

102 Ss. 1, 8, 24, 54 Police and Criminal Evidence Act 1984.
103 S. 1 Coroners and Justice Act 2009; A Sanders, above n11 at 87–88.
104 D Griffiths, A Sanders, above n40 at 139.
105 A Sanders, above n10 at 88.
106 Ibid.
107 P Thornton (Chief Coroner), 'The Coroner System in the 21st Century', The Howard League for Penal Reform–Parmoor Lecture 2012, October 2012, 7.
108 A Sanders, above n10 at 88.
109 Williams Review, above n24 at 24.
110 A Sanders, above n10 at 89.

'pursued at length because of family pressure on the police and/or because of media interest'.[111]

Although 'the combination of human rights culture with victim awareness seems to be a major influence increasing the volume and thoroughness of police investigations', the police have less means and resources or do not gather as much evidence as JIs in France, and may not investigate certain cases that would be pursued in France. For example, the police closed a case where there was evidence that the death of the patient was a result of the doctor's negligence, because 'it was likely to take up more resources that [they] could bring to bear on it'.[112] Furthermore, in England and Wales, 'the police are not obliged to investigate everything, nor anything in particular, nor refer to other authorities if they decide to take no action about something they believe to be criminal',[113] whereas once a victim of medical negligence becomes a *partie civile* in France, there is a strong chance that a JI will push for the case to be investigated.

French criminal procedure also includes an interesting feature used in systemic healthcare negligence cases, called *pôles de santé publique*[114] (PSPs), created in 2003. There are two PSPs in France, one in Paris and one in Marseille. Victims of 'systemic' healthcare negligence may turn to either of the PSPs after their complaints have been received by the MP. PSPs were created specifically to treat cases of healthcare accidents and environmental disasters which involve systemic error, or corporate failure, where there are a great number of victims; such as exposure to asbestos or the contamination of the human growth hormone with vCJD (variant Creutzfeldt-Jakob disease), or more recently the Mediator scandal.[115] PSPs were created to facilitate proceedings in that area. In PSPs, all *constitutions de parties civiles* regarding the same case and alleged negligence are gathered into one case file, and the evidence is analysed altogether. However, as well as the case file which applies to the case as a whole, each victim has his/her own case file assessing the level of harm and the causal link between the negligence and the harm.[116] This can result in very complex procedures.[117] PSPs include prosecutors, JIs and specialised assistants (*assistants-*

111 D Griffiths, A Sanders, above n40, at 139.
112 Ibid at 137; A Sanders, above n10 at 89.
113 A Sanders, above n10 at 86–87.
114 *Pôles de santé publique* are authorities within criminal courts which are in charge of investigating cases of dangerous health products, foods or substances which have caused multiple victims. Article 706-2 CPP; M Obadia, 'L'expérience d'un pôle de santé publique', (2008) *Revue de droit sanitaire et social* 44; M-O Bertella-Geffroy, 'Justice Pénale, Santé Individuelle et Santé Publique', (2008) 128(2) *Droit de la Santé* 14.
115 This is a non-exhaustive list; 'Scandale de l'amiante: 705 nouveaux dossiers de victimes', *Le Point* (4 Avril 2012); P Gand, 'Les pôles de santé publique, une organisation adaptée aux contentieux en matière de securité sanitaire', (2013) *RDSS* 813.
116 M-O Bertella-Geffroy, above n114 at 14.
117 M Obadia, above n114 at 44.

specialisés) who can be medical doctors, pharmacists or veterinarians.[118] They are said to fill in the gap between the judiciary and their professional fields, which can be an issue in 'individual' cases of medical negligence (although medical experts can help in that matter).

Specialised assistants are not themselves experts, but they have a determinant role in designating experts and witnesses in such procedures.[119] Their notes on the case can be added to the investigative file, they can attend witness hearings, they can assist the investigative judges and police officers during searches, and they can also make recommendations as to whether or not to prosecute.[120] It is argued that the specialised assistants' contribution to criminal investigations has led to considerable savings because it avoids getting numerous expert reports.[121]

The SCCTD of the CPS is now in charge of all 'medical manslaughter' cases in England and Wales and should be consulted by the police at any early stage.[122] However, in practice, research has shown that they do not always do so.[123] The SCCTD bears some resemblance to the PSPs in France as they are both specialised bodies in charge of specific criminal cases. However, PSPs specialise only in cases of healthcare negligence that result from systemic failure, and would not usually be involved in cases of 'individual' medical negligence, or other alleged crimes outside healthcare negligence cases. Their work is thus focused on healthcare systemic failings which have caused multiple victims, and they have specifically been set up to investigate these cases, which reflects a stronger willingness to deal with healthcare systemic cases in the criminal setting in France than in England and Wales.

The trial phase: the role of judges and juries

The jury is another important difference between the French and English systems of criminal procedure in healthcare negligence cases. Whilst in England and Wales juries are an essential feature of the criminal process, they have a much lesser role in France. Only the *Cour d'Assises* which deals with *crimes* (the most serious offences in the French criminal hierarchy) in France involves a jury. The other criminal courts (*Tribunal de police* and *Tribunal correctionnel*), which deal with healthcare negligence cases (because they are cases of either *délits* or *contraventions*), do not involve a jury. Thus, cases of healthcare negligence are not decided in front of a jury in France.

As is made clear in *Adomako* and in the Corporate Manslaughter and Corporate Homicide Act 2007 (CMCHA 2007), in England and Wales, the question

118 P Gand, 'Le Pôle de Santé Publique face à un contentieux technique et des délits "sériels"', (2014) 198(4–5) *Bulletin de l'Académie Nationale de Médecine* 717.

119 Ibid.

120 Ibid at 717–718.

121 Ibid.

122 Williams Review, above n24 at 23.

123 Ibid.

of whether the alleged negligent conduct was gross and amounted to a criminal offence is left to jurors for both individual GNM and corporate manslaughter. GNM is the

> [i]ndifference to an obvious risk of injury to health, actual foresight of the risk coupled with the determination nevertheless to run it, an appreciation of the risk coupled with the intention to avoid it but also coupled with such a high degree of negligence in the attempted avoidance *as the jury consider justifies conviction.* (emphasis added)[124]

Further,

> [g]ross negligence . . . depends . . . on the seriousness of the breach of the duty committed by the defendant in all the circumstances in which he was placed when it occurred and whether, having regard to the risk of death involved, the conduct of the defendant was so bad in all the circumstances *as to amount in the jury's judgment to a criminal act or omission.* (emphasis added)[125]

Similarly, the CMCHA 2007 provides that 'it falls to the jury to decide whether there was a gross breach' of a relevant duty of care.[126] In England and Wales, the jury decides whether the defendant is guilty, but the question of the sentence is entirely decided by the judge.[127] Juries make their decision based on issues of fact.[128] They give no reason for their decision, and therefore it may be difficult to challenge a verdict. In England and Wales, 'juries are free to independently evaluate the competing expert evidence'.[129] Thus, whereas in France the decision on whether a health practitioner or official, or a health institution, is criminally liable for negligent conduct rests on judges, in England and Wales the decision on whether their conduct amounted to gross negligence rests on the jury.

This raises an issue as 'juries are frequently incapable of critically evaluating expert testimony, are easily confused, give inordinate weight to expert evidence, are awed by science [and] defer to the opinions of unreliable experts'.[130] This means that the involvement of the jury and the current test of gross negligence can lead to inconsistencies and variations in convictions of medical professionals for GNM, as 'juries are not asked to assess different scientific theories but instead,

124 *Adomako* [1994] 3 WLR 288 at 295.
125 Ibid.
126 S. 8(1) Corporate Manslaughter and Corporate Homicide Act 2007.
127 N Padfield, above n61 at 343.
128 Ibid at 376.
129 O Quick, 'Expert Evidence and Medical Manslaughter: Vagueness in Action', (2011) 38 *Journal of Law and Society* 503.
130 N Vidmar, R Lempert, S Seidman Diamond, V Hans, S Landman et al., 'Amicus brief: *Kumho Tire v Carmichael*', (2000) 24 *Law and Human Behaviour* 387, 388.

to consider contrasting opinions on how excusable or inexcusable certain conduct was', and this has been argued to be 'a moral, not a medical, matter'.[131] Moreover,

> juries would be expected to have the same feelings of sympathy towards the healthcare professionals in question that the prosecutors expressed (e.g., 'tragic mistake by a dedicated professional'). Acquittals would therefore have been likely even if all the elements of *Adomako* were satisfied.[132]

Like the CPS, jurors are generally reluctant to convict medical professionals when there is no evidence of subjective recklessness.[133] On the other hand, in France, it is claimed that judges have increasingly been more severe in the conviction of medical professionals in that they admit the conviction of doctors more easily than before.[134] It was found that the conviction rate of juries in 'medical manslaughter' cases in England and Wales is 39%, which is 'considerably lower that of manslaughter prosecutions generally'.[135] Although a lower rate of conviction suggests a lesser impact on medical professionals, variations in prosecution rates demonstrate that medical professionals' careers can still be severely impacted even if prosecution is not successful. In Chapter 5, I will suggest therefore that a more appropriate test for the criminalisation of manslaughter is recklessness, to eliminate variations in judgements and the negative impact a prosecution for GNM can have on medical professionals.

Conclusion

French criminal procedure comprises features which help to explain the wider use of criminal proceedings in healthcare negligence. Victims who act as *parties civiles* in France may be greatly involved in the proceedings and thus have a significant impact on the number of prosecutions against medical professionals for negligence. Most cases of healthcare negligence are prosecuted following complaints from victims who have become *parties civiles*, as the MP would not otherwise prosecute many of these cases.

The French inquisitorial process presents advantages for victims of medical negligence. In particular, criminal investigations conducted by the JI, who has wide coercive powers of investigation, provide victims with an explanation and transparency on what happened and makes the burden of proof easier for victims. In England and Wales, victims have a more passive role and cannot be actively involved in the launching of prosecutions against healthcare professionals;

131 O Quick, above n129 at 501.

132 D Griffiths, A Sanders, above n40, at 144.

133 Ibid at 145.

134 P Hennion-Jacquet, 'Quelques aspects de l'ambivalence des responsabilités pénale et civile du praticien', (2004) 14 *Revue générale de droit médicale* 286.

135 O Quick, above n70 at 161.

although victims in England and Wales may sometimes influence the decision of the police to investigate.

JIs in France have wider powers of investigation and are often in favour of victims in prosecuting medical professionals for negligence. In both France and England and Wales, prosecutors are reluctant to prosecute and convict medical professionals for involuntary conduct. However, in France, the MP might prosecute for simple negligence, whereas in England and Wales, the CPS would, until recently, only prosecute healthcare professionals for GNM, and the CPS applies a high threshold in considering what is 'gross'.

The role of the jury in England and Wales is also a major factor which explains why healthcare negligence is less criminalised in England and Wales, as the jury have difficulty in interpreting the test of gross negligence and are generally reluctant to convict medical professionals, whereas judges in France are keener to convict. In the next chapter, we will see how the various factors identified so far have impacted on a well-known case of healthcare malpractice: the contaminated blood scandal.

4 Contaminated blood

A tale of two scandals

Introduction

In the 1970s and 1980s, thousands of patients were infected with HIV[1] and hepatitis C (HCV)[2] from using contaminated blood products provided by UK[3] national health services. Once the infected patients and their families became aware of the failings of the authorities, the tainted blood scandal led to demands for justice and accountability for victims. Many victims in the UK called unsuccessfully for criminal prosecutions of the individuals and organisations responsible. Only in July 2017, over 40 years after the beginning of the scandal, was a full public inquiry, the 'Infected Blood Inquiry', chaired by a retired High Court judge, Sir Brian Langstaff, established by UK Prime Minister Theresa May. This inquiry aims to 'examine the circumstances in which men, women and children treated by national Health Services in the [UK . . .] were given infected blood and infected blood products'.[4] As explained in Chapter 1, the UK was not the

1 HIV stands for human immunodeficiency virus. This virus attacks the body's immune system, and it is the virus responsible for the acquired immunodeficiency syndrome (AIDS). A HIV-positive person might not necessarily go on to develop AIDS if s/he gets the appropriate treatments. To this day, no known cure has been found to get rid of HIV in the human body.

2 Hepatitis C is a virus which can infect and damage the liver. If left untreated, it can cause serious and potentially life-threatening damage to the liver.

3 The episode affected the UK as a whole. In this chapter, my analysis of the responses and the law applicable to actions and omissions committed by health authorities during the scandal will be confined to England and Wales. However, I will sometimes make reference to 'the UK scandal' where relevant. It must be noted here that two separate inquiries were opened over a decade ago to look into the contamination: the 'Archer Inquiry' covered events in the UK, apart from Scotland, and the 'Penrose Inquiry' covered the situation in Scotland during the relevant period. See Rt Hon Lord Archer of Sandwell QC et al., *Independent Public Inquiry report on NHS-Supplied Contaminated Blood and Blood Products*, February 2009 (Archer Report); Rt Hon Lord Penrose, *The Penrose Inquiry Final Report*, March 2015 (Penrose Inquiry).

4 P Walker, A Topping, 'Theresa May Orders Contaminated Blood Scandal Inquiry', *The Guardian* (11 July 2017); *Infected Blood Inquiry*, Terms of Reference, July 2018, 1. www.infectedbloodinquiry.org.uk/sites/default/files/Terms-of-Reference-Infected-Blood-Inquiry.pdf, accessed 20 January 2020. Throughout this chapter, the Infected Blood Inquiry will be referred to as 'the Langstaff Inquiry'.

DOI: 10.4324/9781315099170-4

only country affected by contaminated blood; in particular, across the Channel, a scandal of the same magnitude, *Le scandale du sang contaminé*, would agitate French politics for years to come. In France in contrast to England and Wales, several prosecutions were brought, and two medical professionals were jailed.

This chapter will demonstrate that although similar, and in some cases, culpable failings occurred in the decision-making of health authorities supplying blood in both countries, criminal proceedings ensued in France, but so far there have been no successful criminal prosecutions in England and Wales. It will further show that some of those failings in the decision-making process in England and Wales *were* preventable and foreseeable, and reflected a disregard for the life and health of patients so as to justify the use of the criminal law. The chapter will thus examine why resort to the criminal process was utilised in France but not in England and Wales. This will be done in order to assess what may be learnt from the French response in relation to the particular context of that scandal and how to assist victims of future episodes of healthcare failings and more broadly all patients harmed by healthcare negligence. Finally, the chapter will argue that for the most part, the criminal process in France did not achieve victims' demands fully; thus illustrating my argument that resort to the criminal process is not *on its own* a satisfactory response to negligent failings in the delivery of healthcare. However, it may be useful when disregard for the life and health of patients was committed.

Multiple factors in the background to the episode (i.e. underestimation of the risk, disorganisation of national blood supplies, the uncertainty of scientific evidence on HIV/AIDS at the time) made the episode hard to fit with the criminal process, and for the most part (except for cases where officials acted with disregard for the safety of blood patients for bad motives), the criminal law had little useful to do. Victims, families and the media, however, found it difficult to distinguish between the different failures on the part of health officials and health authorities, and demanded 'justice' via the use of the criminal process. In both France and England and Wales, legal responses given to the contamination scandals have not been able to address the victims' loss of physical integrity, their need for financial support and their loss of autonomy – basic elements which a person needs to achieve a fulfilling life. In this chapter I will suggest how this may be achieved in England and Wales, noting what we might take and reject from the way the criminal law was used in France following the scandal.

Background

The All-Party Parliamentary Group on Haemophilia and Contaminated Blood reported in January 2015 that between 1970 and 1991 an estimated 31,718 people were infected with hepatitis C,[5] and between 1978 and 1985, over 1500

5 But just under 6000 people had been identified; see the All-Party Parliamentary Group (APPG) on Haemophilia and Contaminated Blood, *Inquiry into the Current Support for Those Affected by the Contaminated Blood Scandal in the UK*, January 2015, 12.

people were infected with HIV, 'most of whom were co-infected with HCV also'.[6] Most victims were patients with haemophilia (PWH) who needed injections of blood products, including clotting factor concentrates (FCs), to prevent internal bleeding caused by this disorder. Other victims had become infected with hepatitis C and/or HIV as a result of receiving blood transfusions.

The contamination of the blood supply in both France and England and Wales was exacerbated by the failure of public authorities to achieve self-sufficiency in local blood products. In the 1980s, three types of blood products were used to treat PWH in France and England and Wales: frozen cryoprecipitates, freeze-dried cryoprecipitates and Factor VIII (FVIII) and Factor IX (FIX) concentrates.[7] FCs were made from larger numbers of blood donations, which meant that they were at greater risk of contamination.[8] If one donor was infected, the whole pool of blood used to produce FCs would be contaminated. Cryoprecipitates, on the other hand, were argued to be less at risk of being contaminated, being made from smaller numbers of blood donations, yet not always safe.[9] However, FCs provided PWH with rapid and easy treatment which enabled them to enjoy a 'normal' life, which was made more difficult when using cryoprecipitates.[10] In both countries, there was therefore a growing demand from PWH for FCs (in particular FVIII), but national blood services were not ready to supply demand and had to import blood from foreign countries, including the US, where blood donations were paid and often came from drug users or prisoners.[11] By 1989 in France, 45% of PWH had been infected with HIV.[12] In England, 44% of PWH were reported to be infected with HIV in 1989.[13]

In contrast to limited *ex gratia* payments offered to English and Welsh victims, in France recourse to legal remedies, including criminal proceedings, was sought promptly after the scandal had been uncovered. Victims of the contamination in France filed criminal complaints and became *parties civiles*[14] in the proceedings. They, however, received limited civil compensation at the end of the proceedings. *Le scandale du sang contaminé* featured three sets of criminal proceedings.

6 Ibid at 12.

7 L Greilsamer, *Le procès du sang contaminé* (Paris: Le Monde 1992), 21; Archer Inquiry, above n3, 13.

8 Ibid at 21.

9 Ibid.

10 Ibid at 22; M Lucas, *Transfusion Sanguine et SIDA en 1985, Chronologie des faits et des décisions pour ce qui concerne les hémophiles*, Inspection Générale des Affaires Sociales, Septembre 1991, 27; Archer Inquiry, above n3 at 14–15.

11 AM Casteret, *L'affaire du sang* (Paris: La Découverte 1992), 67–69; Archer Inquiry, above n3 at 15.

12 J Sourdille, C Huriet, *La crise du système transfusionnel français*, Rapport de la commission d'enquête du Sénat (Paris: Economica 1992), 19.

13 Ibid.

14 As explained in Chapter 3, in French criminal procedure, victims of crimes can join civil claims to criminal complaints and obtain civil compensation at the end of the proceedings, after conviction of the defendant(s); Article 10-2 *Code de Procédure Pénale* (CPP).

In the first set of proceedings, four blood centre officials were prosecuted for *tromperie*[15] (deception) and *non-assistance à personne en danger* (failure to rescue someone in danger). At the end of the first set of criminal proceedings, in 1992, Michel Garretta, Director of the *Centre National de Transfusion Sanguine* (CNTS)[16], and Jean-Pierre Allain, Director of the Department of Research and Development of the CNTS, were convicted of *tromperie* and jailed.[17] Jacques Roux, Director General of Health[18], and Robert Netter, Director of the *Laboratoire National de la Santé* (National Health Laboratory),[19] were convicted of *non-assistance à personne en danger* and given suspended sentences.[20]

At the end of the second set of proceedings, in 1999, Laurent Fabius, Edmond Hervé and Georgina Dufoix – respectively the Prime Minister, Health Secretary and Social Affairs Minister between 1984 and 1986 – underwent a trial before the *Cour de Justice de la République*[21] for *homicide involontaire* (involuntary homicide) and *blessures involontaires* (involuntary wounding). Dufoix and Fabius were acquitted whilst Hervé was found guilty but given an absolute discharge.

The third set of proceedings began in 1993, when 26 other medical civil servants and treating doctors, including some who had been prosecuted in 1992, were prosecuted for different offences including *empoisonnement* (poisoning), *violences volontaires* (grievous bodily harm), *non-assistance à personne en danger* and *homicide involontaire*. In the end, in 2003, the third set of proceedings was referred to the *Cour de Cassation*,[22] which discharged all the defendants for lack of intention.[23]

15 *Tromperie sur les qualités substantielles d'un produit* (deception with regard to the substantial qualities of a product) is a type of deception in French criminal law. The offence will be discussed in the section 'Possible Criminal Charges' in this chapter.

16 CNTS was the French national blood centre which supplied blood products in France at the time of the episode.

17 L Greilsamer, above n7 at 304.

18 The *Direction Générale de la Santé* (DGS) is a governmental body within the Ministry of Health in charge of implementing public health policies in France; see https://solidarites-sante.gouv.fr/ministere/organisation/directions/article/dgs-direction-generale-de-la-sante, accessed 7 October 2019.

19 The *Laboratoire National de la Santé* (LNS) was in charge of regulating the licensing of drugs and medical devices, including registering HIV tests; L Greilsamer, above n7 at 28–29, 78.

20 L Greilsamer, above n7 at 304; Cass Crim 22/06/1994 in J Pradel (Dir.), *Sang et droit pénal: A propos du sang contaminé*, Travaux de l'Institut de Sciences Criminelles, Vol XIV (Paris: Editions Cujas 1994), 173.

21 The *Cour de Justice de la République* deals with criminal liability of members of the Government in France. It was created during the contaminated blood scandal in order to try the executive on criminal grounds. It replaced the *Haute Cour de Justice*. O Beaud, *Le sang contaminé* (Paris: Presses Universitaires de France 1999), 3.

22 The *Cour de Cassation* is the highest court in the civil and criminal courts hierarchy. It deals with appeals lodged against lower criminal or civil courts, and looks at points of law only. It can quash or confirm a decision of a lower court. When the lower court's judgement is quashed, another court of the same level in the hierarchy (tribunal or appeal court) will have to follow the *Cour de Cassation*'s decision to make a final judgement. A Beziz-Ayache, *Dictionnaire de Droit pénal général et procédure pénale* (6th edn, Paris: Ellipses 2016), 46.

23 Cass Crim 2/07/1998, Bull Crim n211, JCP 1998 II 10132.

Victims of the tainted blood scandal in England and Wales

The victims' battle for justice and compensation began in 1987 when victims of the contamination (represented by the UK Haemophilia Society) started lobbying Members of Parliament (MPs) to obtain financial compensation for the harm caused.[24] In April 1989, 962 PWH brought civil proceedings to hold health authorities – including the Department of Health (DH), regional health authorities (RHAs) and the Central Blood Laboratory Authority – to account for negligence and breach of statutory duty.[25] The claimants alleged that these authorities had failed to achieve self-sufficiency in blood products, to take appropriate donor screening measures and to undertake HIV-testing soon enough. The claimants also argued that the defendants had failed to make heat-treated products available early enough and had knowingly provided foreign blood products which were at high risk of HIV contamination.[26] In December 1990, the case was settled out of court.[27] Victims were also awarded *ex gratia* payments from various trusts and funds (including the Macfarlane, Eileen and Skipton funds), and more recently the Infected Blood Support Scheme[28] but the Government always denied liability.

In 2008 (20 years after the victims' demands for an inquiry), an independent inquiry was conducted by Lord Archer on the contaminated blood episode. The inquiry aimed to analyse the knowledge on HIV/AIDS and the decision-making process of health authorities at the time of the episode and to give recommendations to the DH to respond to victims' demands. Recommendations made in the report included public health measures such as the creation of a statutory committee which would advise the Government on the management of haemophilia, to which the Government responded that it was better 'to build on existing arrangements and expertise, rather than risk disrupting or duplicating those arrangements via legislation'.[29] The Archer Report further recommended that 'direct financial relief should be provided for those infected, and for carers who have been prevented from working', and that the 'beneficiaries of the scheme should receive their entitlements from the Government and not through intermediate sources such as the Macfarlane or Eileen Trusts, or the Skipton Fund'.[30] The Government responded to this recommendation by explaining that the Macfarlane and Eileen Trusts already provided *ex gratia* payments to

24 Mr Justice Horace Krever, *Commission of Inquiry on the Blood System in Canada*, Final Report Vol 3, 1997, 940–942, 939.

25 *HIV haemophiliac litigation* [1990] 41 BMLR171 at 171.

26 Ibid at 177.

27 Mr Justice Horace Krever, above n24 at 942; AM Farrell, *The Politics of Blood* (Cambridge: Cambridge University Press 2012), 140.

28 Archer Inquiry, above n3 at 73; see https://www.nhsbsa.nhs.uk/sites/default/files/2019-10/EIBSS%20Annual%20Report%202018%2019%20FinalV2.pdf

29 Ibid at 107; UK Government, *Government Response to Lord Archer's Independent Inquiry Report on NHS-supplied Contaminated Blood and Blood Products*, 20 May 2009, 6.

30 Archer Inquiry, above n3 at 108–109.

patients who have contracted HIV through infected blood and blood products, and that Government intended to increase the payments made through these Trusts. The Government further stated that 'the Skipton Fund [would] continue to make payments to people infected with Hepatitis C', thus completely dismissing Archer's recommendations to make payments to victims without the need for intermediaries.[31]

The Archer Inquiry was unable to respond to victims' demands adequately. It suffered from a number of gaps, such as the lack of thorough investigations into the potential liability of health officials and authorities, and the inability to make its recommendations enforceable by the Government. The Government's response to the Archer recommendations was dismissive and unsatisfactory, to say the least. Victims were left dissatisfied by both the Archer Report and the Government's response, as no one had been found to be accountable.[32]

The 'Langstaff Inquiry'

The ongoing Infected Blood Inquiry[33] thus came at the end of a very long battle by victims, their families, some MPs and campaign groups for a public inquiry, which the DH had so far refused to undertake.[34] Victims and some MPs, including Mayor of Greater Manchester Andy Burnham, had for years demanded that investigations be conducted into the scandal to find out what had truly happened and whether there was evidence of criminal conduct, which could potentially be subject to prosecutions at the end of the inquiry, should such evidence be found.

The Langstaff Inquiry aims to examine the treatment of patients who were given infected blood since 1970 by National Health Service (NHS) and to look into what was known at the time about the risk of infection in blood products, the possible warnings which were given to patients about the contamination, and the adequacy of measures undertaken by public authorities to counteract the contamination (for instance the screening of blood donors). It also aims to look into the UK's failure to become self-sufficient in blood products, the actions of public bodies and other stakeholders (e.g. pharmaceutical companies) and whether or not any 'commercial or other interests' might have affected the decision-making process of public authorities.[35]

31 UK Government, above n39 at 8.

32 S Boseley, A Topping, 'A Horrific Human Tragedy': Report Criticises Response to Blood Scandal', *The Guardian* (24 February 2009); *Haemophilia Society React to Government Response to the Archer Report*, date unknown.

33 See www.infectedbloodinquiry.org.uk, accessed 20 January 2020.

34 Archer Inquiry, above n3 at 6.

35 *Infected Blood Inquiry*, Terms of Reference, July 2018. https://3p43ah231u8w1xptng1yprm2-wpengine.netdna-ssl.com/wp-content/uploads/2018/07/Terms-of-Reference-Infected-Blood-Inquiry.pdf, accessed 20 January 2020.

In other words, just as French *juges d'instruction* have done following the blood episode, the inquiry will seek to discover the 'truth' about this scandal and provide the justice that victims have sought for so long and that previous inquiries were unable to achieve. In witness statements gathered so far in the inquiry, victims have expressed their need for answers, recognition of what happened and accountability of those who may be found to be responsible for this tragedy.[36] This chapter will highlight what the Langstaff Inquiry may learn from the criminal proceedings brought in France following the tainted blood scandal, in terms of establishing the accountability of decision-makers, providing transparency and closure to victims and the public about what really happened and preventing further healthcare disasters in the future.

Systemic failings or culpable omissions?

This section will demonstrate that although so far criminal proceedings have not been brought successfully in England and Wales, comparable failings and delays occurred during the episode in both England and Wales and France. It will be shown that some of these failings were preventable, whilst some others were not, given knowledge and measures available at the time to public authorities. This section makes use of available documents on decisions made by health authorities in both countries during the relevant period (1974–1988).[37] Although the Langstaff Inquiry aims to find out information beyond what is already known, as will be explained below there is at the moment sufficient evidence to say that some delays in addressing the contamination of the blood supply were caused by reckless and deliberate omissions by public authorities, including the English Department of Health, which could be subject to criminal prosecutions. This analysis is not meant to be used as the basis for accusations or a criminal prosecution, but is meant to be used as a reflection on the criminal law's potential influence and role in this case and to point out differences and similarities between the use of the criminal law in relation to the French case and the use of the criminal law in relation to the English case. Further research and investigations will need to be done to enquire whether criminal prosecutions may be successful in this case.

The blood supply organisation

A comparative analysis of the blood supply organisation in France and England and Wales at the time of the episode is crucial here because in both countries,

36 See, for instance, Infected Blood Inquiry, Witness Statement of Barry Fitzgerald, WITN2819001, 12 August 2019, 16; Infected Blood Inquiry, Written Statement of Maria Fletcher, WITN1876001, 14 February 2019, 15; Infected Blood Inquiry, First Witness Statement of Graham Manning, WITN1367001, 7 June 2019, 115.

37 This period was chosen as representing the most crucial period in the episode, from the time the risk of hepatitis C contamination became known to scientists to the beginning of criminal proceedings in France.

the decentralisation of blood services 'had led to a lack of institutional and financial incentives for regional directors to engage in cooperative and coordinated policy-making on a national basis'.[38] According to Farrell, 'such an approach was essential for dealing effectively with the threat of HIV/AIDS, which recognised no regional or national boundaries'.[39] The blood supply organisations in both France and England and Wales had a similar structure. In both countries, blood donations were voluntary and unpaid. Blood centres were decentralised and under the supervision and control of health authorities.

In the 1980s in the UK, the blood supply was divided into two services: the National Blood Transfusion Service (NBTS) for England and Wales, and the Scottish National Blood Transfusion Service for Scotland and Northern Ireland.[40] The NBTS collected blood and plasma from voluntary and unpaid donors.[41] Like French blood centres, the NBTS was said to be very decentralised.[42] There were 13 regional transfusion centres in England and Wales, and 5 in Scotland.[43] They were all supervised by the DH.[44] They were funded by RHAs, which were subsidised by the Health Ministry.[45] The institution in charge of plasma fractionation for the NHS in England was the Blood Products Laboratory (BPL),[46] which, as will be shown below, was inadequate to respond to PWH's demands for FCs.[47] The NBTS was said to be 'a fragmented and disorganised shambles'.[48] Blood bankers had a great deal of autonomy regarding policy-making on blood products because of a lack of a centralised structure for the blood supply organisation.[49] Structural and institutional issues in the blood supply organisation contributed to the inability of health authorities to achieve self-sufficiency in blood products and thus led to more contamination than would have occurred if self-sufficiency had been achieved.

In France, apart from the CNTS, around 150 blood centres were decentralised and spread all over the country.[50] There was at least one blood centre in each

38 AM Farrell, 'Contaminated blood, A Comparative Study of Policy-Making Arising out of HIV Contamination of the Blood Supply in France, the United Kingdom and Ireland' (PhD thesis, University of Manchester 2004), 227.
39 Ibid.
40 The present study focuses only on the NBTS; Mr Justice Horace Krever, above n24 at 923; M Setbon, *Pouvoirs contre sida* (Paris: Seuil 1993), 133.
41 Mr Justice Horace Krever, above n24 at 923.
42 M Setbon, above n40 at 134.
43 Mr Justice Horace Krever, above n24 at 923.
44 M Setbon, above n40 at 134.
45 Ibid at 135.
46 The BPL was designed to develop and manufacture therapeutic products derived from human blood for England and Wales; Department of Health, *Self-Sufficiency in Blood Products in England and Wales, A Chronology from 1973 to 1991*, 2006, 4.
47 AM Farrell, above n38 at 119.
48 J Cash, 'The Blood Transfusion Service and the National Health Service' (1987) 295(6599) *British Medical Journal* 617.
49 AM Farrell, above n38 at 136.
50 M Setbon, above n40 at 76–80; Mr Justice Horace Krever, above n24 at 807–808.

département (county).[51] Some were non-profit organisations; others were part of public hospitals.[52] They were placed under the supervision of the Executive. The Health Minister, then Hervé (later charged with *homicide involontaire*), had the power to decide on technical and normative matters.[53] The Health Minister was in charge of regulating blood product prices and reimbursement by *Sécurité Sociale* (National Insurance).[54] The Health Minister could approve the set-up of a blood centre and nominate blood centre directors.[55] The more day-to-day oversight of blood centres was carried out by the *Direction Générale de la Santé* (DGS) and the *Laboratoire National de la Santé*.[56] Roux (later charged with *non-assistance à personne en danger*), as head of the DGS, could intervene in blood centres' technical activity via circulars on issues like prices and policies, although he was said to lack authority to enforce them.[57] The *Laboratoire National de la Santé*, directed by Netter (later charged with *non-assistance à personne en danger*), was in charge of regulating the licensing of drugs and medical devices, including registering HIV tests.[58] Among blood centres, seven centres were in charge of plasma fractionation and produced FCs.[59] The CNTS, run by Doctor Michel Garretta (later jailed for *tromperie*), did not have authority over other blood centres, but it had a monopoly on plasma fractionation and drying for around 40% of French territory, which represented 45% of the total population of France.[60] The CNTS also had a monopoly on clotting factor imports.[61]

Knowledge on HIV and hepatitis C

Analysing the suitability of public health measures relating to blood products provided at the time of the scandal in both countries requires a retrospective examination of scientific knowledge at the time. To inform this section, data were collected from articles, reports and other sources published from the beginning of the contamination to find out the status of scientific and medical knowledge on HIV and hepatitis C at the time of the episode. At the time, scientists were in discussion about how HIV and hepatitis C were transmitted and how the viruses could be inactivated once this was known. I do not argue that public authorities should have taken measures as soon as *some* knowledge was available, but rather

51 O Beaud, above n21 at 11.
52 Ibid; C Bettati, *Responsables et coupables, Une affaire de sang* (Paris: Seuil 1993), 27; Mr Justice Horace Krever, above n24 at 807.
53 L Greilsamer, above n7 at 27.
54 Ibid.
55 M Lucas, above n10 at 5.
56 C Bettati, above n52 at 27; L Greilsamer, above n7 at 27–29.
57 D Starr, *Blood: An Epic History of Medicine and Commerce* (New York, NY: Harper Collins 2000), 288.
58 L Greilsamer, above n7 at 28–29, 78.
59 Ibid at 25; M Lucas, above n10 at 5.
60 C Bettati, above n52 at 27–28; L Greilsamer, above n7 at 25.
61 L Greilsamer, above n7 at 24.

that they should have taken measures as soon as there was unequivocal evidence of hepatitis C and HIV infection in blood products, and as soon as safe and efficient techniques were available to inactivate the viruses when they had the means to take these measures.

In the mid-1970s, 'it became clear that Hepatitis was frequent in Haemophiliacs',[62] and through the 1970s, 'it was recognized that the use of concentrates of coagulation factors made from plasma pooled from several thousands of blood donations was often associated with hepatitis'.[63] In addition, as early as 1981, in both France and England, scientists were aware that AIDS was a transmissible disease.[64] They had found similar symptoms in homosexual males: a loss of immune defences shown by Kaposi's sarcoma and pneumocystis pneumonia.[65]

The first case of AIDS in a homosexual male in England was reported in December 1981.[66] A year later, scientists discovered that AIDS affected people under 60 years of age who had had no prior disease and who had never received previous treatment that could have caused 'immune depression',[67] and that AIDS manifested itself by one or several 'opportunistic' infections.[68] In 1982, there were reports in the US showing evidence that AIDS could be transmitted through blood.[69] The epidemic in 1982 was already known to have affected 750 people in the US, around 100 in Europe and an undetermined number in Africa.[70] Victims were all young and had the same type of immunodeficiency (decrease in T-lymphocytes), and 75% were homosexual or bisexual.[71] The remaining 25% were heterosexual males or females, children, intravenous drug users, Haitians recently immigrated to the US, and PWH.[72]

From March 1983, scientists worldwide were aware that there was a risk of HIV infection through sexual contact.[73] The first reports of AIDS cases in PWH were found in the *Annals of Internal Medicine* in March 1983.[74] At that time, 10 cases of AIDS had already been reported in France, and 6 cases had been

62 PM Mannucci, 'AIDS, Hepatitis and Hemophilia in the 1980s: Memoirs from an Insider', (2003) 1(10) *Journal of Thrombosis and Haemostasis* 2065–2069.
63 Ibid.
64 MV Ragni et al., 'Acquired-Immunodeficiency-like-syndrome in two haemophiliacs', (1983) 321(8318) *The Lancet*, 213–214; L Montagnier, *Des virus et des hommes* (Paris: Odile-Jacob 1994), 44–45.
65 'Acquired Immunodeficiency Syndrome', (1983) 321(8317) *The Lancet*, 162.
66 'Surveillance of the Acquired Immune Deficiency Syndrome in the United Kingdom, January 1982–July 1983', (1983) 287(6389) *British Medical Journal* 407.
67 L Montagnier, above n64 at 46.
68 Ibid.
69 LB Leveton, HC Sox Jr, MA Stoto, *HIV and the Blood Supply* (Institute of Medicine 1995), 20.
70 L Montagnier, above n64 at 46.
71 Ibid at 46–47.
72 Ibid.
73 AP Waterson, 'Acquired Immune Deficiency Syndrome', (1983) 286 *British Medical Journal* 743.
74 KC Davis et al., 'Acquired Immunodeficiency Syndrome in a Patient with Hemophilia', (1983) 98(3) *Annals of Internal Medicine* 284–286.

reported in the UK.[75] Very soon after, in April 1983, the risk of contamination in FCs was being discussed in the scientific world.[76] By the end of July 1983, 14 cases of AIDS were reported to the Communicable Disease Surveillance Centre in England, of which one case was a PWH who had received FVIII imported from the US.[77] In August 1983, a *British Medical Journal* article was reporting that 'the risk from blood products, imported into Britain seems at present very small'.[78] In England and Wales, in the summer of 1983, the transmission of AIDS through blood was reported in medical and scientific journals.[79] Human T-lymphotropic virus III (HTLV-III) was officially recognised as the virus causing AIDS in 1984.[80] Lymphadenopathy associated virus (LAV)/HTLV-III was later renamed HIV.

From 1984, scientists were discussing possible ways to counteract the contamination of blood products with HIV. In 1984, during the International AIDS Conference in Atlanta in the US, scientists explained that heating blood products, including FCs, would eliminate HIV. At the International Congress of Blood Transfusion in Munich in July 1984, inactivation processes were presented, including heat treatment.[81] In October 1984, the Centers for Disease Control (CDC) in the US issued a report in the *Mortality and Morbidity Weekly Report* which confirmed the efficacy of heat treatment in the inactivation of HIV.[82] In October 1984, the National Hemophilia Foundation in the US was recommending that haemophilia doctors who used FCs start using heat-treated FCs, even though effective protection against AIDS still had to be proved.[83] In December 1984, *The Lancet* was recommending the use of heat-treated blood products to treat PWH.[84]

On the 9th of February 1985, the chairman of the Haemophilia Centre Directors Organisation (UKHCDO)[85] in England and Wales wrote to *The Lancet* claiming that 'untreated FVIII of any type must be considered potentially to be infected with HTLV-III [HIV]'.[86] In June 1985, the chairman

75 L Montagnier, above n65 at 48; *British Medical Journal*, above n66 at 407.

76 FCs became available in England from the 1970s and were much appreciated by PWH. Because of the rising demand for FCs, by 1984 the annual requirement of Factor VIII was 80 million units; Archer Inquiry, above n3 at 15; *The Lancet*, above n74.

77 *British Medical Journal*, above n66.

78 Ibid.

79 Mr Justice Horace Krever, above n24 at 927.

80 L Montagnier, above n64 at 68; M Setbon, above n40 at 52; AM Casteret, above n11 at 67–69; Mr Justice Horace Krever, above n24 at 812–814.

81 M Lucas, above n10 at 21.

82 LB Leveton, HC Sox Jr, MA Stoto, above n69 at 258.

83 M Lucas, above n10 at 22.

84 'Blood Transfusion, Haemophilia and AIDS', (1984) 324(8417–8418) *The Lancet* 1433; Mr Justice Horace Krever, above n24 at 936.

85 The UKHCDO was a voluntary association of haemophilia doctors in charge of collecting and coordinating data and giving recommendations to the Government and other bodies on haemophilia patients and their treatment; Archer Inquiry, above n3 at 11.

86 Mr Justice Horace Krever, above n24 at 937.

of the UKHCDO issued another article in the *British Medical Journal* stating that 'the safety of cryoprecipitate and unheated UK blood products with regard to HTLV-III infection can no longer be assumed'.[87] At that time in England and Wales, five cases of PWH infected with AIDS had been reported, and 44% of haemophilia A patients and 6% of haemophilia B patients had been reported to be HIV-positive.[88] By 1989 in France, 45% of PWH had been infected with HIV.[89] In England and Wales, 44% of PWH were infected with HIV in 1989.[90]

This timeline strongly suggests that there was unequivocal evidence about the risk of contamination of blood products with HIV and hepatitis C from the summer of 1983. In both countries, health authorities had the facilities to take measures to address the contamination from the summer of 1983. Heat treatment of FCs should have been achieved from December 1984. It will be shown that HIV-testing was made compulsory in August 1985 in France and started in October 1985 in England and Wales. Heat treatment of FCs started in June 1985 in both countries. This means that both measures were delayed by over a year in both France and England and Wales.

Self-sufficiency

From the 1970s, French and English health authorities had aimed for self-sufficiency in FCs following the recommendations of the World Health Organisation and the Council of Europe. Achieving self-sufficiency would have meant that there was no need to import FCs which could be at risk of non-A-non-B hepatitis contamination from countries which allowed paid donations, for instance the US, with the aim of guaranteeing the safety of FCs.[91] However, in both countries, self-sufficiency was never completely achieved.

This issue was raised in later criminal investigations by blood victims in France. They claimed that authorities had knowingly imported contaminated blood products from foreign countries. In the *HIV Haemophiliac Litigation*, plaintiffs in England and Wales claimed that the DH had failed to achieve self-sufficiency in blood products early enough, which increased the number of blood imports, which were at risk of contamination.[92]

In France, the purpose of the CNTS's monopoly on fractionation and imports was to improve the quality of FCs and to achieve self-sufficiency.[93] On 22 November 1984, Netter announced that France was self-sufficient in FVIII, although

87 AL Bloom, CD Forbes, CR Rizza, 'HTLV-III, Haemophilia and blood transfusion', (1985) 290(6485) *British Medical Journal* 1901; Mr Justice Horace Krever, above n24 at 938.
88 Mr Justice Horace Krever, above n24 at 928.
89 J Sourdille, C Huriet, above n12 at 19.
90 Ibid.
91 Mr Justice Horace Krever, above n24 at 815; Department of Health, above n46 at 1.
92 41 BMLR 171 at 176.
93 M Lucas, above n10 at 6.

it was said that self-sufficiency had actually been achieved thanks to commercial imports of FCs (two-thirds were imported from abroad).[94]

Before 1975 in England and Wales, the BPL was not producing sufficient FCs to supply demand (only 20% of England and Wales' need for FCs) because it did not have adequate processing facilities, and there was a risk of contamination of the blood supply, especially blood products coming from the US.[95] From 1975, departmental minutes showed that funds were allocated to increase the production of FVIII, and it was claimed that the blood supply should become self-sufficient within 2 to 3 years.[96] In 1975, the DH granted half a million pounds to the NBTS to increase plasma production to permit England and Wales to become self-sufficient in FVIII by 1977.[97] The increased demand for FVIII in the late 1970s did not allow this to happen, and the decision to develop a new fractionation plant at Elstree was made in 1979, even though Margaret Thatcher's newly elected government had shown little interest in achieving self-sufficiency.[98] On 30 September 1980, at a meeting of the UKHCDO, £1 million was authorised by ministers to improve BPL facilities; the work was completed in July 1982.[99] Thus, the DH decided to give £1.3 million to develop BPL facilities and £21 million to build a new plant with the capacity to produce 100 million units of FVIII.[100] However, 'the government kept slogging away at building' this new fractionation plant, and it was not until 1987 that the construction was complete, and England and Wales relied heavily on American imports.[101] England and Wales became almost self-sufficient in FVIII by the end of the 1980s, when the NHS was importing only 20% of FVIII used by PWH, but like France, it never became fully self-sufficient in FCs.[102] In March 1984, England and Wales was still importing two-thirds of its FVIII.[103]

Public health measures

When the risk of HIV contamination was known to scientists and public authorities from the summer of 1983, measures against contamination in blood products such as donor screening, HIV-testing and heat treatment could have been taken

94 Ibid at 29.
95 V Berridge, *AIDS in the UK: The Making of Policy, 1981–1994* (Oxford: Oxford University Press 1996), 41; Archer Inquiry, above n3 at 26.
96 Archer Inquiry, above n3 at 30–36.
97 Department of Health, above n46 at 1; DD Lindholm, 'Freeze-dried Factor VIII Concentrates and the NHS', (1978) 2(6150) *British Medical Journal* 1451.
98 S Garfield, *The End of Innocence: Britain in the Time of AIDS* (London: Faber and Faber 1995), 61; Department of Health, above n46 at 2; Archer Inquiry, above n3 at 38.
99 Archer Inquiry, above n3 at 38.
100 Department of Health, above n46 at 2; Mr Justice Horace Krever, above n24 at 924.
101 D Starr, above n57 at 301.
102 Mr Justice Horace Krever, above n24 at 924.
103 Supraregional Haemophilia Reference Centre, Royal Free Hospital, London, 'Blood Products and Their Problems', March 1984.

at an early stage, but as will be shown, in both countries, public authorities chose to run an unacceptable risk to safety and caused unnecessary delays, which significantly increased the rate of contamination.

a) Donor screening and HIV-testing

In September 1983, the DH in England and Wales issued the first pamphlet which contained guidelines for blood centres on the exclusion of high risk donors.[104] It was entitled 'AIDS and How It Concerns Blood Donors'.[105] Persons at risk of HIV infection were listed and asked not to donate blood.[106] People at risk were homosexual men with many sexual partners, intravenous drug users and people who had had sexual contacts with persons suffering from AIDS.[107] In January 1985, a second pamphlet was published, and a circular was sent to RHAs, stating that it was 'essential that the revised leaflet be brought to the attention of each donor on an individual basis'.[108] It included as people at risk of HIV infection people who had bisexual or homosexual intercourse even on an occasional basis.[109] Following these, three other leaflets were issued between August 1985 and July 1987, which were based on the second one but were updated based on the scientific knowledge at the time.[110] Some regional blood centres' directors considered the information given to donors insufficient and inappropriate, as all HIV-positive people were not necessarily detected by this.[111]

The failure to take necessary measures to screen blood donors early enough was used as a ground for the liability of Hervé in the second set of proceedings in France but was not addressed in civil proceedings in England and Wales.[112] On 20 June 1983, in France, Roux, then Director General of Health, had issued a circular to inform blood centres that the AIDS agent could be transmitted through blood.[113] The circular was ordering blood centres to identify high risk donors: homosexuals or bisexuals with multiple partners, intravenous drug users, people from Haiti and equatorial Africa, and the sexual partners of all these persons.[114] The circular also demanded donors who thought they were in the 'people at risk'

104 Mr Justice Horace Krever, above n24 at 929.
105 Ibid.
106 Ibid.
107 Ibid.
108 Ibid.
109 M Setbon, above n40 at 140.
110 Ibid at 140–141; Mr Justice Horace Krever, above n24 at 230–231.
111 M Setbon, above n40 at 140–141.
112 Commission d'instruction de la Cour de Justice de la République (CJR), Arrêt portant renvoi devant la CJR, 17 juillet 1998, D6137, 85, 213.
113 M Lucas, above n11, Annexe 5: Ministère des affaires sociales et de la solidarité nationale, Secrétariat d'Etat chargé de la santé, Direction générale de la santé, *Circulaire relative à la prévention de l'éventuelle transmission du syndrôme d'immunodépression acquise (SIDA) par la transfusion sanguine*, DGS/3B n° 569, 20 juin 1983.
114 Ibid; L Greilsamer, above n7 at 36.

category to refrain from donating blood.[115] In August 1983, the DGS enacted another circular in which PWH were added to the 'people at risk' category.[116] But it was later shown in a report, sent by the DGS to the CNTS in November 1984, that blood centres had not implemented the circulars properly.[117]

In January 1985, Roux issued another circular which provided that blood centres should closely implement the provisions of the initial circular; otherwise, blood centres could be liable for not implementing it.[118] However, these circulars 'never became rigorously enforced'.[119] Roux's behaviour did not show any disregard for patient safety. He acted promptly, but there was a lack of enforcement mechanisms. Blood centres did not realise the scale of the danger at the time. Secretary of State for Health Edmond Hervé was said to have failed to take effective measures for the implementation of Roux's circular when he had the power to do so.[120] But no causal link was found between Hervé's negligence and the victims' deaths.[121] Even though Hervé had the power to implement the circular, no evidence was found that he might have been aware that the circular was not being applied.

In both countries, donor screening was done on a voluntary basis. The main difference was that in France the screening was done by medical professionals, and in England and Wales it was done by donors themselves. This raised the question of the efficacy of the screening. Although it seems that screening should have been more efficient when done by medical professionals, it had to be implemented properly, and yet it was shown that the first two circulars were not implemented properly by blood centres in France. The efficiency of screening in England and Wales was not assessed. Hence, donor screening in both countries was achieved through instruments and procedures available at the time of the contamination. The process of screening was not 100% efficient and not always realised properly. This, however, does not help to establish culpability on the part of French and English and Welsh medical professionals and officials.

When laboratories started manufacturing HIV tests, the next step in HIV-screening in France and England and Wales was the screening of blood donations, and the issue was to get reliable HIV test kits to start the screening.[122] Failures in implementing HIV-testing soon enough took place in both France and England and Wales. The failure to set up an HIV test earlier on was used as a ground for

115 M Lucas Annexe 5, above n113.
116 Mr Justice Horace Krever, above n24 at 815.
117 Tribunal de Grande Instance de Paris, Ordonnance de transmission du dossier et des pièces à conviction au procureur général et de non lieu partiel, D20917, 154; M Lucas, above n10 at 24.
118 M Lucas, above n10 at 33.
119 D Starr, above n57 at 289.
120 Commision d'instruction de la CJR, above n112 at 213.
121 Cour de Justice de la République, arrêt 9 mars 1999, affaire n° 99-001, 20.
122 Ibid at 168.

criminal liability of health officials in France and civil liability of health authorities in England and Wales.[123] Netter was convicted of *non-assistance à personne en danger* for having failed to authorise HIV-testing early enough.[124] Fabius, Dufoix and Hervé were prosecuted for *homicide involontaire* in part because they had negligently delayed HIV-testing.[125] So in both countries, health officials had failed to set up HIV-testing early enough, but only in France did this failure give rise to prosecutions of health officials and ministers.

In England and Wales, as in France, the concern was to evaluate screening tests which were on the market.[126] Because of the decentralised nature of the blood supply organisation, blood bankers had great autonomy in the choice of HIV test kits.[127] From June to September 1985, evaluations of screening tests were carried out.[128] In both England and Wales and France, there was reluctance to use the US Abbott Laboratories test, claimed to be unreliable. According to one source, 'when Abbott Laboratories applied for a British licence in March 1985, their British competitor, the Burroughs-Wellcome, was lagging. That circumstance made the government's response to the Abbott test suspicious'.[129] In other words, English health authorities rejected Abbott to give priority to their local laboratory's test. The DH delayed the approval of the American test for another 5 months, claiming that it was unreliable.[130] On 1 August 1985 (when HIV-testing was made compulsory for every blood donation in France), the DH announced that the Organon and Wellcome tests were 'particularly suitable'.[131] In September 1985, all the evaluations of HIV test kits were completed, and the DH announced that testing would begin in mid-October 1985 in blood transfusion centres.[132] On 14 October 1985, the NHS began screening blood donations using Organon and Wellcome tests.[133]

The Archer Inquiry found that HIV-testing proved to be a slow process, and the practice of testing was different from one hospital or treatment centre to another.[134] Archer stated that 'there was no one moment when a conclusive breakthrough for reducing or eliminating AIDS was achieved'.[135] Even though HIV tests were available at an earlier date, it was only licensed in the UK in October 1985, and all donations processed by the BPL were screened from

123 41 BMLR 171 at 177.
124 L Greilsamer, above n7 at 79.
125 O Beaud, above n21 at 62–63.
126 J Sourdille, C Huriet, above n12 at 103.
127 AM Farrell, above n38 at 136.
128 Mr Justice Horace Krever, above n24 at 933–934.
129 D Starr, above n57 at 301–302.
130 Ibid at 302.
131 Mr Justice Horace Krever above n24 at 933.
132 Ibid at 934.
133 Ibid; V Berridge, above n95 at 486.
134 Archer Inquiry, above n3 at 58.
135 Ibid at 59.

June 1986.[136] It was said that the delay in adopting a screening test in England and Wales

> gave the British firm the chance to step into the business of producing diagnostic kits for AIDS, a market which could be worth 100–200 million pounds world-wide by the late 1980's and which is now dominated by the US companies, chiefly Abbott Laboratories.[137]

In both countries, health authorities could have set up a HIV test earlier, but they did not because they wanted to give priority to the local market. Starr states that

> like their British colleagues, the French had valid reason to proceed cautiously, since the Abbott test produced a slight false-positive rate that policy-makers had to consider. Unlike the British, however, the French left an unmistakable record of their motives.[138]

b) Heat treatment (and supply) of contaminated blood stocks

As noted earlier, the necessity of heat-treating FCs was known from at least December 1984. The failure on the part of blood authorities in France and England and Wales to heat-treat FCs early enough had serious consequences for the number of PWH who would become infected with HIV. The comparison shows that in both countries, there was a serious failure to provide heat-treated products to PWH soon enough and to stop the supply of contaminated FCs to patients. In France, these failures led to the prosecution of doctors, health officials and ministers for *empoisonnement* and other offences, including *homicide involontaire.* The supply of contaminated FCs for a period of time after heat-treated FCs were available to blood centres was also invoked as a ground for the DH's liability by PWH in England and Wales in civil litigation.[139]

In both countries, blood authorities had to evaluate heat-treated FCs from different firms. From September 1983 in England and Wales, haemophilia centre directors were informed of the types of heat-treated FVIII available for trial. They were those of Travenol Laboratories Inc., Armour Pharmaceutical Company, Miles Laboratories Inc., Alpha Therapeutic Corporation, Behringwerke AG and the NHS.[140] It was said that all these products except NHS FVIII were made from imports from the US and could therefore be at risk of transmitting AIDS.[141]

136 Ibid.
137 D Starr, above n57 at 302.
138 Ibid at 311.
139 41 BMLR 171 at 177.
140 Oxford Haemophilia Centre, *Trials of 'Hepatitis Reduced' Factor VIII-an Update*, 29 March 1984; Mr Justice Horace Krever, above n24 at 931.
141 Oxford Haemophilia Centre, above n140.

On 19 November 1984, the BPL declared that it would begin heat-treating FCs by April 1985. The NHS's heat-treated FVIII was said to give satisfactory yields. However, FIX free from HIV would have cost the NHS between £2 million and £3 million a year.[142] Former Health Minister Lord Owen declared that the DH had 'failed to spend money allocated to stop the import of blood and blood products from abroad', but he claimed that he did not know about it at the time.[143] He also stated that 'there was resistance at the DH at the time to putting in the money'.[144] As an example, 'a batch of Australian-made Tuta blood bags with faults stretching from faulty seals to inadequate labelling was bought in defiance of local wishes just in order to save the NHS £700,000; a tiny fraction of its annual £32 billion budget'.[145] It was said that 'there is bound to be suspicion that the blood transfusion service is being run by accountants and penpushers rather than experienced medical professionals for whom the welfare of patients and donors has always come first'.[146] The Archer Report also states that 'it is difficult to avoid the conclusion that commercial interests took precedence over public health concerns'.[147]

England and Wales had started importing heat-treated FVIII from 1984, and heat-treated blood products were manufactured in England and Wales from April 1985. However, non-heat-treated blood products were still supplied in certain transfusion centres until June or August 1985 (dates vary depending on the source).[148] Heat-treated FCs processed by the BPL were released from April 1987.[149] Imported heat-treated FCs were still used in England and Wales until 1988.[150] English blood products became completely free from HIV only from 1988.[151] Even after England and Wales had started donor screening measures, blood stocks obtained from plasma collected before donor screening were not withdrawn because it would have caused a 'crisis of supply'.[152] It was shown that until 1986 England and Wales supplied a batch of heat-treated FVIII manufactured by Armour Pharmaceuticals from the US named H.T. Factorate, which was contaminated with HIV.[153] In September 1986, health authorities discovered that two patients who had received blood from this

142 Research and Development department, BPL, annual report to December 1984, 1.
143 'Haemophiliac HIV Tragedy "Needless"', *BBC News* (3 August 2001).
144 Ibid.
145 'Blood Scandal That Cannot Go Unpunished', *Mail on Sunday* (9 July 1995).
146 Ibid.
147 G Katz, 'No Individual Blame in UK's Tainted Blood Scandal', *ABC News International* (23 February 2009).
148 Mr Justice Horace Krever, above n24 at 932; M Setbon, above n40 at 153; J Sourdille, C Huriet, above n12 at 128, 130; Archer Inquiry, above n3 at 45.
149 Archer Inquiry, above n3 at 58.
150 Ibid.
151 Ibid at 59.
152 Ibid at 52, 53.
153 Mr Justice Horace Krever above n24 at 932–933.

batch had seroconverted.[154] In October 1986, the batch was withdrawn from the market.[155]

There is thus a great deal of evidence that health authorities could have heat-treated blood products much earlier and, as in France, could have stopped the supply of contaminated batches. French and English health authorities thus chose to run an unacceptable risk to patient safety by failing to allocate funds to the heat treatment of blood products. This disregard for the health and life of patients is something which, I argue in this book, should justify the use of criminal law.

Information to patients

In both France and England and Wales, patients were not informed of the risk of contamination in the products they were supplied with. The failure of health professionals to inform their patients of the risk of contamination in FCs was a crucial issue in criminal proceedings in France and was discussed in the Archer Inquiry report, which made recommendations to the DH to that effect.[156] Several witnesses in the Langstaff Inquiry have stated that they were not informed of the risk of contamination in products they were using at the time: that there was 'no proper information in relation to hepatitis C' or 'no adequate information about the risk of infection', and patients were not warned that they might infect others.[157] For instance, one witness recalls that she had 'been treated and tested without [her] knowledge, without [her] consent, and without being given adequate or full information', and that she was 'never informed of the risk of infection'.[158]

Similarly, in France, victims claimed that they were not informed of the risk of HIV infection from FCs they were treated with until it was too late. They argued that if they had been informed, they would have chosen not to use the products and would have relied on other, safer, blood products such as cryoprecipitates, or they would have put pressure on health authorities to act on screening, testing and heat treatment.[159] In the first set of criminal proceedings in France, the use of the offence of *tromperie*, a product liability-type offence, partly aimed to represent the failure to inform patients of the risk of contamination in the products

154 Ibid; V Berridge, above n95 at 47.

155 Ibid.

156 Archer Inquiry, above n3 at 60.

157 See, for instance, Infected Blood Inquiry, Written Statement of Louise Marsden, WITN1371001, April 2019, 4; Infected Blood Inquiry, Written Statement of Annette Hill-Stewart, WITN1001001, 12 July 2019, 12; Infected Blood Inquiry, Written Statement of Susan Threakall, WITN1564001, December 2018, 3; Infected Blood Inquiry, Written Statement of Barry Fitzgerald, WITN2819001, 12 August 2019, 6; Infected Blood Inquiry, Written Statement of Mr L, WITN0148001, 16 October 2018, 2; Infected Blood Inquiry, Written Statement of Maria Fletcher, WITN1876001, 14 February 2019, 6.

158 WITN1876001, above n157 at 6.

159 L Greilsamer, above n7 at 292; Réquisitions de Joseph Perfetti, Avocat général près la chambre criminelle de la cour de cassation in J Pradel (Dir.), above n20 at 117.

that were supplied to them.[160] Doctors were also prosecuted for *empoisonnement* (poisoning) and *violences volontaires* (voluntary wounding) in the third set of proceedings for failing to inform their patients of the risk of HIV infection from FCs and for prescribing contaminated FCs to their patients.

In England and Wales, the question of the information given to patients by medical professionals at the time of the contamination was also addressed in the Archer Inquiry.[161] Lord Archer stated that in the 1970s and 1980s, patients were not informed of the risk of infection with viruses through blood products and the risk of contamination in cryoprecipitates and FVIII.[162] The inquiry also highlighted that HIV-testing was often used without the patient's consent, and test results either were not passed on to patients or were disclosed with inappropriate advice or no advice at all.[163] But Lord Archer also argued that at the time, the doctor-patient relationship was very paternalistic and that 'a significant number of patients with haemophilia received advice and information from their doctors in ways that today would be unacceptable'.[164]

In a 1988 document entitled 'HIV Infection and Aids: The Ethical Considerations', the General Medical Council did recognise that 'a doctor should treat a patient only on the basis of the patient's informed consent', and that this principle was particularly important in the case of testing for HIV infection 'because of the possible serious social and financial consequences which may ensue for the patient from the mere fact of having been tested for the condition'.[165]

Although the Archer Report does not argue that the failure to inform patients of the risk of contamination amounts to criminally wrongful conduct, serious failures were committed in relation to the lack of information given to patients at the time of the contamination. In both countries, the failure to inform patients of the risk of infection from blood products reflected the same level of culpability, caused further harm to patients and seriously threatened patient safety.

The question of whether this could form the basis of an action for negligence in England and Wales is a difficult one. The leading decision of *Bolam v Friern Hospital Management Committee* provides that 'a doctor is not guilty of negligence if he has acted in accordance with a practice accepted as proper by a responsible body of medical men skilled in that particular art'.[166] In *Sidaway v Bethlem Royal Hospital Governors*, Lord Diplock held that the failure to disclose a risk in a particular medical procedure should be approached in the same way as other cases of medical negligence, i.e. using the *Bolam* standard.[167] The *Sidaway* test

160 L Greilsamer, above n7 at 71.
161 Archer Inquiry, above n3 at 60–67.
162 Ibid at 60.
163 Ibid at 61.
164 Ibid.
165 General Medical Council, *HIV Infection and Aids: The Ethical Considerations*, 1988, PEN0161165, 2–3.
166 [1957] 2 All ER 118, 121.
167 [1985] 1 All ER 643.

did provide that if there was a significant risk to patient safety, the patient should have been informed of it by the medical professional.[168] However, *Sidaway* would allow medical professionals to retain information if 'a reasonable medical assessment of the patient would have indicated to the doctor that disclosure would have posed a serious threat of psychological detriment to the patient' (i.e. the therapeutic privilege).[169] Over the years, English courts became more protective of patients' rights, [170] ultimately culminating in the case of *Montgomery v Lanarkshire Health Board* in 2015, which provided that 'the doctor is under a duty to take reasonable care to ensure that the patient is aware of any material risks involved in any recommended treatment, and of any reasonable alternative or variant treatments'.[171]

In the tainted blood case, the risk of HIV contamination in FCs was known by medical professionals and scientists to be significantly high, and it was in the interest of patients as well as public safety to disclose the information on the risks of contamination in FCs as soon as possible. The failure to inform patients of the risk of infection in blood products they were using as treatment for haemophilia could form the basis of an action for negligence if it is found that the risk to patient safety and public health was high enough for the medical professionals to have had an obligation to disclose the risks of contamination to the patients and that this caused harm to patients, but criminal culpability may be difficult to establish on those grounds.

Blood collected from French prisons

So far I have shown that the flawed decision-making process in responding to the contamination was in most respects rather similar in France and England and Wales. In this section, it will be demonstrated, however, that there was one substantial difference in the decision-making process which arguably suggests that French officials were more culpable than English officials. The failure to stop blood collection in prisons was used in the second set of proceedings against Hervé in France. He was found to have failed to take measures to implement the 20 June 1983 circular in prisons, but no causal link was found, and his liability was not established on this ground.[172]

In France, the high levels of contamination were also due to widespread collection of blood in prisons.[173] Even though from 1985 doctors and scientists

168 *Sidaway v Board of Governors of the Bethlem Royal and the Maudsley Hospital* [1985] 1 All ER 643 at 654.

169 Ibid at 654. Please note that the claim of privilege was patient specific rather than a blanket plea: *AB v Leeds Teaching Hospital Trust* [2014] EWHC 644.

170 See, for instance, *Pearce v United Bristol Healthcare NHS Trust* [1999] PIQR 53.

171 [2015] UKSC 11 at [87].

172 Commission d'instruction de la CJR Arrêt portant renvoi devant la CJR, 17 juillet 1998, D6137213; CJR arrêt 9 mars 1999, affaire no 99-001, 20. Ibid at 88.

173 Ibid at 88.

had warned of the risk of HIV contamination of blood collected from high risk donors, blood was still collected from prisons until the end of 1985 and the beginning of 1986 in France.[174] The June 1983 circular was not implemented in prisons.[175] Even when the January 1985 circular was issued, prison blood collections were not banned.[176] The reason for continuing to collect blood in prisons was that stopping it would have caused CNTS's profit to decline.[177]

In England and Wales, no evidence has yet been found on collection of blood in prisons. Interestingly, although health officials and ministers' failure to stop blood collections in prisons once they knew of the high risk of HIV infection in prison was an obvious disregard for healthcare safety, these failures did not lead to any convictions in France. The following section explores possible criminal charges which should be brought in England and Wales in response to the above conduct of health officials.

Possible criminal charges

As argued throughout this book, conduct which reflects a disregard for the life and health of patients should give rise to criminal prosecutions. On the other hand, conduct which falls short of that degree of culpability should not attract criminal liability but may give rise to a civil claim for compensation. As we have seen above, in some facets of the decision-making process in both France and England and Wales, there was disregard for the life and health of patients, in particular in the form of unnecessary delays in authorities' adoption of existing methods to counteract the contamination. At the time, saving money was seen as more important than saving the lives of patients. There are various criminal offences in England and Wales which could be used to prosecute both decision-makers and health authorities as corporate bodies in this context. I argue here that fatal and non-fatal offences against the person could be used, as well as health and safety offences and corporate manslaughter.

Fatal and non-fatal offences against the person

In theory, two offences could be used to bring prosecutions for failures which had shown disregard for the life and health of patients in England and Wales. These two offences are gross negligence manslaughter (GNM) and inflicting grievous bodily harm (GBH) in s. 20 of the Offences Against the Person Act 1861 (OAPA 1861).

As explained in Chapter 2, in England and Wales, since the *Adomako* decision in 1995, the requirements for GNM are that a breach of duty took place which

174 J Ruffié, JC Sournia, *La transfusion sanguine* (Paris: Fayard 1996), 314.

175 Mr Justice Horace Krever above n24 at 816.

176 Ibid.

177 Ibid at 817.

caused the victim's death and that the breach of duty must be gross.[178] Sadly, many victims of the scandal have now died from the contamination, which means that it would be possible to prosecute health professionals and health officials for GNM in England and Wales. Depending on whether the contamination caused the death of the victim, or life-threatening harm, either GNM or causing GBH could be used in criminal proceedings.

a) GNM

The *Adomako* test requires gross conduct, and subsequently, in *Rose* and *Rudling*, the Court of Appeal held that gross negligence required foreseeability of a serious and obvious risk of death.[179] According to the *Adomako* test for gross negligence, and even if the Supreme Court was to uphold the decisions of the Court of Appeal in *Rose* and *Rudling*, culpable wrongdoings which were committed during the tainted blood scandal could be subject to prosecution, as decision-makers had recklessly taken unnecessary risks which then caused the death of patients – conduct which *they knew* would cause harm to patients or a serious and obvious risk of death.

After establishing the culpability of decision-makers during the events which led thousands of patients to be infected with HIV and/or hepatitis C, causation will also need to be established. What is interesting to note is that in 2002–2003, after infected PWH demanded a criminal action, police investigations of health officials were conducted with regard to the contaminated blood episode. But Crown Prosecution Service (CPS) legal experts affirmed that it would be impossible to prove culpability on the part of health officials.[180] Unfortunately, no further information on the decision of the CPS is accessible. What can be said, however, is that *but for* the health officials' and authorities' failure to stop the contamination in blood products, some patients would not have been infected. Further, what will need to be proved is that health officials' acts or omissions were a substantial and operating cause of the deaths of the patients.[181] As seen above, health officials' failure to stop the contamination contributed to the death of patients to a significant extent and was the operating cause of their death.

In France, following the scandal, Ministers Fabius, Dufoix and Hervé were charged with *homicide involontaire* in the second set of criminal proceedings. They were said to have failed to enact proper regulations to guarantee the safety of blood products supplied to PWH and blood recipients, in particular regarding compulsory donor screening.[182] Hervé was convicted of *homicide involontaire*

178 *R v Adomako* [1994] 3 WLR 288.

179 See Chapter 2.

180 D Black, 'Police Drop 'Bad Blood' Scandal', *The Journal* (7 July 2003).

181 *R v Mellor* [1996] 2 Cr App R 245.

182 Cour de justice de la République (CJR) arrêt 9 mars 1999, affaire no 99-001, 17–20.

and *blessures involontaires* because the court held that he had the responsibility to implement effective regulations to ensure the safety of blood products.[183] He was nevertheless given an absolute discharge as the court considered that given that the trial had taken place 15 years after the episode and 5 years after the prosecution, 'numerous arguments had been conflicting, bringing charges on the action and responsibility of ministers, without any possible defense'.[184] The court argued that 'in such context, Edmond Hervé could not totally benefit from the presumption of innocence, by being subject, before trial, to excessive judgment, as it is too frequently the case for many other accused'.[185] The court considered that Hervé's case had already been pre-judged by the public and the media, and so there was no fair trial.

The use of *homicide involontaire* required lengthy investigations to establish culpability on the part of each defendant and a causal link with each victim's infection and death.[186] It is worth noting therefore that a prosecution for manslaughter raises substantial practical problems in the sense that in each case the patient's death has to be linked to the defendant's negligence. Nevertheless, GNM is the only offence that can at present reflect the harm done to patients and address the need for fair labelling.

b) Inflicting GBH

If an infected victim has survived but is now suffering a life-threatening disease, the offence of inflicting GBH could be used in England and Wales. S. 20 of the OAPA 1861 provides that 'whoever shall unlawfully and maliciously wound or inflict any grievous bodily harm upon any other person, either with or without a weapon or instrument, shall be guilty of a misdemeanor'.[187] Liability for maliciously causing GBH does not require proof of an assault,[188] and the alleged wrongdoer has to foresee that his/her conduct would result in physical harm to another.[189] What is also particularly relevant here is that the offence has been used in the context of people infecting their sexual partners with HIV. In *R v Dica*,[190] a defendant was convicted of a charge of causing GBH for knowingly and recklessly transmitting HIV to his successive partners through sexual intercourse. The wrongful conduct of a person failing to warn his partner that he was HIV-positive

183 Ibid at 20.

184 Ibid at 20–21; F Gremy, 'Contaminated Blood: The State's Renunciation and Incompetence in the Public Health Domain, a Long Tradition', (2002) 2(14) *Santé Publique*, 179–186.

185 CJR arrêt 9 mars 1999, above n179 at 20–21; F Gremy, above n183 at 179–186.

186 M Bernard-Requin, 'SIDA et transfusion sanguine ou l'affaire du sang contaminé. Les difficiles qualifications pénales' (1998) 28(1) *Médecine et Maladies Infectieuses*, 20.

187 Ibid.

188 *R v Wilson, R v Jenkins* [1984] AC 242.

189 *R v Savage, R v Parmenter* [1992] 1 AC 699.

190 [2004] 3 All ER 593 at 594.

can be compared to the conduct of doctors and health officials failing to warn patients of the risk of contamination in blood products. However, medical treatment is very different from sexual intercourse, in which case policy considerations could mean that *Dica* (in which the defendant took risks for his/her own sexual enjoyment) may not apply to medical treatment (in which any defendant was carrying out a public service). This is a question which will need to be answered when and if the case reaches the courts.

Health and safety offences

As explained in Chapter 2, under the Health and Safety at Work Act 1974 (HSWA 1974), employees at work who fail 'to take reasonable care for the health and safety . . . of other persons who may be affected by [their] acts or omissions at work' may be criminally liable.[191] This piece of legislation was in force before the tainted blood scandal occurred. Blood centre officials could in theory be found criminally liable for failing to take reasonable care for the health and safety of haemophilia patients at risk of HIV or hepatitis C infection from FCs under the HSWA 1974. The blood supply organisation or the DH could also be prosecuted for offences under the HSWA 1974.[192]

Corporate manslaughter

Prior to the coming into force of the Corporate Manslaughter and Corporate Homicide Act 2007 (CMCHA 2007), the common law offence of corporate manslaughter applied, and imposing criminal liability for the common law offence is arguably more difficult than for the new offence under the CMCHA 2007 for the following reasons. For deaths which occurred prior to the coming into force of the Act in 2008, the common law offence of corporate manslaughter would apply.

Before 2008, to use common law corporate manslaughter, courts would apply direct corporate liability, vicarious liability or the identification doctrine.[193] According to the doctrine of vicarious liability, a company could be criminally liable for the acts of senior managers and employees.[194] The identification doctrine provided that if only the governing authority of a corporation had committed an offence, then the whole corporation was liable for the offence.[195] The

191 S. 7(a), s. 33(1)(a) HSWA 1974.

192 S. 7, s. 33(1)(a) HSWA 1974.

193 S Parsons, 'The doctrine of identification, causation and corporate liability for manslaughter' (2003) 67 *Journal of Criminal Law* 69; N Allen, 'Medical or Managerial manslaughter', in C Erin, S Ost, *The Criminal Justice System and Health Care* (Oxford: Oxford University Press 2007), 60–62.

194 J Gobert, 'Corporate Criminality: Four Model of Fault', (1994) 14(3) *Legal Studies* 396.

195 N Allen, above n192 at 56; *Lennards Carrying Co. Ltd v Asiatic Petroleum Ltd* [1915] AC 705, HL; *DPP v Kent and Sussex Contractors* [1944] KB 146, DC; *R v ICR Haulage Ltd* [1944] KB 551, CCA; *Tesco Supermarkets Ltd v Nattrass* [1972] AC 153 (HL).

identification doctrine therefore provided limited scope for the criminalisation of corporations as it had to be proved that the controlling minds or senior managers of the corporation had the required *mens rea* for the offence to be established.[196] Demonstrating that senior managers had a sufficient level of culpability would be required. As we have seen, there is clear evidence that in some parts of the decision-making process, health officials did have the required level of culpability, and imposing corporate liability on the part of relevant health institutions would be possible.

Deaths which occurred after 2008 would be covered under the CMCHA 2007. As explained in Chapter 2, under this Act, a corporation can be criminally liable 'if the way in which its activities are managed or organised (a) causes a person's death and (b) amounts to a gross breach of a relevant duty of care owed by the organisation to the deceased'.[197] The condition is that the way in which the corporation's activities are 'managed or organised by its senior management must be a substantial element in the breach'.[198] S. 1(4)(b) indicates that 'a breach of a duty of care by an organisation is a "gross" breach if the conduct alleged to amount to a breach of that duty falls far below what can reasonably be expected of the organisation in the circumstances'.[199] This implies that institutions which do not owe a duty of care to the individual would not be covered by the Act. In the HIV litigation case in England and Wales, a breach of duty towards patients was not recognised on the part of the DH. Liability under the CMCHA 2007 may therefore be difficult to establish. The use of the CMCHA 2007 may nevertheless assist prosecutors in this context following a decision allowing victims to launch action in court for damages against the Government in September 2017.[200]

Product liability offences

Garretta and Allain in France were convicted of '*tromperie sur la marchandise avec la circonstance que le délit a eu pour conséquence de rendre l'utilisation de celle-ci dangereuse pour la santé de l'homme*' (deception about merchandise with the aggravated circumstance that the use of the product was dangerous to human health).[201] They were accused of failing to stop the supply of contaminated blood products to PWH and to inform them of the risk of contamination of the

196 S Parsons, above n192; P Blair, M Germain, 'Corporate Criminal Intention in the Enforcement of Environmental Law', (2012) 24(1) *Environment Law and Management* 20.

197 S. 1(1) CMCHA 2007.

198 S. 1(3) CMCHA 2007.

199 S. 1(4)(b) CMCHA 2007.

200 'Contaminated Blood: Victims Can Launch Court Damages Action', *BBC News* (26 September 2017). Note that the court action has been put on hold while the Langstaff Inquiry takes place.

201 Cass Crim 22/06/1994 in J Pradel (Dir.), above n20 at 171; Article 1 Loi du 1er août 1905 sur les fraudes et falsifications en matière de produits ou de services; L213-1 Code de la consommation.

'inadequate', as victims felt they had to beg to receive payments, and emphasised the need for proper compensation.[241] In 2017, additional payments were made by the England Infected Blood Support Scheme to victims of the contamination and their families. The annual payments from the scheme were due to increase from £46 million to £75 million in 2019.[242] Although the scheme aimed to provide further support to victims of the contamination, the process of obtaining compensation still seems overly complex for victims and their families, and easy and quick access to compensation is still much needed.[243] Sadly, calls for the creation of a national compensation scheme have recently been rejected by UK ministers.[244]

The criminal process did not provide compensation at the level of what compensation funds could have granted in France. Victims in both countries were dissatisfied with the compensation or payments they received from various funds. It was imperative for victims of the contamination in England and Wales to receive compensation for the harm they had suffered, rather than mere 'payments'. In Chapter 6, I claim that compensation and moral support should be provided promptly to compensate victims for the harm suffered following healthcare disasters, but I argue that this cannot be achieved through the criminal law but rather through compensation schemes which can provide easy and prompt access to compensation, like the ONIAM scheme aims to do in France.

Conclusion

During the contaminated blood episode, failures which were found to amount to criminal conduct in France (for instance the provision of contaminated blood products or the failure to heat-treat blood products) led to three sets of criminal proceedings involving several individual stakeholders in the blood product organisation, including ministers and blood centre directors. The same failures were observed in England at the same time, but did not lead to any criminal prosecutions. This chapter has argued that some of these failures, which amounted to reckless and deliberate endangerment, are serious enough to warrant a criminal law response.

Prosecutions for criminal charges are possible, subject to finding culpability on the part of each individual decision-maker or relevant institutions. Depending on

241 See, for instance, Infected Blood Inquiry, Written Statement of Louise Marsden, WITN1371001, April 2019, 20; Infected Blood Inquiry, Written Statement of Susan Threakall, WITN1564001, December 2018, 16; Infected Blood Inquiry, Written Statement of Gaynor Lewis, WITN2368001, 15 February 2019, 11; Infected Blood Inquiry, Written Statement of Maria Fletcher, WITN1876001, 14 February 2019, 14; Infected Blood Inquiry, First Witness Statement of Graham Manning, WITN1367001, 7 June 2019, 12.

242 See https://www.gov.uk/government/news/infected-blood-scandal-increased-financial-support-for-victims-confirmed, accessed 12 March 2020

243 S Gorman, 'Those left behind by the contaminated blood scandal shouldn't have to fight for support', *The Guardian* (16 April 2019).

244 O Bowcott, 'Ministers reject calls for immediate compensation for infected blood victims' *The Guardian* (28 January 2020).

the time of the contamination and the result of the contamination (death or life-threatening disease), the outcome of criminal proceedings will also be different for each victim, and it might be thought that different levels of justice are being offered to victims and/or the public. Nevertheless, from the discussion above, several criminal offences could and should be used in relation to the harm caused to victims of the contamination scandal. GNM and causing GBH can be used depending on whether the victim died from the contamination or suffered life-threatening harm. Offences found at s. 7 or s. 33 of the HSWA 1974 may also be used against public health authorities, who may be found criminally responsible for providing contaminated blood products to thousands of people.

The chapter also strongly recommended that ways to provide compensation to victims of the contaminated blood scandal should be reconsidered in England and Wales. Payments made via different funds merely helped victims cope with the immediate aftermath of the contamination, but failed to provide them with moral support or to give them a sense that their level of harm had been acknowledged by public authorities.

Finally, what this analysis has shown is that it is imperative for public authorities to acknowledge and provide information and explanations about this tragedy to victims and patients, take the necessary steps to ensure accountability of those responsible, and address any future failings within the healthcare system, as this is one way further healthcare disasters will be prevented.

5 Is criminal law the answer to individual healthcare negligence?

Introduction

> Criminal prosecution does not achieve the objectives of an appropriate response to unintended harm to a patient; notably it is expensive, it does not reliably identify correctable faults in the system, does not necessarily reduce the likelihood of recurrence, and does not usually address the need for compensation.[1]

At present, in England and Wales, medical professionals can be criminally liable for causing the death of a patient if their negligence was gross, and for ill-treating or wilfully neglecting a patient.[2] Liability under the offence of gross negligence manslaughter (GNM) in the healthcare context has been criticised, as it has been shown that cases of individual healthcare negligence can often be the result of a number of factors, including systemic issues within the healthcare institution. For instance, a healthcare professional may be charged with GNM, even when his/her error was caused by external factors.[3] Examples include several cases where an individual healthcare professional was the subject of a criminal prosecution but systemic issues which surrounded the error were not explored or addressed by the courts; the danger is that one individual professional can be used as a scapegoat and blamed for an error which in fact resulted from a faulty and dangerous system.[4]

Healthcare professionals have also expressed concerns that the overuse of criminal law or other types of liability may obstruct transparency and openness within the healthcare setting as professionals may fear to admit any error they have made

1 A Merry, 'When Are Errors a Crime?-Lessons from New Zealand', in C Erin, S Ost (eds), *The Criminal Justice System and Heath Care* (Oxford: Oxford University Press 2007), 96.

2 See Chapter 2.

3 M Kazarian, 'Who Should We Blame for Healthcare Failings? Lessons from the French Tainted Blood Scandal', (2019) 27(3) *Medical Law Review* 390–405.

4 See, for instance, A Merry, W Brookbanks, *Merry and McCall Smith's Errors, Medicine and the Law* (2nd edn, Cambridge: Cambridge University Press 2017), 4; see my analysis of the use of criminal offences in several healthcare scandals in M Kazarian, above n3.

DOI: 10.4324/9781315099170-5

in their practice out of fear of repercussions.[5] One particular concern which the healthcare community expressed was the use of their reflective practice in the evidence put forward in criminal proceedings for GNM.[6] Concern was also raised that a rise in prosecutions and convictions for GNM would hinder a just and learning culture, which is vital for healthcare safety.

Furthermore, a prosecution for GNM may have considerable repercussions for an individual healthcare professional even if it does not result in an actual conviction. Notably, as has been explained in Chapter 2, contrary to French offences against the person, GNM has a much more severe maximum sentence of life imprisonment, whereas the maximum sentence for a conviction for *homicide involontaire* is 5 years imprisonment.

It follows that the consequences of being convicted of GNM may be much more serious than the consequences of being convicted of the French equivalent, *homicide involontaire*, or of wilful neglect/ill-treatment, as will be more fully explored in this chapter.

The question that arises in the present chapter is whether and to what extent lessons can be learnt from the French approach in the context of individual healthcare negligence. As evidence is lacking that the criminal process effectively deters healthcare practitioners from committing errors, the chapter firstly argues that the criminalisation of 'simple' negligence – which does not reflect a culpable state of mind – should not be followed in England and Wales. The criminal law should be used only where there is evidence of a high level of culpability: where the defendant has shown obvious disregard for the life and health of another. Punishment should be proportionate to the conduct of the defendant for the criminal law to have an effective expressive function.[7]

Secondly, it suggests an abandonment of the use of the gross negligence test, which suffers from notorious flaws – notably circularity and lack of precision. A great deal can be learnt from the clarity and precision of French offences against the person contained in the Penal Code, which help experts involved in investigations of medical professionals for negligence. I suggest here that the GNM test be replaced by a better worded recklessness test.

Thirdly, as Chapter 2 highlighted, causation is difficult to establish in cases of medical manslaughter, and a medical professional 'unlucky' enough to have caused the death of a patient may be subject to criminal prosecution under the GNM offence. On the other hand, a medical professional would not be subject to criminal prosecution if there was no proof of a causal link between his/her fault and the damage caused to the patient, however culpable the professional's

5 General Medical Council, *Independent Review of Gross Negligence Manslaughter and Culpable Homicide*, June 2019 (Hamilton Review), 29.

6 Department of Health, *Gross Negligence Manslaughter in Healthcare, The Report of a Rapid Policy Review* (Department of Health, June 2018) (Williams Review), 7; Hamilton Review, above n5 at 8.

7 N Lacey, C Wells, O Quick, *Reconstructing Criminal Law* (Cambridge: Cambridge University Press 2010), 12.

conduct might be. It follows that the criminalisation of medical negligence under GNM exacerbates *moral luck* issues present in this context. As the French experience shows, the use of conduct offences, which do not require proof of any harm caused, will be very useful in avoiding the effects of *moral luck* issues on the medical profession, and punish truly wrongful conduct, when causation is otherwise difficult to establish.

Finally, the chapter highlights that the use of GNM in this context contributes to making 'front-line' staff more vulnerable to criminal prosecution, whereas managers and directors are less likely to be the subjects of criminal prosecution. Blaming front-line staff may hinder effective deterrence and the improvement of safety, because the systems which led an individual care professional to make a mistake are not corrected, and the possible culpability of senior professionals or decision-makers in contributing to that error is overlooked. Healthcare decision-makers should not be excluded from the scope of criminal liability if they have made decisions which they knew could harm patients. And I will explain that, similarly to French conduct offences, s. 20 and s. 21 of the Criminal Justice and Courts Act 2015 (CJCA 2015) allow the criminalisation of senior care professionals and decision-makers in this context.

No accountability for error/'simple' negligence

Errors cannot be deterred

Drawing on the arguments made so far in this book, I argue in this section that it is morally wrongful conduct that should be subject to criminal liability. The criminalisation of healthcare negligence should not depend on the chance of death, and the level of moral culpability required for criminalisation of health professionals should be neither the French test of simple negligence nor gross negligence but the higher test of recklessness.

Errors cannot generally be deterred.[8] The simple negligence test is hence not sufficient to establish criminal liability in the healthcare negligence context as 'when serious accidents follow unintentional errors on the part of well-motivated people trying to do the right thing, the law, as a minimum, should not add to the harm that has already been done'.[9] In other words, an extensive punitive response which would include the criminalisation of mere errors would do more harm than good to healthcare safety and to healthcare professionals. As recognised in the 2018 Williams Review and the 2019 Hamilton Review, medical professionals have expressed fear that criminalisation of simple errors could have a negative

8 A Merry, W Brookbanks, above n4 at 6; MS Moore, HM Hurd, 'Punishing the Awkward, the Stupid, the Weak, and the Selfish: The Culpability of Negligence', (2011) 5(2) *Criminal Law and Philosophy* 148; A Ashworth, 'Is the Criminal Law a Lost Cause?' (2000) 116 *Law Quarterly Review* 14.

9 A Merry, W Brookbanks, above n4 at 2.

effect on openness and transparency within a healthcare setting[10] and could then have a devastating impact on healthcare practice.

All well-intentioned and competent healthcare professionals may commit slips or errors at times, but these can have particularly serious consequences given the type of hazardous environment in which they work.[11] For instance, injecting the wrong drug could be seen as a 'sort of mistake a reasonable practitioner might make', whereas 'leaving an anaesthetised patient unattended' would not be the sort of mistake a reasonable practitioner would make.[12] It is therefore important to precisely distinguish between 'mistakes' which should attract a criminal response and 'mistakes' which should not. Merry and Brookbanks argue that in the first example, the use of a punitive response could be counterproductive, whereas in the second example, a punitive response might be necessary.[13] They suggest that only 'violations' – actions which involve choice and may show deliberate risk taking, as opposed to mere 'errors' – may be reprehensible.[14] Violations occur when 'the person concerned *knows* that an alternative is both reasonably available and more likely to achieve the given objective safely, and yet *deliberately chooses* the less satisfactory option',[15] as was the case in some parts of the decision-making process relating to the provision of blood products in the tainted blood scandal. As Moore and Hurd have argued, 'choice . . . is the touchstone of both culpability and deterrability'.[16] Errors are more akin to failures 'to carry out a planned action as intended or application[s] of an incorrect plan'.[17]

The criminal law makes a distinction between merely negligent behaviour, grossly negligent behaviour and reckless and deliberate conduct. In the healthcare context, a reckless state of mind would be shown where the defendant was aware of a risk associated with a particular procedure but nevertheless went on and carried out that procedure.[18] Mere errors do not usually attract criminal liability in England and Wales, but serious errors do, under the offence of GNM. There have been cases where a medical professional would be investigated and/or prosecuted for GNM even when s/he had not shown any awareness of a risk.[19] Errors are typically the domain of civil liability under the law of negligence, but the criminal law has little to do in the prevention of those errors.

The question of whether negligence is gross and therefore criminal can be tricky. The assessment of whether a particular course of action does, or does not,

10 Williams Review, above n6 at 7; Hamilton Review, above n5 at 29.
11 A Merry, W Brookbanks, above n4 at 4.
12 Ibid.
13 Ibid.
14 Ibid.
15 Ibid at 141.
16 MS Moore, HM Hurd, above n8 at 150.
17 W Runciman et al., 'Towards an International Classification for Patient Safety: Key Concepts and Terms', (2009) 21 *International Journal for Quality in Health Care* 21.
18 MS Moore, HM Hurd, above n8 at 149.
19 See *R v Bawa-Garba* [2016] EWCA Crim 1841; *R v Prentice; R v Sullman* [1993] 4 All ER 935.

amount to criminal conduct is done retrospectively and depends on many things, for instance experts' or jurors' views on what amounts to criminal conduct. Yet the 'person making the appraisal is in possession of facts that the defendant would not have been in possession of at the time', and this has the 'potential for hindsight bias'.[20] It has been found that experts often struggle with the definition of GNM in medical cases. Juries have no role in criminal proceedings for offences against the person in France, but in England and Wales, the jury will also have a crucial role in proceedings involving charges for GNM, which adds to the adverse effects caused by the uncertainty over the offence. The question of whether a healthcare professional has committed GNM will depend on the jury's judgement of what amounts to criminal conduct. Although not a problem in itself, this has proved to cause variations in prosecutorial decision-making relating to 'medical manslaughter' cases.

In France and in England and Wales, the healthcare professional's conduct is tested against what a reasonable professional would have done.[21] Negligence is thus a 'disparity between the actual conduct of the actor and the standard of conduct expected'.[22] However, given the vagueness of the gross negligence test, prosecutions for GNM have the potential to be unfair to healthcare professionals, especially because they work in a high risk environment.[23] An interesting comparison can be made here. If a lecturer fails to deliver on his/her teaching duties, s/he will have failed to act as a reasonable competent lecturer, yet s/he will not be held to account in either civil or criminal proceedings, as the delay which was caused by his/her negligence would have caused no harm which justifies civil or criminal liability. In contrast, a healthcare professional's failure to attend to a patient soon enough may often cause the patient harm or even cause his/her death. In both cases, negligence is committed, in the sense of a conduct which falls below the required standard expected in the relevant profession, but in the latter case, the negligence is likely to cause harm.

Prosecuting individuals for negligence seems therefore unhelpful in deterring errors, and thus the level of culpability required from a defendant healthcare professional should demonstrate the awareness of a risk. Only healthcare professionals who showed obvious disregard for the welfare of their patient(s) should be criminally liable. In other cases, healthcare professionals should be subject to civil liability when the error did not involve moral culpability but may have caused serious harm, and disciplinary proceedings when the professional's behaviour was contrary to reasonable standards of practice required by the General Medical Council.

20 A Merry, W Brookbanks, above n4 at 219.

21 D Papanikolaou, 'La responsabilité pénale des membres d'une équipe médicale', (2004) 14 *Revue générale de droit médical* 80.

22 A Merry, A McCall Smith, *Errors, Medicine and the Law* (Cambridge: Cambridge University Press 2013), 133.

23 See Chapter 2; also see O Quick, *Regulating Patient Safety: The End of Professional Dominance* (Cambridge: Cambridge University Press 2017), 112.

It follows that the criminal law should have a role when a medical professional was aware of a risk but was indifferent to it. McCall Smith indicates that

> the person who decides not to take a particular precaution, or who decides to omit to do something which he knows to be necessary to prevent harm to others, is negligent in a way which is also morally culpable. He has made an unacceptable choice, and is legitimately called to account for it.[24]

He adds, '[T]he actor should be aware of all the relevant implications of his action. If he feels, for example, that what he is doing imports no potential wrong to others, then the choice, from his perspective, does not prefer his own interests to that of another'.[25] Only in the first case should the person be criminally liable, as for deterrence to be effective, defendants have to realise that what they have done was wrong, or that they have done something that the law forbids.[26]

Understanding errors in the broader systemic context

By focusing on one individual's error or negligence, we tend to overlook the broader context which surrounds the error, as has been seen in some recent GNM cases. It has been argued that 'decisions and their consequent actions should be judged only on the basis of information and events that were reasonably accessible or foreseeable at that time'.[27] To acknowledge concerns about over-criminalisation in recent years in England and Wales[28] and to avoid the risk of over-criminalising healthcare activities, we must therefore explore medical errors in their broader systemic context. We must acknowledge that 'the delivery of healthcare today is typically dependent on the combined efforts of many people, working to a greater or lesser extent as a team, within a complex social and technological system'.[29]

The Williams Review has acknowledged that 'a just culture considers wider systemic issues where things go wrong, enabling professionals and those operating the system to learn without fear of retribution'.[30] It follows that when establishing a healthcare professional's state of mind, surrounding circumstances should be taken into account, and the healthcare professional's negligence should be evaluated in light of the broader systemic context. Factors such as the organisation and quality of the healthcare service, the supervision and physical state of

24 A McCall Smith, 'Clinical Negligence and the Incompetent Doctor', (1993) 1(3) *Medical Law Review* 344.
25 Ibid at 345.
26 MS Moore, HM Hurd, above n8 at 150.
27 A Merry, W Brookbanks above n4 at 108.
28 J Chalmers, F Leverick, 'Tracking the Creation of Criminal Offences', (2013) 7 *Criminal Law Review* 559.
29 A Merry, W Brookbanks above n4 at 14.
30 Williams Review, above n6 at 9.

the defendant medical professional, or failures in communication between staff members should be considered by prosecutors and courts to determine where the negligence originated and whether the healthcare professional's conduct was blameworthy enough to justify a criminal conviction.[31] Hall considers that 'one must always ask whether the actor knew he was creating an unwarranted, unreasonable risk'.[32] In fact, it would seem unfair to prosecute a healthcare professional whose conduct was the result, for instance, of another healthcare professional's negligence or of disorganisation of the service.[33]

Several cases of GNM reflect the impact that systemic issues have on medical practice and on care professionals' perceived vulnerability to criminal prosecutions, and courts have at times considered these systemic issues in their judgements. For instance, a junior doctor had been charged with GNM because he had injected penicillin into the brain of the patient instead of intravenously but was acquitted, because he had been working 14 hours in the same day and 110 hours the week before.[34] The victim's widow declared that the doctor 'had paid the price for the long hours demanded from untrained doctors'.[35] Similarly, judges recognised that Drs Prentice and Sullman had made a mistake, but because they were not trained and supervised properly, they were 'far from being bad men'.[36] The Court of Appeal later decided that their conduct was not gross in all the circumstances.

At other times, however, systemic issues were not considered by courts.[37] This illustrates once again that the simple test of negligence, or the gross negligence test, is not sufficient to establish culpability in this context because the negligence of a healthcare professional might result from factors outside of his/her control and the courts may choose to consider systemic factors or not, hence reinforcing variations in judgements. The Bawa-Garba case particularly illustrates the need to reconsider the criminalisation of individual medical professionals in the systemic context. The Bawa-Garba case featured evidence of systemic issues, but a single doctor and a nurse were blamed and convicted, which the use of GNM facilitated. I have argued elsewhere that blaming one individual for the death or injury of a patient, when systemic factors had clearly played a considerable role in the events leading to the injury or death, is dangerous and unwarranted.[38] As Ash and Jo Samanta have argued, 'this could impact detrimentally on honesty and the duty of candour, with negative implications for patient safety'.[39] Furthermore, as

31 J Hall, *General Principles of Criminal Law* (Clark, NJ: The Lawbook Exchange 2010), 637.
32 Ibid.
33 A McCall Smith, above n24 at 349.
34 RE Ferner, 'Medication Errors That Have Led to Manslaughter Charges', (2000) 321(7270) *British Medical Journal* 1424.
35 Ibid.
36 See chapter 2.
37 *R v Bawa-Garba* [2016] EWCA Crim 1841.
38 M Kazarian, above n3.
39 A Samanta, J Samanta, 'Gross Negligence Manslaughter and Doctors: Ethical Concerns Following the Case of Dr Bawa-Garba', (2019) 45(1) *Journal of Medical Ethics* 10.

the Hamilton Review found, healthcare professionals are working under significant pressure, with one medical professional confessing that 'there are too many patients for one person to deal with and things get missed'. This reinforces the fear that healthcare professionals have of making a mistake which will cause harm to a patient; a situation which can lead to defensive medicine where medical professionals refuse 'to engage in learning and reflection following incidents for fear that this could be used in evidence against them'.[40]

Accountability for reckless and/or deliberate behaviour – abandoning the gross negligence test?

In Chapter 2, I highlighted concerns about the test of gross negligence, which is circular and unclear. Here I argue that a better test is a form of recklessness inspired by the definition of the French *faute caractérisée* and *mise en danger délibérée*. As illustrated by several cases of healthcare negligence, including the contaminated blood episode, some thought needs to be given to using offences which can more fairly represent the harm caused to victims of healthcare negligence: the awareness of a serious risk and disregard for the health and safety of the victim, which GNM fails to explicitly recognise. Thought also needs to be given to using offences which can provide legal certainty to all those involved in criminal proceedings, e.g. investigators, experts, prosecutors, juries, judges, and victims and defendants.

As explained above, recklessness and deliberate conduct involve an element of choice and can thus be deterred *in theory*. There is at the moment a thin line between recklessness and gross negligence in English law, and I propose therefore that the law on manslaughter be at least clarified. Amongst others, Quick explains that 'the current test for liability (gross negligence) is unclear, unprincipled, often unfair and ought to be abolished'.[41] He further argues that 'committing to a form of subjective reckless liability would likely lead to a decrease in individual prosecutions'.[42] The Williams Review also found that the 'bar for the offence is set too low'.[43] The definition of *faute caractérisée* in French law, as described in Chapter 2, could be used as an example of clarity in order to improve or replace the definition of gross negligence in England and Wales. It is defined in France as 'exposing another person to a particularly serious risk of which [one] must have been aware'.[44] This definition acknowledges the element of culpability: the awareness of exposing someone to a risk and the choice to do so.

40 Hamilton Review, above n5 at 17–18.

41 O Quick, 'Medicines, Mistakes and Manslaughter: A Criminal Combination?' (2010) 69(1) *Cambridge Law Journal* 186.

42 O Quick, 'Medical Manslaughter: The Rise (And Replacement) of a Contested Crime?' in C Erin, S Ost (eds), *The Criminal Justice System and Health Care* (Oxford: Oxford University Press 2007), 46.

43 Williams Review, above n6 at16.

44 121-3 al 4 CP.

The offence of GNM is too broad and leaves great scope for prosecutorial and jury discretion. Although only the most serious cases of 'medical manslaughter' will generally lead to prosecutions, 'investigations that have little prospect of conviction cause uncertainty and distress' for both victims and defendants.[45] The Williams Review and many scholars have highlighted these flaws. Quick argues that

> the offence is too broad for prosecutorial judgment to be consistently applied, and this translates into particular harshness for those operating in error-ridden activities who are exposed to risk of prosecution by virtue of their socially vital work, and are often at the mercy of moral luck.[46]

Tadros notes that 'the offence of manslaughter is very broad indeed. It includes defendants who are very seriously culpable, but also defendants who, in one way or another, lack a high degree of blameworthiness for killing'.[47] Similarly, McCall Smith has claimed that 'the only respect in which gross negligence should be treated as being more culpable than ordinary negligence is if it demonstrates an awareness on the part of the accused of the risk to which he is subjecting others'.[48]

The *Rose* and *Rudling* decisions have attempted to clarify the GNM test.[49] In these two decisions, the Court of Appeal added a requirement of 'reasonable foreseeability of serious and obvious risk of death' to the definition of GNM, which raised the threshold of culpability for GNM. In other words, to convict a defendant of GNM, there will need to be evidence that the defendant could have reasonably foreseen a serious and obvious risk of death. These decisions have therefore made the gross negligence test close to a recklessness test. But I feel it would be worthwhile for the courts to draw a clear line and lean towards a more certain subjective recklessness test, rather than risking creating more confusion.

The Law Commission has previously discussed the adoption of new offences to replace GNM and address problems arising from its application.[50] The offence of 'reckless killing' in particular could address issues related to the application of GNM, as it requires that

> reckless killing would be committed if: (1) a person by his or her conduct causes the death of another; (2) he or she is aware that his or her conduct will cause death or serious injury; (3) it is unreasonable for him or her to take that risk, having regard to the circumstances as he or she believes them to be.[51]

45 Williams Review, above n6 at 7. Also see Hamilton Review, above n5 at 16–18.

46 O Quick, above n42 at 38.

47 V Tadros, 'The Limits of Manslaughter', in CMV Clarkson, S Cunningham (eds), *Criminal Liability for Non-Aggressive Death* (Aldershot: Ashgate 2008), 42.

48 A McCall Smith, above n24 at 344.

49 *R v Rudling* [2016] EWCA Crim 741; *R v Rose* [2017] EWCA Crim 1168.

50 The Law Commission, *Legislating the Criminal Code: Involuntary Manslaughter* (Law Com No 237) Item 11 of the Sixth Programme of Law Reform: Criminal Law, 4 March 1996.

51 Ibid at 45.

It thus contains the element of awareness and the choice of taking the risk, as in *faute caractérisée*, and could reduce the scope for uncertainty and circularity. Similarly, a definition proposed by Tadros of a form of reckless manslaughter could be an option. It would require that '(a) the action was of a kind that might carry risks with it according to the beliefs of the individual; and either (b) (i) given those beliefs the agent failed to fulfil his duty of investigating the risks; or (ii) the agent wilfully blinded himself to the existence of the risks'.[52] I have previously argued that only behaviour which put the life of patients at risk, or which represented a disregard for the health of patients, should be subject to criminal liability in the healthcare context. Thus, a 'reckless' manslaughter offence would more fairly represent this level of culpability than the current GNM offence.

Furthermore, the current criminalisation of healthcare negligence suffers from a mismatch between the level of moral culpability required in the GNM offence ('gross' negligence) and the level of culpability required in wilful neglect/ill-treatment by care professionals[53] (reckless or deliberate conduct). This means that prosecutors may use GNM more successfully than wilful neglect or ill-treatment because of a lesser level of culpability required for GNM. The consequences of being prosecuted for GNM will nevertheless be more serious than being prosecuted for wilful neglect or ill-treatment. In particular, this is because a charge of GNM can lead to a sentence of life imprisonment, whereas the maximum punishment for a charge under s. 20 of the CJCA 2015 is 5 years imprisonment, and the courts have at times punished medical professionals 'far beyond their culpability'.[54] The stigma attached to a prosecution for GNM can have damaging consequences for a healthcare professional, and even unsuccessful investigations for a charge of GNM may have the effect of preventing the defendant healthcare professional from engaging in open and transparent practice in the future.[55] This provides a further reason for raising the threshold for liability for manslaughter, and I suggest that this offence should therefore be used in the most serious cases of healthcare professionals' behaviour which was proved to be reckless or where there was disregard for the health and safety of patients, and where causation can be proved.

Conduct offences

As demonstrated by the French approach, criminal liability in the context of healthcare negligence should put more emphasis on the conduct of the defendant rather than on the harm caused. A severe injury may have consequences as

52 V Tadros, 'Recklessness and the Duty to Take Care', in S Shute, AP Simester (eds), *Criminal Law Theory: Doctrines of the General Part* (Oxford: Oxford University Press 2002), 255.

53 S. 20 and s. 21 CJCA 2015.

54 H Quirk, 'Sentencing White Coat Crime: The Need for Guidance in Medical Manslaughter Cases', (2013) 11 *Criminal Law Review* 888.

55 D Husak, 'The Criminal Law as Last Resort', (2004) 24(2) *Oxford Journal of Legal Studies* 219.

tragic as death for the victim or his/her family, as it may lead to very expensive lifelong treatment and require moral support. As an example, Jamie Merrett had been severely injured in a car accident and needed intensive care and a life support machine to live.[56] A camera installed by his bed caught a nurse switching off his ventilator by mistake and failing to resuscitate him as she did not know how to use the resuscitation equipment. Mr Merrett was left with severe brain damage.[57] Until April 2015, a victim could be left with severe injury short of death no matter how reckless the behaviour of a medical professional (A) was, and could not benefit from the use of the criminal process against him/her as the CPS would not prosecute conduct resulting in injury in the medical context; although the charge of causing grievous bodily harm could, in theory, be used. On the contrary, another medical professional (B) whose negligence had caused the death of a patient would have been subject to the criminal process even though his/her level of culpability had not reached A's level of culpability. The nurse who had turned off Mr Merrett's life support machine was thus not subject to criminal prosecution. Quick called this gap an unsatisfactory '"all or nothing" scenario, often hinging on moral luck and prosecutorial (and expert witness) performance'.[58]

The offences of wilful neglect and ill-treatment at s. 20 and s. 21 of the CJCA 2015, so far only used in relation to children or patients lacking capacity, can now be used in relation to all patients to allow the prosecution of conduct resulting in injury in the healthcare setting.[59] As Yeung and Horder have argued, wilful neglect and ill-treatment would target 'conduct that harms patients or unjustifiably poses risks to patients'.[60] Offences under s. 20 and s. 21 of the CJCA 2015 would therefore add more fairness to prosecutions involving 'negligent' healthcare professionals. Although there have been cases where patients were harmed by healthcare professionals who had recklessly or deliberately mistreated or neglected them (e.g. during the Mid-Staffordshire scandal), these cases were not subject to prosecution – thus offering no justice to patients who had been recklessly or deliberately harmed by healthcare professionals.

The wilful neglect/ill-treatment offences also have the potential to resolve issues of causation which may arise in prosecutions for offences against the person. Being conduct offences, wilful neglect and ill-treatment do not require any proof of harm. The offences focus on conduct rather than outcome, 'with no threshold of harm'.[61] In theory, a care worker may therefore be criminally liable

56 'Tetraplegic Man's Life-support Turned Off by Mistake', *BBC News* (25 October 2010).

57 Ibid.

58 O Quick, 'Expert Evidence and Medical Manslaughter: Vagueness in Action', (2011) 38 *Journal of Law and Society* 496.

59 See Chapter 2.

60 K Yeung, J Horder, 'How Can the Criminal Law Support the Provision of Quality in Healthcare?' (2014) 23 *BMJ Quality and Safety* 519.

61 Department of Health, *New Offence of Ill-treatment or Wilful Neglect, Government Response to Consultation*, June 2014, 14.

for either wilfully neglecting or ill-treating a patient, even if no harm was caused to the patient. In reality, of course, it is likely that a care worker would be prosecuted only if s/he has caused harm.[62] Nevertheless, this aspect of s. 20 of the CJCA 2015 merits our attention. In particular, the offence of GNM requires proof of causation – that the negligence caused the death – which means that many cases of gross negligence or even recklessness may not be prosecuted if causation cannot be proved.

Proving causation can result in lengthy proceedings, which are not helpful for either victims or defendants, or the wider system, which hopes to learn from errors. Whether a health professional causes death or only injury to his/her patient is often a matter of luck, as the same act could have different effects on the human body.[63] Moral luck and thus causation issues are even more complex in healthcare cases than in many other cases of negligence due to the nature of the profession and the complexity of events leading to injury or death, as many patients who are the victims of healthcare negligence are already terribly ill before the medical professional's intervention.[64] The extension of these two offences to all patients is a welcome development as it has the potential to reduce moral luck issues and aims to 'close the gap in the current legislation' in this area.[65] The offences also present other advantages, for instance less severe prison sentences than GNM or other offences against the person, which can help in the rehabilitation of medical professionals, who then have a better chance of going back to practice.

The offences of wilful neglect and ill-treatment can also catch a wide range of conduct as they can be constituted by either an act or an omission. As explained in Chapter 2, these offences bear similarities with some French offences against the person (notably *mise en danger délibérée*) because they do not require proof of harm, and the maximum punishment applicable for s. 20 of the CJCA 2015 reminds us of the maximum sentence for *homicide involontaire:* 5 years when there is proof of deliberate conduct.[66] The existence of both GNM and s. 20 CJCA 2015 offences means that injustice remains. A medical professional who has caused a patient's death may be prosecuted for conduct which is less blameworthy than that which is required by the 2015 Act for wilful neglect and ill-treatment, hence my suggestion to raise the threshold of culpability for manslaughter.

62 K Laird, 'Filling a Lacuna: The Care Worker and Care Provider Offences in The Criminal Justice and Courts Act 2015', (2016) 37(1) *Statute Law Review* 8.

63 A McCall Smith, above n24 at 348.

64 D Griffiths, A Sanders, 'The Road to the Dock: Prosecution Decision-Making in Medical Manslaughter Cases', in D Griffiths, A Sanders (eds), *Medicine, Crime and Society* (Cambridge: Cambridge University Press 2013), 189.

65 Department of Health, *Criminal Offence of Ill-treatment or Wilful Neglect, Impact Assessment*, June 2014, 1.

66 See Chapter 2.

Including individual decision-makers in the scope of criminal liability

It has been argued that 'to be effective, deterrence must be directed at those who are able to effect change within the system'.[67] This is another lesson which can be learnt from the French approach in this context, in particular the experience of the contaminated blood scandal. Whilst I am rejecting the wider criminalisation of healthcare negligence as in France, I argue that the criminal justice system in England and Wales has so far been unable to ensure the accountability of key decision-makers following healthcare scandals which had caused multiple victims; even where there was evidence of culpable conduct which deserves a criminal response. Whilst the criminalisation of health institutions can be achieved via the use of corporate or health and safety offences, which, I will show in the next chapter, might sometimes be helpful to address some issues within the broader healthcare organisation and ensure safety, I argue here that criminalisation under GNM in the healthcare context prevents senior decision-makers from being included in the scope of liability, even when they may have recklessly or deliberately shown disregard for patient safety.[68] This is because prosecutions will generally target the person 'holding the "smoking gun"'.[69]

It was shown that between 2005 and 2009 at the Mid-Staffordshire NHS Foundation Trust, in what has been labelled one of England's worst healthcare scandals, hospital staff had treated 400 to 1200 patients with the most appalling care.[70] It appeared that health officials and regulators claimed that concerns had not been raised by staff members in the hospital, although it was later shown that concerns had actually been raised.[71] Health officials and regulators had failed to prevent the neglect of these patients, and severe failures had occurred in several areas of the decision-making process.[72] This scandal reflected the lack of accountability of decision-makers when something goes wrong in the healthcare setting. The offences of wilful neglect/ill-treatment in s. 20 of the CJCA 2015 can be used against an individual care provider and could therefore be used to penalise decision-makers who have recklessly or wilfully put patients at risk of harm, without having to prove causation. The new offences in fact aim to 'incentivise providers to take further action to put in place systems to monitor and ensure that service users are not subject to ill-treatment or wilful neglect in order to avoid a potential prosecution'.[73]

67 A Merry, W Brookbanks, above n4 at 4.
68 S Tombs, D Whyte, *The Corporate Criminal, Why Corporations Should Be Abolished* (London: Routledge 2015), 86.
69 A Merry, W Brookbanks, above n4 at 18.
70 C Smyth, 'New NHS Scandal Is Inevitable, Mid Staffs Inquiry Chief Warns', *The Times* (10 February 2017).
71 P Gooderham, B Toft, 'Involuntary Automaticity and Medical Manslaughter', in D Griffiths, A Sanders (eds), above n64 183.
72 M Kazarian, above n3.
73 Department of Health, Impact Assessment, above n65 at 13.

I recognise that this approach may seem to have the potential for wider criminalisation of healthcare negligence, but this would be mitigated by restricting the use of the criminal law to reckless and/or deliberate behaviour. It must also be made clear that I am not arguing in favour of an approach which would lead to 'scapegoating' individuals, as was the case in some prosecutions arising out of the blood contamination scandal in France. I am suggesting instead that decision-makers should not be able to escape liability, and front-line staff should not always be the ones who are blamed for medical mishaps. I recognise that this approach has limits; 'individual' criminal liability may not easily fit with the complexity of healthcare delivery, which features the 'combined efforts of many people',[74] and it may sometimes be difficult to identify culpable individuals.[75] As I show elsewhere, in several healthcare scandals, 'a number of reckless failures and deliberate decisions resulting in harm to patients [are], in part, caused by the prioritization of cost calculation over the safety of patients'.[76] As explained in Chapter 4, these failures do sometimes reflect disregard for the safety of patients, which should justify the use of a criminal response.

The Hamilton Review states that 'if blaming individual clinicians is seen as unfair and a barrier to candour and learning, shifting the blame in order to criminalise managers is no better'.[77] Here I am not arguing that the blame should shift from individual medical professionals to individual managers who have not shown the required level of *mens rea*. At the moment, if an individual medical professional commits gross negligence, s/he may be prosecuted for GNM, but if an individual manager commits gross negligence, s/he is unlikely to be prosecuted predominantly because of the difficulty of proving a causal link between his/her negligence and the harm caused. More fairness is therefore needed to treat everyone equally, rather than blaming particular individuals if they have not reached the required threshold of culpability.

It follows therefore that *both* individual medical professionals *and* managers should be subject to criminal investigations and prosecutions if there is evidence that they have recklessly put patients in danger or if they have demonstrated disregard for the life and health of patients. Blaming front-line staff whilst overlooking the potential culpability of managers is in itself an obstacle to candour and learning. I will, however, argue in the following chapter that where there is no proof of individual culpable conduct, corporate criminal liability could be a useful tool to address healthcare negligence at the systemic level, to investigate systemic failings, whilst highlighting the current flaws of corporate offences which can be used in this context.

74 A Merry, W Brookbanks, above n4 at 14.

75 P Gooderham, 'No-one Fully Responsible': A 'Collusion of Anonymity' Protecting Health Care Bodies from Manslaughter Charges?' (2011) *Clinical Ethics* 75.

76 M Kazarian, above n3 at 396.

77 Hamilton Review, above n5 at 32.

Improving our prosecutorial policy?

A change in the law may not be necessary to address the problems discussed so far in relation to GNM, and using conduct offences in the form of wilful neglect and ill-treatment would be an answer to some of the issues raised. In very serious cases of death caused by a medical professional, a conviction of manslaughter is appropriate, but the threshold of culpability must be raised to reflect reckless conduct or a disregard for the life and health of a patient. The Williams Review has made some useful propositions on how to address some problems linked to the criminalisation of medical manslaughter, and has in particular pointed out that there exists 'a sense of arbitrariness in which cases result in prosecution', proposing that a working group be set up 'to set out a clear explanatory statement of the law on gross negligence manslaughter'.[78] This is a much-needed and useful proposition, but this may not be sufficient to address some of the problems raised by GNM for the reasons explained above. In addition to clarifying the law on manslaughter, prosecution policy should be focused more on cases which have shown reckless behaviour or a disregard for the life and health of patients, which a prosecution for reckless manslaughter or wilful neglect/ill-treatment would rightly achieve.

The support given to victims of 'medical manslaughter' during and after investigations is another issue which needs to be given more thought. As has been made clear throughout, I do not endorse wider criminalisation of healthcare negligence; giving victims a stronger role in criminal procedure could encourage a more punitive response. French criminal procedure has often been seen as a way to satisfy victims' demands for accountability and retribution. This approach would be counterproductive. Nevertheless, French criminal procedure does offer victims of crime more transparency and closure than does English criminal procedure, as 'the adversarial nature of the criminal trial does not lend itself to the task of identifying what lessons can be learned from a tragic and unexpected medical death'.[79] The Hamilton Review noted that victims and their families often have the perception that the truth of wrongdoing is sometimes concealed and often do not obtain the answers they are seeking.[80] Transparency during investigations and prosecutions for healthcare 'negligence' should be improved for victims, as this would go a long way to assist them with obtaining answers and gaining a sense of closure. Victims and their families must be more involved and supported throughout the proceedings and be given some opportunities to be informed more regularly of the progress of the prosecution.

Lastly, lessons can be learnt from the experience of French *juges d'instruction* and *pôles de santé publique* (PSPs) in dealing with healthcare negligence cases, in particular, in investigating systemic and human factors which have a role in

78 Williams Review, above n6 at 18, 23.

79 M Brazier et al., 'Improving Healthcare Through the Use of "Medical Manslaughter?" Facts, Fears and the Future', (2016) 22(5–6) *Clinical Risk* 92.

80 Hamilton Review, above n5 at 7.

healthcare failings.[81] The PSPs' specialisation in healthcare cases and focus on multi-level institutional failings could inform us on how to address issues linked to experts' unfamiliarity with medical negligence cases, as well as the investigative costs and delays which we observe currently in England and Wales.[82]

The Williams Review proposes that

> where a suspected [GNM] case in a healthcare setting has been referred to the CPS, the CQC [Care Quality Commission] must be informed so that it can consider whether to carry out a parallel, but separate, investigation of the healthcare provider to determine the role of systemic and human factors in the incident and to identify any changes which might need to be made.[83]

This illustrates that there is a need to investigate systemic failings in a coordinated manner with the aim to improve safety in healthcare services. This type of reform could face some resistance from prosecutors and other bodies involved in criminal investigations and prosecutions. As Griffiths and Quick's research found, this particular proposal in the Williams Review was not welcomed by the police, and they suggested instead that regional leads within the police be created and trained by specialist prosecutors from the Special Crime Unit, which could address problems highlighted in CPS prosecutions for medical manslaughter.[84]

Conclusion

Because 'error will never be completely eliminated, and there will always be some doctors whose behaviour is frankly culpable',[85] criminal law should only be used to criminalise conduct which showed obvious *disregard* for or *indifference* to a risk to the life and health of another. The French model of criminalising doctors for simple negligence is not to be followed in England and Wales. This chapter has demonstrated that the criminal law may have a useful role only when an individual defendant has shown a reckless or deliberate state of mind, i.e. where an individual medical professional or decision-maker has recklessly or deliberately put patients at risk of harm or death. The French experience shows that the criminal law may have a useful expressive function in these cases.

At present, the use of the offence of GNM in cases of alleged healthcare negligence is not desirable for several reasons. Firstly, the gross negligence test is unclear and may lead to unfair prosecutions of individual medical professionals, who will often be front-line staff. Decision-makers, however, may more easily

81 See Chapter 3.
82 D Griffiths, O Quick, 'Managing Medical Manslaughter Cases: Improving Efficiency and Transparency?' Law Research Paper Series, May 2019, Paper No 007 2019, University of Bristol, 18–19; see Chapter 3.
83 Williams Review, above n6 at 30.
84 D Griffiths, O Quick, above n82 at 24.
85 A Merry, W Brookbanks above n4 at 5.

escape criminal liability owing to the lack of a causal link between their failure and the harm caused to patients. I have shown that the gross negligence test should be abandoned and replaced by a recklessness test to ensure that conduct which can be deterred is punished.

Secondly, the difficulty of proving causation in GNM cases has meant that many instances of wrongful conduct may not be subject to prosecution for manslaughter because it may be difficult to prove a causal link between the wrongful conduct and the death of a patient. I have argued therefore that conduct offences which do not require proof of causation should be used to respond to many instances in this context. The offences of wilful neglect and ill-treatment at s. 20 and s. 21 of the CJCA 2015 allow the criminalisation of wrongful conduct which may result in injury or death, or no harm at all. They have the advantage of allowing the prosecution of truly wrongful conduct at the individual level without having to prove the existence of a causal link. These offences thus have the potential to provide justice and retribution to victims who were harmed as a result of reckless or deliberate conduct by healthcare professionals.

Finally, I have highlighted the need to include decision-makers and senior medical professionals in the scope of liability if they have shown the required level of culpability. Drastic changes to the law are not needed to achieve this. S. 21 of the CJCA 2015 permits the criminalisation of such individuals if there is proof of at least reckless conduct. I suggest therefore that offences under s. 20 and s. 21 of the CJCA 2015 be used to prosecute individuals in the healthcare context when injury has been caused and the defendant has the required level of culpability, and reckless manslaughter when death resulted from the conduct.

In the next chapter, I explore issues relating to the criminalisation of healthcare corporations for failings which have caused harm or death. I argue that corporate liability can be a useful alternative to criminalising individual conduct when there is no proof of individual reckless or deliberate conduct but the corporation itself has failed to provide safe care to patients.

6 Institutions in the dock and alternatives to the criminal process

Introduction

With 1.5 million employees, the National Health Service (NHS) is the largest UK employer, and one of the largest employers worldwide.[1] Compared to other corporations and given the nature of the core role of the NHS, it also 'runs a greater than average risk that harm may result from its procedures'.[2] Should this greater risk of harm prompt a greater emphasis on and justify the use of the criminal process against NHS institutions and so help in promoting healthcare safety?

In both England and Wales and France, health institutions can be liable for various types of criminal offences when patients have suffered harm as a result of institutional failings. In England and Wales, corporate offences which can be used in this context require different thresholds of liability, however, and in this chapter I emphasise this inconsistency. The corporate manslaughter offence requires gross negligence which has caused death, whilst offences under the Health and Safety at Work Act 1974 (HSWA 1974) do not require any level of blameworthiness – a breach of health and safety legislation is sufficient; further, the offences of wilful neglect and ill-treatment at s. 21 of the Criminal Justice and Courts Act 2015 (CJCA 2015) require a 'gross breach' of a relevant duty of care owed to the patient. Only corporate manslaughter necessitates proof of a causal link between negligence and death.

In France, the *Code Pénal* admits an even wider scope for criminalisation than offences in England and Wales in the context of corporate healthcare negligence. Under French criminal law, health institutions can be charged with any of the negligence offences set out in Chapter 2. A health institution can thus be prosecuted for a failure which amounts to mere negligence and which either has or has not caused injury or death. French criminal law thus makes it possible to prosecute and secure convictions of hospitals and other health institutions much more easily than English criminal law.

1 L Rolewicz, B Palmer, 'The NHS Workforce in Numbers', *The Nuffield Trust* (8 May 2019).
2 C Wells, 'Medical Manslaughter-Organisational Liability', in D Griffiths, A Sanders (eds), *Medicine, Crime and Society* (Cambridge: Cambridge University Press 2013), 192.

DOI: 10.4324/9781315099170-6

The relevant academic literature has previously argued that an effective alternative to the use of criminal law against individuals is corporate criminal liability in the context of healthcare 'negligence', in particular under the Corporate Manslaughter and Corporate Homicide Act 2007 (CMCHA 2007).[3] In this chapter, I argue against the trend which advocates corporate criminal liability as an alternative to problems arising from individual criminal liability in the context of healthcare 'negligence'. Corporate criminal liability should be used *alongside* individual liability and where appropriate.

Many cases of healthcare failings in England and Wales have demonstrated that corporate criminal offences are underused in this context. Victims of such mishaps have therefore limited recourse to legal remedies. This chapter examines how the criminalisation of health institutions can be improved following the French experience. Corporate liability can provide useful remedies to harmed patients, and thus should be used more often than it is in this context. To this end, I demonstrate that existing corporate offences have more potential than has previously been thought in the healthcare context. This is not to argue that corporate liability should be seen as an alternative to individual liability, but it should be seen as an additional mechanism to be used to achieve a number of different aims, including contributing to healthcare safety, ensuring retribution and deterring future harmful actions. However, I point out the limitations of corporate criminal liability in the achievement of some of these goals, and suggest that there are other ways in which some of these goals, in particular safety defined as 'the reduction of risk of unnecessary harm to an acceptable minimum',[4] can be better achieved outside the criminal law framework. Furthermore, in order to ensure that harmed patients get quick access to compensation and explanations, I explain the benefits which a compensation scheme – similar to the French ONIAM scheme – can offer in the context of healthcare failings.

Systemic failings and criminal liability

Chapter 5 argues that when an individual healthcare professional and/or decision-maker has shown a sufficient level of culpability, the criminal law should be invoked. This is in theory easy, but reality is quite different. As is seen throughout this book, in the healthcare setting, culpability may sometimes be hard to

3 P Brearey-Horne, 'The Corporate Manslaughter and Corporate Homicide Act 2007 and Maternal Death: An Opportunity to Address Systemic Deficiencies in Maternity Services?' in D Griffiths, A Sanders (eds), above n2; O Quick, 'Medicine, Mistake and Manslaughter: A Criminal Combination', (2012) 69(1) *Cambridge Law Journal* 186; N Allen, 'Medical or Managerial Manslaughter', in C Erin, S Ost (eds), *The Criminal Justice System and Health Care* (Oxford: Oxford University Press 2007), 50–66; C Wells, above n2; P Gooderham, 'No-One Fully Responsible: A "Collusion of Anonymity" Protecting Health Care Bodies from Manslaughter Charges?' (2011) *Clinical Ethics* 68.

4 W Runciman et al., 'Towards an International Classification for Patient Safety: Key Concepts and Terms', (2009) 21 *International Journal for Quality in Health Care* 21.

establish for one or several individuals because roles and duties are shared within an institution. In these instances, the role and effect of the criminal law would be limited because no one has actually *caused* the harm; instead, several people may have *contributed* to the same harm. If the liability of one individual cannot be established, however, it would seem that the criminal law would have no effective role in ensuring retribution or deterrence and would thus be unable to offer justice to victims of these mishaps and their families.

Logically, then, when patients have been harmed as a result of healthcare failings, criminal liability should fall on the institution itself, but only *if* the institution has *itself* reached the threshold of criminal culpability, which should be consistent with the level of culpability required for individuals. A healthcare institution should be criminally liable only if it has disregarded patient safety or deliberately put patients at risk of harm or death. However, establishing culpability on the part of a corporation is not that simple. The key question here is how to determine when an institution has been reckless or has committed deliberate wrongdoing. The difficulty in assessing that level of culpability is that a corporation does not have a 'mind' *per se*, in the same way as an individual human being. Reckless or deliberate wrongdoing at the corporate level is therefore more difficult to assess than for individual wrongdoers. When determining a corporation's culpability, an appropriate test to impose liability is therefore needed.

The blood episode has shown that the failure to respond to the contamination of the blood supply was in part a result of diffused levels of responsibility in the decision-making process. The blood episode also illustrated that a common problem in this area is that healthcare failings sometimes appear at first to result from individual failure. Among many others, the *Sullman and Prentice* case and the *Ubani* case fall into this category.[5] In these cases, the criminal charges picked out just one or two individuals at the end of a long chain of failures to protect the patient – including understaffing and lack of resources. Criminal proceedings arising out of the blood episode in France illustrated the preference of the victims and the *juge d'instruction* for using individual criminal liability rather than corporate liability. *Juges d'instruction* looked for culpability on the part of each person involved in the decision-making process leading to the contamination, even though it was sometimes difficult to prove causation, or even culpability, on the part of each defendant, which explains the lack of success of most of these prosecutions.

Several healthcare scandals have shown that it is difficult to hold to account individuals, as well as institutions, for mishaps which have caused patients to die or suffer harm. Several healthcare disasters in England and Wales demonstrate the lack of accountability of decision-makers and corporations in this matter.[6] In

5 P Gooderham, above n3.

6 See, for instance, *Gosport War Memorial Hospital: The Report of the Gosport Independent Panel*, 20 June 2018 (Gosport Inquiry); R Francis, *Independent Inquiry into Care Provided by Mid Staffordshire NHS Foundation Trust January 2005–March 2009*, Vol I and II (2010).

England and Wales, there are only a few examples of prosecutions and convictions of health institutions for causing harm to patients or the death of patients, using either offences under the HSWA 1974 or corporate manslaughter.[7] I express several concerns about using corporate criminal liability as an *alternative* to individual criminal liability. Holding *only* healthcare institutions to account may not necessarily deliver justice to patients, ensure effective deterrence or contribute to safety when individuals who have made unsafe decisions remain unaccountable.

The danger in using *only* corporate liability is the reinforcement of the corporate veil, or the impunity of individual decision-makers, and several healthcare scandals are a testament to this impunity.[8] Individual decision-makers are shielded from liability because they hide in large institutions which feature complex and shared decision-making. Instead, corporate liability should be used alongside individual liability when the required level of culpability is established.

The corporate 'person' in the healthcare context

In comparison to other enterprises, healthcare is unique because it runs a greater risk of causing harm and death than do many other corporations. Many of its 'users' are also vulnerable, in the sense that they are already ill or injured when they receive treatment, thus making it more probable that harm may result from a healthcare procedure. In both France and England and Wales, the healthcare system is also specific because, unlike many other enterprises, it is mostly publicly funded; therefore, its resources are more limited and scarce than in other corporations. This means that criminal liability will affect health institutions in a different way than it does other corporations. In particular, criminal sanctions will have a different impact on health institutions than on other enterprises, as will be explained later in the chapter. It is therefore necessary to first look at how criminal law can relate to the various institutions within the NHS.

The French and English healthcare systems, unlike other healthcare systems such as that of the US, are largely funded by taxation. The difference between the two systems is that the NHS is based on the Beveridge model of healthcare, and the French healthcare system is based on the Bismarckian model. Both systems provide universal access to healthcare, but the French healthcare system is a mix of private and public sector involvement for both service provision and financing of healthcare.[9] French healthcare is financed through both taxation and insurance fees. Patients are therefore expected to contribute to healthcare provision

7 See, for instance, *R v Errol Cornish and Maidstone and Tunbridge Wells NHS Trust* [2015] EWHC 2967 (QB); *R v Mid Staffordshire NHS Foundation Trust*, Sentencing Remarks of the Hon Mr Justice Haddon-Cave, 28 April 2014.

8 S Tombs, D Whyte, *The Corporate Criminal, Why Corporations Should Be Abolished* (London: Routledge 2015), 92; S Tombs, 'The UK's Corporate Killing Law: Un/fit for Purpose?' (2018) 18(4) *Criminology and Criminal Justice* 500.

9 L Chambaud, 'How Healthy Is the French Health System?' *The Conversation* (21 September 2017).

through a 'modest out-of-pocket co-payment'.[10] In the Bismarckian model, the medical profession 'has higher levels of autonomy'[11] than in the Beveridge model, which may explain the greater willingness of courts to use criminal liability for healthcare 'negligence' in France, as healthcare professionals represent private interests rather than the interests of a state institution.

In the NHS, a distinction is drawn between institutions which *commission* care and institutions which *provide* care. These institutions are at different levels of the decision-making process in the health service and face different levels of risk. Institutions providing care confront a higher and more immediate risk to patient safety than those which commission care, because providers are in direct contact with patients. Clinical commissioning groups (CCGs) are responsible for commissioning secondary care, such as hospital care, and have control over the vast majority of NHS expenditures. Secondary care is generally provided by NHS Trusts or Foundation Trusts and other institutions, including private sector organisations.

The NHS is also regulated by various bodies, including the Care Quality Commission (CQC), which are responsible for ensuring that good quality service and care are provided to patients. The CQC aims to 'protect and promote the health, safety and welfare of people who use health and social care services'.[12] Given that institutions which provide care are in direct contact with patients, they are more likely to commit errors, or failures which may cause harm to those patients, and this may lead to some form of liability, whilst institutions which commission care are more distant from risk and therefore liability. Later in the chapter, I explore how criminal sanctions may affect NHS institutions and whether criminal sanctions are effective in ensuring what the criminal law aims to achieve, including deterrence.

Establishing the culpability of a health institution

The difficulty raised by corporate personality and responsibility is the determination of any *mens rea* when a criminal offence is committed.[13] The following questions are thus raised: should a health institution be liable for mere errors/negligence, or should the threshold of culpability be consistent with that applied to individual defendants? And what model of criminalisation is the most appropriate for healthcare corporations?

In France, for a corporation to be prosecuted for a criminal offence, that offence has to have been committed by one of its bodies or representatives on its behalf.[14] If the corporation's representative has committed an offence, the

10 J Beckfield, S Olafsdottir, B Sosnaud, 'Healthcare Systems in Comparative Perspective: Classification, Convergence, institutions, Inequalities and Five Missed Turns', (2013) 39 *Annual Review of Sociology* 130–131.

11 Ibid.

12 S. 3(1) Health and Social Care Act 2008.

13 J Gobert, 'Corporate criminality: Four Models of Fault', (1994) 14(3) *Legal Studies* 395.

14 Article 121-2 Code Pénal (CP); Cass Crim, 11/07/2017, n°16-86.092; Cass Crim, 17/12/2003, n°00-87.872; Cass Crim, 13/04/2010, n°09-86.429; Cass Crim, 16/10/2013,

corporation may be subject to criminal liability.[15] In the previous chapter, I have argued that if one of the controlling minds of the institution (i.e. an individual) has committed a reckless action, or omission, or has disregarded the health and life of a patient, which then caused the patient to die or suffer injury, s/he should be convicted of a criminal offence. This follows from Toft and Gooderham's argument that 'where managers have been warned of an unsafe system, and reasonable action has not been taken, then liability, particularly criminal liability for manslaughter, should fall more upon managers'.[16]

When there is a culture of conscious risk-taking with awareness that serious harm may be caused to people in the corporation, this is, in my view, sufficient to show that an institution is culpable in the criminal sense.[17] Corporations should be prosecuted when harm or death has resulted from an unsafe system, where there is evidence that there was a generalised culture of conscious and harmful risk-taking. This is not to say that individuals should not be prosecuted as well. Individuals should be prosecuted when they have committed reckless or deliberate wrongdoing. For instance, what would justify the use of criminal sanctions against individual decision-makers are decisions which prioritise profit-making over health and safety, as we have seen in the contaminated blood episode or the Mid-Staffordshire (Mid-Staffs) scandal. The appropriate test to establish an institution's culpability would therefore follow the French *faute caractérisée*: 'exposing another person to a particularly serious risk of which the defendant ought to have been aware'.[18] If there is evidence that decision-making bodies within the institution were aware of that risk, this is evidence that the institution has sufficient culpability. If both the corporation and individuals within the corporation have the required level of culpability, i.e. if they have shown disregard for the health and safety of patients, then they should both be prosecuted for criminal offences.

In previous chapters, we have seen examples of healthcare negligence caused by systems errors. For instance, in *Prentice and Sullman*, vincristine was wrongly injected into a patient's spine. The negligence was in part the result of a lack of supervision of the two junior doctors and a misunderstanding of each doctor's responsibility, as well as the failure to read the drug's label, which indicated how vincristine was to be administered. It was also shown that the cytotoxic drugs

---

n°12-81.532; B Bouloc, H Matsopoulou, *Droit pénal général et procédure pénale* (21e edn, Paris: Sirey 2018), 153; Assemblée Nationale, *Rapport n° 2266 fait au nom de la commission des lois constitutionnelles, de la législation et de l'administration générale de la République sur la proposition de loi, adoptée par le Sénat, tendant à préciser la définition des délits non intentionnels*, par M René Dosière (22 mars 2000), 53.

15 But French courts have admitted that even if the directing mind of the corporation was not found guilty in the proceedings, the corporation could still be convicted of a criminal offence; see, for instance, CA Grenoble, 12/06/1998, affaire du Drac.

16 P Gooderham, B Toft, 'Involuntary Automaticity and Medical Manslaughter', in D Griffiths, A Sanders (eds), above n3 at 188.

17 S Tombs, D Whyte, above n8 at 88.

18 Article 121-3 al 4 CP.

had been placed on the lumbar-puncture trolley without the manufacturer's data sheet, which misled the two doctors.[19] The judge sentencing the two doctors thus affirmed that they 'could have been helped more than [they] were helped'. Prosecuting two junior medical professionals for a fault which had been caused by systemic factors 'simply sets the stage for the same thing to happen again to someone else', as we would be 'removing the last person in the chain of errors without fixing the predisposing factors'.[20] Similarly, Dr Ubani had prescribed an inappropriate dose of diamorphine to a patient who died as a result. The causes of his failure were said to be his poor English, his unfamiliarity with the product and his fatigue. Gooderham made an analysis of all the agencies involved in the appointment of Ubani as an out-of-hours General Practitioner. He discovered that six institutions could potentially have been held to account for Ubani's error.[21]

In the contaminated blood episode, failure to respond to the contamination had resulted in part from the disorganisation of the healthcare system and misunderstanding of each actor's role and responsibility, which was acknowledged in the various inquiries into the episode.[22] Several cases of healthcare failings demonstrate that individual prosecutions would be inappropriate when the causes of the harm suffered by the patients were in fact systemic, resulting from corporate mismanagement. A healthcare corporation's culpability could be established if documents, witness statements and other evidence of standards used by the institution all point to a disregard for patient safety, and where warnings had been given but not followed for too long. One particular difficulty which arises with regard to the criminalisation of healthcare corporations is the proof of a causal link between the failings of the institution and the harm suffered by patients. I argue below that some criminal offences could provide an answer to this problem.

Using corporate offences in the healthcare context

Although the CMCHA 2007 has aimed to address issues regarding corporate liability which arose under the common law, it will be demonstrated here that it is still difficult to hold health institutions to account under the CMCHA 2007, and so far no healthcare institution has been successfully prosecuted for corporate manslaughter.[23]

19 [1993] 4 All ER 935 at 945.

20 A Merry, 'When Are Errors a Crime?-Lessons from New Zealand', in C Erin, S Ost (eds), above n3 at 81.

21 P Gooderham, above n3 at 69.

22 See Chapter 4; J Sourdille, C Huriet, *La crise du système transfusionnel français*, Rapport de la commission d'enquête du Sénat (Paris: Ecomonica 1992), 43–44; Assemblée Nationale, *Rapport de la commission d'enquête sur l'état des connaissances scientifiques et les actions menées à l'égard de la transmission du sida* (Union générale d'édition 1993), 14.

23 General Medical Council, *Independent Review of Gross Negligence Manslaughter and Culpable Homicide*, June 2019 (Hamilton Review), 32.

Liability under the CMCHA 2007

Under the CMCHA 2007, a gross breach is required on the part of the corporation for criminal liability to be established.[24] The condition is that the way in which the corporation's activities are 'managed or organised by its senior management must be a substantial element in the breach'.[25] S. 1(4)(b) indicates that 'a breach of a duty of care by an organisation is a "gross" breach if the conduct alleged to amount to a breach of that duty falls far below what can reasonably be expected of the organisation in the circumstances'.[26] This offence does not apply to an institution which does not owe a duty of care to an individual patient. 'Senior management' refers to the 'persons who play significant roles in (i) the making of decisions about how the whole or a substantial part of its activities are to be managed or organised, or (ii) the actual managing or organising of the whole or a substantial part of those activities'.[27]

Gooderham argued that 'the Act offers more guidance to a jury on what constitutes a breach of duty than [gross negligence manslaughter (GNM)]'.[28] The Act, however, is not clear on what is to be considered 'substantial'. The Act would be apt to embrace many cases where an NHS body which owed a duty of care to an individual had been grossly negligent and caused the death of that individual patient. Nevertheless, it could not be used to hold liable regulators who do not owe a duty of care to individual patients. For instance, it could not apply to regulators of the NHS, such as the CQC, which regulates hospitals to check whether they meet safety standards.

Another criticism which can be made is that the Act admits a large range of exceptions.[29] First, included in the 'relevant duty of care' of an organisation are

> (a) a duty owed to its employees or to other persons working for the organisation or performing services for it; (b) a duty owed as occupier of premises; (c) a duty owed in connection with (i) the supply by the organisation of goods or services, (ii) the carrying on by the organisation of any construction or maintenance operations; (iii) the carrying on by the organisation of any other activity on a commercial basis, or (iv) the use or keeping by the organisation of any plant, vehicle or other thing.[30]

This would mean that if an NHS Trust commissions a clinical service, it would be considered to be supplying a service and will thus owe a duty of care and be included in the scope of the CMCHA 2007.[31]

24 S. 1(1) CMCHA 2007.
25 S. 1(3) CMCHA 2007.
26 S. 1(4)(b) CMCHA 2007.
27 S. 1 (4)(c) CMCHA 2007.
28 P Gooderham, above n3 at 71.
29 C Wells, above n2 at 202; P Gooderham, above n3 at 71.
30 S. 2 CMCHA 2007.
31 C Wells, above n2 at 202–203.

Nevertheless, according to s. 3(1) of the Act, 'any duty of care owed by a public authority in respect of a decision as to matters of public policy (including in particular the allocation of public resources or the weighing of competing public interests) is not a "relevant duty of care"'.[32] For example, an institution might decide not to provide patients a particular drug for financial reasons.[33] Similarly, 'any duty of care owed in respect of things done in the exercise of an exclusively public function is not a "relevant duty of care"', unless the duty is 'owed to its employees or to other persons working for the organisation or performing services for it'; the duty is 'owed as occupier of the premises'; or it is 'owed to a person who . . . is someone for whose safety the organisation is responsible'.[34] On that basis, it would have been difficult to prosecute the UK national blood centre for corporate manslaughter following the tainted blood scandal under the CMCHA 2007 had the Act been in force at the time.

Lastly, a duty 'owed by a public authority in respect of inspections carried out in the exercise of a statutory function' is not a 'relevant duty of care' unless the duty is 'owed to its employees or to other persons working for the organisation or performing services for it', or it is 'owed as occupier of premises'.[35] This would then also not apply to the CQC or other regulators of the NHS.

The Act notes that an 'exclusively public function' is one that 'falls within the prerogative of the Crown or is, by its nature, exercisable only with authority conferred (a) by the exercise of that prerogative, or (b) by or under a statutory provision', which is a 'function conferred by or under a statutory provision'.[36] The Ministry of Justice Notes on the Act provide that this includes licensing drugs.[37] Wells indicates that this excludes a function which required a licence or 'took place on a statutory basis', and this means that 'NHS liability that previously existed under common law manslaughter would be removed altogether'.[38]

The Act also admits a large number of exceptions in the area of emergencies. S. 6 of the Act provides that 'any duty of care owed by an organisation . . . in respect of the way in which it responds to emergency circumstances is not a "relevant duty of care"' unless it is 'owed to its employees or to other persons working for the organisation or performing services for it', or is 'owed as occupier of premises'.[39] This includes 'relevant NHS' bodies (NHS England, CCGs, NHS Trusts, Special Health Authorities or NHS Foundation Trusts), organisations 'providing ambulance services' or 'providing services for the transport of organs, blood, equipment or personnel in pursuance of arrangements (i) made by, or at the request of, a relevant NHS body, or (ii) made with the Secretary of State or with the Welsh

32 S. 3(1) CMCHA 2007.
33 P Gooderham, above n3 at 71.
34 S. 3(2), s. 2(1)(a), (b), (d) CMCHA 2007.
35 S. 3(3), s. 2(1)(a), (b) CMCHA 2007.
36 S. 3(4) CMCHA 2007.
37 Para 27 Explanatory Notes to CMCHA 2007.
38 C Wells, above n2 at 202.
39 S. 6(1) and s. 2(1)(a), (b) CMCHA 2007.

Ministers', and organisations 'providing a rescue service'.[40] S. 6(7) of the Act further indicates that 'emergency circumstances' include circumstances which '(a) are causing, or are likely to cause, serious harm or a worsening of such harm, or (b) are likely to cause the death of a person'.[41] Hence, if an ambulance comes to rescue a patient and causes the death of that person by treating him/her with gross negligence, the ambulance trust would not be criminally liable under the Act.[42]

The Act excludes from liability a substantial proportion of health institution activities that might cause harm as a result of serious failure. As Wells argues, 'the Act is complex and the offence definition itself is full of ambiguities and interpretive uncertainty' and does not provide a satisfactory and efficient criminalisation of healthcare institutions.[43] Gooderham also noted that in a case such as *Ubani*, 'the fragmented nature of the corporate NHS . . . makes it difficult to apply elements of the offence contained in the Act to anyone of the corporate bodies involved'.[44] Moreover, the Act's 'overwhelming targets have thus far been micro or small organizations with "hands-on" directors who are clearly identifiable as the controlling mind of the company and who could have been prosecuted (and convicted) under existing common law'.[45]

Corporate manslaughter under the Act has so far never been used successfully against a health institution. This is mainly due to the need to prove a causal link between the gross breach and the death of a patient.[46] In most cases of healthcare failure, this will be extremely difficult to prove, even though there might be evidence of a gross breach. As an example, it still remains impossible to prove whether the Mid-Staffordshire NHS Foundation Trust did actually cause the death of between 400 and 1200 patients between 2005 and 2009 as many of these patients were already extremely weak and in poor health before receiving treatment at the hospital. As I have argued for individual healthcare negligence, using conduct offences in relation to corporate negligence would therefore be more helpful than using offences which require proof of a causal link. Offences under the HSWA 1974 do not require any proof of a causal link and would therefore be very useful in this context.

Liability under the HSWA 1974

The criminalisation of healthcare failure requires consistency, and therefore, following on what the French experience has taught us, corporate conduct resulting in injury short of death should also be criminalised, in the same way as it is at the individual level. Luck and outcome should not be taken into account when criminalising healthcare negligence, and this should apply to health institutions as well.

40 S. 6(1), (2)(e), (f), (g), (h) and s. 6(7)(a) CMCHA 2007.
41 S. 6(7)(a)(b) CMCHA 2007.
42 C Wells, above n2 at 203.
43 C Wells, above n2 at 200.
44 P Gooderham, above n3 at 75.
45 S Tombs, above n8 at 498.
46 Hamilton Review, above n23 at 32.

Reform would not be necessary to achieve this, as what the HSWA 1974 and the CJCA 2015 offer could respond to the need to criminalise conduct resulting in injury short of death and to address problems linked to proving a causal link in healthcare failure cases.

Offences under the HSWA 1974 offer a more appropriate criminalisation of corporate healthcare malpractice for several reasons: the Act specifically targets healthcare safety; it does not contain exceptions in relation to health institutions; it permits the criminalisation of conduct resulting in injury and not only death; and offences under the HSWA 1974 also do not require the proof of any causal link between breach and harm, which means that proving the elements of the offences is much easier than proving a charge of corporate manslaughter. Under s. 3(1) of the HSWA 1974, every employer has the duty to 'conduct his undertaking in such a way as to ensure, *so far as is reasonably practicable*, that persons not in his employment who may be affected thereby are not thereby exposed to risks to their health or safety' (emphasis added).[47] There is therefore no need to prove a gross breach or a causal link. Proving the failure to comply with this provision will be sufficient for criminal liability to be imposed.

Healthcare services including CCGs, NHS Hospital Trusts, mental care services and NHS Ambulance Services Trusts may be criminally liable under s. 3(1) of the HSWA 1974 for exposing their employees or other persons (patients and members of the public) to 'risks to their health and safety'.[48] Offences under this Act offer advantages over corporate manslaughter in the context of healthcare breaches. HSWA 1974 offences are more appropriate than the 'more unusual offence of manslaughter' as they are 'wide-ranging' and the criteria on which the jury decides on a conviction are based on health and safety regulations and guidance.[49] Furthermore, there is no need to prove that any injury or death resulted from the breach of health and safety legislation, although it seems that it would be easier to prosecute an institution if death or injury had ensued. Quick notes that HSWA 1974 focuses 'squarely on safety, and particularly the contribution of flawed systems'.[50]

Furthermore, the use of both corporate manslaughter and health and safety offences against a corporation may 'present some problems in relation to investigation procedures, enforcement policies and of potential overlap in punishment'.[51] However, this may be mitigated by the definitive guideline on health and safety offences, corporate manslaughter and food safety and hygiene offences, effective from February 2016.[52] The risk remains that 'corporate manslaughter cases

47 S. 3 HSWA 1974.

48 Ss. 2–3 HSWA 1974.

49 C Wells, above n2 at 196.

50 O Quick, 'Patient Safety and the Problem and Potential of Law', (2012) *Journal of Professional Negligence* 97.

51 C Wells, above n2 at 193.

52 The Sentencing Council, Health and Safety Offences, Corporate Manslaughter and Food Safety and Hygiene Offences, Definitive Guideline, 2015; sentencingcouncil.org.uk, accessed 31 January 2020.

continue to look messy and are likely to give rise . . . to multiple charges in relation to the same incident'.[53]

Liability under the CJCA 2015

These offences aim to criminalise conduct which results in harm short of death, and this applies equally to individuals and to institutions. Under s. 21 of the CJCA 2015, a 'care provider', which includes a 'body corporate . . . which provides or arranges for the provision of (i) health care for an adult or child', could be liable for the offences of ill-treatment or wilful neglect which also apply to individual 'care workers'.[54] This section applies to any NHS or private institution providing healthcare. Hence, an NHS Hospital Trust could be liable under s. 21 if a nurse working in the hospital wilfully neglects or ill-treats a patient, the Trust's 'activities are managed or organised in a way which amounts to a gross breach of a relevant duty of care owed' by the Trust to the patient who is ill-treated or neglected, 'and, in the absence of the breach, the ill-treatment or wilful neglect would not have occurred or would have been less likely to occur'.[55] The Mid-Staffordshire NHS Foundation Trust could therefore have been prosecuted under s. 21 for neglecting patients, had the Act been in force at the time of the episode. Offences at s. 21 require a gross breach on the part of the institution, and according to the information available on what had occurred at the Mid-Staffordshire NHS Foundation Trust between 2005 and 2009, gross breach would have been proved, as what the Trust did fall far below what can reasonably be expected of an NHS Trust in the circumstances. I have shown elsewhere that the Mid-Staffs scandal had displayed disregard for the health and safety of patients.[56] The Trust was convicted of offences under the HSWA 1974 for the deaths of five victims which were found to be 'wholly avoidable deaths'.[57]

Offences at s. 21 of the CJCA 2015 also address the issue of fair labelling, which English prosecution services and courts have so far been unable to properly address in relation to healthcare failure cases. The offences are able to represent the disregard for the safety of patients on the part of the defendant institution, which can provide an appropriate degree of retribution to harmed victims.

The effect of criminal sanctions on health institutions

When considering the effect of criminalisation on healthcare institutions, one must explore the effect and impact of criminal sanctions on healthcare safety, staff and patients. Criminal sanctions aim to satisfy the purposes of the criminal

53 C Wells, above n2 at 194.

54 S. 21 CJCA 2015; see Chapter 2.

55 S. 21 CJCA 2015.

56 M Kazarian, 'Who Should We Blame for Healthcare Failings? Lessons from the French Tainted Blood Scandal', (2019) 27(3) *Medical Law Review* 402.

57 *R v Mid Staffordshire NHS Foundation Trust*, Sentencing Remarks of the Hon Mr Justice Haddon-Cave, 28 April 2014, 12.

law, which include the need for deterrence, incapacitation, rehabilitation, retribution and prevention of harm. But can this always be possible following a case of healthcare failure? These aims will be explored in turn.

Deterrence

Although corporations do not have a 'soul' or 'conscience', criminal sanctions may have an effect on the safety of people working in the institution and of users of the services provided by the institutions. For instance, it has been argued that

> the threat of criminal sanctions alone has the power to compel corporate decision-makers to abandon their exclusively economic calculus of thought and action and, for the first time, to begin to base their behaviour on a serious consideration of the human consequences of their actions.[58]

Furthermore, it is argued that managers and directors in commercial corporations may be deterred by the prospect of corporate punishment and should therefore weigh the costs and benefits of the consequences of a decision.[59] However, this point is disputed by scholars who argue that there is no empirical evidence that decision-makers may be deterred by the threat of corporate punishment. Rather, there is evidence to argue that the threat of corporate punishment might actually make decision-makers less affected by the threat of criminal punishment, if corporate liability is used instead of individual liability.[60] Furthermore, the prospect of corporate punishment is more likely to deter decision-makers in small companies than in large companies where corporate sanctions would rarely affect them personally. Consequently, decision-makers in health institutions may not be directly affected or deterred by corporate punishment.

Financial penalties against corporations can act as effective deterrents, but only if certain conditions are met.[61] Financial sanctions need to be sufficiently substantial to discourage the institution from taking an unjustified risk.[62] Quick claims that 'the fact that trusts are unable to insure against the payment of criminal fines may be an important factor in terms of helping to incentivise compliance with safety standards'.[63] Yet imposing large fines on publicly funded NHS institutions is likely to impact negatively on patient safety. The cost of a fine could reduce the institution's income, weaken the performance of the service and result in more accidents due to reductions in staff numbers or necessary healthcare equipment,

58 R Engineer, 'Punishing Corporate Negligence, Industrial Disasters and Criminal Law', (1989) 24(14) *Economic and Political Weekly* 711.

59 Ibid at 713.

60 S Tombs, above n8 at 500.

61 JC Coffee, 'No Soul to Damn: No Body to Kick: An Unscandalized Inquiry into the Problem of Corporate Punishment', (1981) 79(3) *Michigan Law Review* 389.

62 Ibid.

63 O Quick, above n50 at 98.

for instance.[64] Fines may, however, be an effective deterrent against privately funded healthcare companies.

Publicity orders could be seen as more effective in deterring harmful action or inaction by publicly funded health institutions than fines.[65] For example, extensive media coverage of the French tainted blood episode and public outcry eventually led to several reforms of the blood supply organisation following the scandal, such as reorganisation of regulatory processes to improve blood safety.[66] Some of the CMCHA 2007 orders can be effective deterrents against health institutions. The Act provides that a court may order an organisation convicted of corporate manslaughter to publicise '(a) the fact that it has been convicted of the offence; (b) specified particulars of the offence; (c) the amount of any fine imposed; (d) the terms of any remedial order made'.[67]

Wells highlights the limits of the CMCHA 2007 in ensuring deterrence of harmful action or inaction by health institutions. She argues that because of the 'time lag between the event and the trial', any remedial order might not be effective.[68] But this may also be the case with HSWA 1974 offences. As an example, the Mid-Staffordshire NHS Foundation Trust had already gone into administration when it was sentenced to pay fines, and so the fines were eventually paid by the 'public purse', and it seems therefore that the fines imposed had no deterrent effect on the Trust at this stage.[69]

Incapacitation and rehabilitation

One way of ensuring safety in the healthcare environment would be to try and incapacitate and/or rehabilitate unsafe health institutions. Incapacitation is generally seen as a means to protect the public from the alleged criminal. The aim would be to partially or completely disable the institution. Financial penalties can, for instance, be used to make the institution go bankrupt. An institution could be suspended and prohibited from providing services. This would be a more powerful tool than financial sanctions to ensure safety in the healthcare environment. For instance, the Health and Safety Executive (HSE) can enforce improvement or prohibition notices on an institution which has been found in breach of their obligations under the HSWA 1974. These can force the institution to either improve safety or stop a part of their activities if they are considered unsafe.[70]

64 M Childs, 'Medical Manslaughter and Corporate Liability', (1999) 19(3) *Legal Studies* 316, 333.

65 JC Coffee, above n61 at 425, 427, 433; CMV Clarkson, 'Kicking Corporate Bodies and Damning Their Souls', (1996) 59(4) *The Modern Law Review* 557, 562.

66 AM Farrell, M Kazarian, 'The Role of the Criminal Law in Healthcare Malpractice in France: Examining the HIV Blood Contamination Scandal', in D Griffiths, A Sanders (eds), above n2 at 278.

67 S. 10(1) CMCHA 2007.

68 C Wells, above n2 at 207.

69 M Kazarian, above n56.

70 See www.hse.gov.uk/enforce/enforcementguide/notices/notices-intro.htm, accessed 31 January 2020.

In a healthcare setting, rehabilitation would entail considering near-misses and correcting systems which had originally led to the harm. We should note that 'fines at whatever level do not aid rehabilitation – and, indeed, the higher they are set, they may actually hinder more effective systems of health and safety being developed in the aftermath of a conviction since they impose costs on the company'.[71] Moreover, 'such costs may not at all be borne by the offending company itself – many argue that the costs of fines tend to be counter-productive since they are dispersed to the "innocent" '.[72] In particular, they may be 'inappropriately borne by employees, through worsening working conditions, cuts to, or deferred increases in, wages, or even potential redundancy'.[73]

In terms of rehabilitating corporations, particular individuals should be 'removed' or 'disciplined'.[74] There is no evidence that the use of the criminal law would help in 'rehabilitating' health institutions as such, although within the NHS a conviction could lead to new management or transfer of functions. But disqualification orders would help to remove particular decision-makers who may have put the organisation and people within it at risk of harm. Under s. 2 of the Company Directors Disqualification Act 1986, a disqualification order can be made against a person convicted of an indictable offence 'in connection with the promotion, formation, management, liquidation or striking off of a company or with the management of a company's property'.[75] This may apply if, for example, directors or managers are convicted of an offence under s. 7 of the HSWA 1974, where the offence relates to the management of a company's affairs, activities or business. The HSE further indicates that 'such offences are indictable and may call into question that person's suitability to fulfil the role of director'.[76] Following the Mid-Staffs scandal, the Berwick Report had recommended that

> [o]rganisational sanctions might involve removal of the organisation's leaders and their disqualification from future leadership roles, public reprimand of the organisation and, in extremis, financial sanctions but only where that will not compromise patient care. Individual sanctions should be on a par with those in Section 44 of the Mental Health Capacity Act 2005.[77]

The role of the CQC may also be useful here. The CQC has the capacity to prosecute health institutions for non-compliance with the essential standards of quality

71 S Tombs, above n8 at 502.
72 Ibid.
73 Ibid.
74 CMV Clarkson, above n67 at 562.
75 S. 2 Company Directors Disqualification Act 1986.
76 See www.hse.gov.uk/enforce/enforcementguide/court/sentencing-penalties.htm, accessed 31 January 2020.
77 D Berwick, *Improving the Safety of Patients in England, A Promise to Learn-A Commitment to Act*, National Advisory Group on the Safety of Patients in England, August 2013, 34.

and safety required under the Health and Social Care Act 2008.[78] But before it actually prosecutes an institution, it can issue a requirement or warning notice for the institution to comply promptly, restrict the services offered by the institution, stop admissions into the service, issue fixed penalty notices, or suspend or cancel the service's registration.[79] These measures may ensure rehabilitation/incapacitation before an actual prosecution takes place. It may also contribute to prevention of accidents and improved safety if the institution enforces the standards of quality and safety expected from the relevant regulations. This can in theory be a very useful tool to use alongside traditional criminal liability, as compliance with fundamental standards of quality and safety could be achieved even before the use of the criminal process becomes necessary. However, I point out later that CQC processes have been criticised for their lack of effectiveness in ensuring safety and should therefore be improved.

Retribution and demands of victims

The victims' demand to see one person, 'a scapegoat', held liable might not be satisfied when criminalising health institutions.[80] Questions remain about whether families and victims would wish to know exactly who was responsible for the injury or death as individuals rather than as institutions. Victims of the tainted blood episode in both France and England and Wales expressed the need to see someone held accountable for what had happened. At the moment, in England and Wales, neither senior decision-makers nor healthcare corporations have been properly held to account for many instances which would be qualified as disregard for the health and safety of patients, and it is therefore important that appropriate criminalisation in this matter takes the views of victims and the public into account.

There have been arguments in favour of retribution as an aim for corporate liability.[81] For instance, Wells argues that the CMCHA 2007 might offer more by way of retribution than the HSWA 1974, which 'aims at minimising risk directly'.[82] However, the CMCHA 2007 excludes a large number of cases where health institutions could be held liable, and it has been used against a health institution only once so far. Moreover, in reality, penalties imposed against health

78 See www.cqc.org.uk/guidance-providers/regulations-enforcement/offences, accessed 31 January 2020.

79 See www.cqc.org.uk/what-we-do/how-we-do-our-job/taking-action, accessed 31 January 2020; Care Quality Commission, *Registration Under the Health and Social Care Act 2008, Warning Notices, Guidance for Registered Providers and Managers*, October 2015, 4.

80 See Chapter 4.

81 RC Ausness, 'Retribution and Deterrence: The Role of Punitive Damages in Products Liability Litigation', (1985) 74(1) *Kentucky Law Journal* 40; RA Robson, 'Crime and Punishment: Rehabilitating Retribution as a Justification for Organizational Criminal Liability', (2010) 47(1) *American Business Law Journal* 124.

82 C Wells, above n2 at 207.

institutions are unlikely to have the retributive effect expected by the victims, especially if the institution has already been liquidated and is therefore unable to pay any fine. Many victims have also expressed that they did not want to see this type of disaster happen again in the future, and therefore prevention of harm would be key in ensuring this.

Prevention and transparency

The contaminated blood episode illustrates the pressing need of victims of such disasters for transparency. Criminal investigations in France in part addressed this issue but were limited in evaluating systemic error. The question of whether the use of the criminal law contributed to the prevention of further healthcare accidents remains unanswered, but it seems unlikely that the criminal process does much to ensure healthcare safety when used on its own.[83] There is no empirical evidence to say that reforms made in France following the contaminated blood scandal – i.e. the creation of ONIAM, the creation of new medicine and blood agencies and the expansive use of the precautionary principle – were principally a result of the use of criminal proceedings against health officials, doctors and ministers. The use of the criminal process may, however, have an effect in the making of preventive measures, as it has been argued that politicians tend to protect themselves from criminal liability by acting on prevention, for instance by using the precautionary principle.[84]

Some CMCHA 2007 provisions may help to ensure prevention of harm in the healthcare malpractice context. The CMCHA 2007 states that a court may order an organisation that has been convicted of corporate manslaughter to remedy

> (a) the breach of a 'relevant duty of care'; (b) any matter that appears to the court to have resulted from the relevant breach and to have been a cause of the death; (c) any deficiency, as regards health and safety matters, in the organisation's policies, systems or practices of which the relevant breach appears to the court to be an indication.[85]

The Act also indicates that 'an organisation that fails to comply with a remedial order is guilty of an offence, and liable on conviction on indictment to a fine'.[86] These orders are interesting and could help prevent healthcare error and harm to patients. Similarly, notices issued by the HSE or the CQC could help in this matter. It is therefore not the traditional criminal process on its

83 J Guigue, 'Les inconvénients de la pénalisation du droit de la santé', (2008) *Revue de droit sanitaire et social* 36.

84 Interview with B (Paris, France, 17 January 2011), 7; P Rimbault, 'La responsabilité pénale des décideurs et des personnes morales', XXXIVe Congrès Français de criminologie, 14 septembre 2005, 41–42.

85 S. 9(1) CMCHA 2007.

86 S. 9(5) CMCHA 2007.

own which can have an effective influence on healthcare safety, as will be seen in the next section.

Alternatives to the criminal process

After highlighting the limits of the criminal process in addressing healthcare failure, we must now discuss more effective ways in which systemic healthcare error can be dealt with which would rightly, and promptly, engage to promote patient safety and provide reparation and support for victims of healthcare failings.

Regulatory mechanisms

Regulation has been understood as 'the sustained and focused attempt to alter the behaviour of others according to standards or goals with the intention of producing a broadly identified outcome or outcomes, which may involve mechanisms of standard-setting, information-gathering and behaviour-modification'.[87] More specifically in the healthcare context, although regulatory mechanisms have aimed to set standards, they have not always been effective in preventing (avoidable) deaths or injuries caused to patients. What the various episodes of systemic failings in both France and England and Wales have in common is that regulatory mechanisms were either ineffective or not properly complied with; there was no transparency from management to staff, and from staff to patients; there was a 'protective "club" culture among professionals which inhibit[ed] criticism or learning';[88] and profit-making or cost-cutting were given priority when the minimum standard of care expected from the health institution could not even be reached.

There are various ways in which medical harm can be prevented more effectively. The first is to make sure that decision-making in healthcare institutions is focused on patient safety rather than on cutting costs. The second is to encourage a stronger reporting culture and transparency mechanisms. Openness, transparency and whistleblowing should be strongly encouraged in healthcare institutions, and not restricted or shut down as was the case in the Mid-Staffs scandal, the Bristol Royal Infirmary Hospital, or the Gosport War Memorial Hospital scandal.[89] Regulatory bodies must conduct timely and regular inspections to identify flaws in healthcare institutions. Lastly, tools such as the precautionary principle can help to formulate safe and cautious healthcare decisions. For instance, in France, following the contaminated blood episode, the use of the precautionary

87 J Black, 'What Is Regulatory Innovation?' in J Black, M Lodge, M Thatcher (eds), *Regulatory Innovation* (Cheltenham: Edward Elgar 2005), 11.

88 K Walshe, *Regulating Healthcare: A Prescription for Improvement* (Maidenhead: Open University Press 2003), 3.

89 Eleanor Grey QC, Professor Sir Ian Kennedy, *The Report of the Independent Review of Children's Cardiac Services in Bristol*, June 2016, 7, 85, 130; C Dyer, 'Bristol Inquiry Condemns Hospital's 'Club Culture', (2001) 323(7306) *British Medical Journal* 181; Gosport Inquiry, above n6 at 81.

principle led to the creation of regulatory agencies in charge of preserving safety in health institutions. They offer risk assessment and expert reports on adverse events in health institutions.[90] More broadly, regulation should be 'responsive' in that 'government should be attuned to the differing motivations of regulated actors'.[91]

Various regulators in England and Wales are responsible for making sure that healthcare institutions comply with safety standards, in what has been called 'regulatory pluralism'.[92] These include the CQC, the General Medical Council (GMC) and the HSE. The CQC and the HSE have the power to inspect health institutions and issue warning notices if there is a breach of safety regulations. The GMC regulates doctors, set standards for medical practice and can investigate complaints against individual doctors, which can then lead to fitness to practise proceedings.[93] The Medical Practitioners Tribunal Service (MPTS) is then in charge of making decisions about whether or not a doctor is fit to practise medicine. Members of the MPTS can have a medical or non-medical background.[94] If a doctor's practice is found to be impaired, the tribunal can issue warnings or sanctions against the individual doctor, such as suspension or erasure from the medical register.[95] Other professional regulators such as the Nursing and Midwifery Council, the General Optical Council and the General Dental Council have similar roles in relation to their respective profession, and can investigate complaints and impose sanctions on individual professionals.[96] These professional regulators are supervised by the Professional Standards Authority for Health and Social Care, created by the NHS Reform and Health Care Professions Act 2002.[97] The Professional Standards Authority takes the approach of 'right-touch regulation', which involves, for instance, proportionality – 'regulators should only intervene when necessary' – and transparency – 'regulators should be open and keep regulations simple and user friendly'.[98]

90 JF burgelin, 'La médecine saisie par le principe de précaution', (2000) 184(5) *Bulletin de l'Académie Nationale de Médecine* 873, 898.

91 I Ayres, J Braithwaite, *Responsive Regulation: Transcending the Deregulation Debate* (Oxford: Oxford University Press 1992), 4.

92 LG Trubek et al., 'Health Care and New Governance: The Quest for Effective Regulation', (2008) 2 *Regulation and Governance* 5.

93 See www.gmc-uk.org/about/what-we-do-and-why/our-mandate, accessed 11 November 2019.

94 See www.mpts-uk.org/hearings-and-decisions/who-makes-the-decisions, accessed 11 November 2019.

95 MPTS, GMC, Sanctions guidance for members of medical practitioners tribunals and for the General Medical Council's decision makers, April 2017, 22.

96 See www.nmc.org.uk/concerns-nurses-midwives/hearings/sanctions-info/; www.optical.org/en/Investigating_complaints/Hearings/How_hearings_work/Sanctions.cfm; www.gdc-uk.org/raising-concerns/handling-concerns-about-dental-practice/hearings-and-decisions.

97 S. 25 NHS Reform and Health Care Professions Act 2002.

98 Professional Standards Authority for Health and Social Care, *Right-touch Regulation*, October 2015, 4.

There are therefore mechanisms which aim to regulate and contribute to safety both at the individual level and at the institutional and systemic level. At times, because of this plurality of regulatory mechanisms, regulators may 'struggle to persuade all regulatees as to the legitimacy of their position and practices',[99] and this may affect their effectiveness in preserving safety. The effectiveness of these mechanisms in ensuring safety has been questioned, as the current regulatory framework 'lacks cohesion and is unfortunately unable to demonstrate its effectiveness',[100] and performance may vary from institution to institution or even within institutions.[101]

It has been found, for instance, that the GMC has become more punitive of doctors and is 'more proactively seeking to restrict a doctor's practice' and that pre-hearing investigations can have a very harmful effect on doctors.[102] This can in turn have a negative impact on the healthcare system as a whole as doctors who have been through a complaint proceeding are more likely to suffer health problems, including psychological illness.[103] Doctors may also act defensively out of fear of disciplinary or legal sanctions, which can then cripple healthcare institutions.

The standard of proof required to strike off a doctor from the medical register has lowered from the criminal standard of proof (beyond reasonable doubt) to the civil standard of proof (on the balance of probabilities),[104] but there is no evidence that the number of doctors being struck off has risen significantly.[105] Some research shows that the GMC has in fact been biased towards and protective of doctors.[106] Furthermore, concerns have been reported that certain groups of doctors were disproportionately targeted by complaint proceedings, including Black, Asian and minority ethnic doctors.[107] Research also shows that following high profile healthcare scandals, such as Mid-Staffs, doctors are unlikely to face action by the GMC, which raises concerns about the ability of fitness to practise proceedings to effectively contribute to safety and to restore the confidence of victims and the public in the healthcare profession. For instance, following the Mid-Staffs scandal, half of the doctors investigated by the GMC actually faced no

99 R Brownsword, *Rights, Regulation and the Technological Revolution* (Oxford: Oxford University Press 2008), 10.

100 O Quick, *Regulating Patient Safety, The End of Professional Dominance?* (Cambridge: Cambridge University Press 2017), 85. Also see AL Beaussier, D Demeritt, A Griffiths, H Rothstein, 'Accounting for Failure: Risk-Based Regulation and the Problem of Ensuring Healthcare Quality in the NHS', (2016) 18(3–4) *Health, Risk & Society* 206.

101 K Walshe, above n88 at 1.

102 JM Chamberlain, 'Risk-Based Regulation and Reforms to Fitness to Practice Tribunals in the United Kingdom: Serving the Public Interest?' (2016) 18(5–6) *Health, Risk & Society* 323.

103 Ibid.

104 S. 112 Health and Social Care Act 2008, amending s. 60 Health Act 1999.

105 JM Chamberlain, above n102 at 324.

106 G McGivern, M Fischer, 'Medical Regulation, Spectacular Transparency and the Blame Business', (2010) 24 *Journal of Health Organisation and Management* 597.

107 General Medical Council, *Fair to refer? Reducing Disproportionality in Fitness to Practise Concerns Reported to the GMC*, June 2019, 3.

action.[108] Similarly, following the Gosport War Memorial Hospital scandal, which had seen around 650 elderly patients die after being given unnecessary and lethal doses of opioid drugs between 1989 and 2000, only one doctor, Dr Barton, was the subject of investigations. Although it was shown that she had had a central role in the prescriptions and decisions about provision of these drugs to patients, she was able to keep her medical license.[109] The GMC had found Dr Barton guilty of serious professional misconduct, but the GMC did not erase her name from the register and instead gave her an order for 3 years with 11 conditions which she had to comply with, including notifying the GMC of any post she may accept which requires registration with the GMC, and not prescribing or administering opiate drugs by injection.[110] No other medical professional was the subject of a fitness to practise proceeding following the scandal.[111]

At the institutional level, the CQC and its predecessor, the Healthcare Commission, have been heavily criticised for failing to prevent the Mid-Staffs scandal, and the CQC has since revised its regulatory approach by, for instance, conducting regular inspections of hospitals, but 'its latest system for prioritizing hospital inspections was found not to work',[112] as its system could not 'detect risks to care quality in hospitals'.[113] The CQC's 'risk-based' regulatory approach is said to have been hard to implement, as the CQC has only limited resources to conduct on-site inspections, and 'regulators have hesitated to deploy enforcement sanctions', in part 'for fear of undermining the continuity of healthcare provision'.[114] More broadly, Beaussier et al. have criticised 'risk-based' approaches for their lack of effectiveness in ensuring healthcare safety, stating that 'the language of risk is a powerful way of deflecting blame by rationalizing adverse events as outcomes that were in principle acceptable ex ante, given limited resources and competing demands upon them'.[115] Overall, CQC inspections of healthcare services were found not to be effective in raising standards and improving safety.[116] It is worth noting, however, that in 2018–2019 the CQC has increased the use of its civil and criminal powers, whilst decreasing its use of warning notices, from 1343 in 2017–2018 to 1089 in 2018–2019.[117] Although these 'enforcement powers are clearly designed to respond to public concern following failures such as those at

108 C Dyer, 'Half of Doctors Investigated Over Mid Staffs Have Faced no Action, Says GMC', (2013) 346 *British Medical Journal* 872.
109 Gosport Inquiry, above n6 at 37, 76.
110 Ibid at 209.
111 Ibid at 213.
112 AL Beaussier et al., above n100 at 206.
113 Ibid.
114 A Griffiths, AL Beaussier, D Demeritt, H Rothstein, 'Intelligent Monitoring? Assessing the Ability of the Care Quality Commission's Statistical Surveillance Tool to Predict Quality and Prioritise NHS Hospital Inspections', (2017) 26 *BMJ Quality and Safety* 120; AL Beaussier et al., above n100 at 215.
115 AL Beaussier et al., above n100 at 218.
116 G Lacobucci, 'CQC-Style Inspections Don't Raise Standards or Improve Patient Safety, Say RCGP Members', (2018) 363 *British Medical Journal* 4216.
117 Care Quality Commission, *Annual Report and Accounts 2018/19*, July 2019.

Mid-Staffordshire and bolster the accountability of healthcare organisations',[118] the CQC must be cautious that an over-punitive approach may in turn prevent the development of an open and learning culture.

Improvements therefore need to be made to GMC proceedings to ensure both fairness and efficiency in contributing to safety at the level of the individual medical professional, and likewise improvements to mechanisms which aim to ensure safety at the institutional level are needed, such as CQC inspections and their quality control processes. It must be made clear that a more punitive approach in this matter is not necessarily the answer, unless justified, as 'punitive responses to non-compliance can compromise the quality and continuity of healthcare delivery'.[119] However, a more consistent, open and transparent approach should be encouraged in healthcare institutions, from management to staff, and from staff to patients, as well as from regulators to professionals and patients.[120] The Hamilton Review notes that doctors must 'feel able to engage constructively with their regulator, confident that its culture and processes will be proportionate, fair and just'.[121] Furthermore, the review recommends that there should be 'close adherence to the professional and statutory duty of candour to be open and honest with the family of' a deceased patient.[122] Further, whistleblowing and speaking up should be more strongly encouraged within healthcare institutions.[123] This is likely to involve a 'major culture change' in healthcare institutions.[124]

According to Regulation 20 of the Health and Social Care Act 2008 (Regulated Activities) Regulations 2014, the CQC can prosecute for breaches of the duty of candour provided for in the regulation.[125] In France, a duty of candour was introduced in 2002 and is provided for in Article 1142-4 of the Public Health Code, which states that

> anyone who is a victim or who considers himself or herself to be the victim of an injury attributable to a prevention, diagnosis or treatment activity or his or her successors, if the person has died, or, where appropriate, his/her legal representative, must be informed by the health facility, the health services or the body concerned on the circumstances and causes of the damage.[126]

This information must be given within 15 days of the harm or discovery of the harm, and during an interview where the victim can be assisted by a doctor or

118 O Quick, above n100 at 81.
119 AL Beaussier et al., above n100 at 218; O Quick, above n100 at 84.
120 L Leape, D Berwick, 'Five Years After to Err Is Human: What Have We Learned?' (2005) 293(19) *Journal of the American Medical Association* 2388.
121 Hamilton Review, above n23 at 22.
122 Ibid at 26.
123 O Quick, above n100 at 149–150.
124 L Leape et al., 'Transforming Healthcare: A Safety Imperative', (2009) 18 *Quality and Safety Health Care* 425, 427.
125 Regulation 20 of the Health and Social Care Act 2008 (Regulated Activities) Regulations 2014.
126 Article L1142-4 Public Health Code.

any other person of his/her choice.[127] The duty can be enforced in civil proceedings, but there is at present no evidence that this has been effectively enforced for patients in France.[128] Although a legal duty of candour is not sufficient on its own to promote healthcare safety, it is one of many tools which can be used as a step towards a more balanced and more open doctor-patient relationship, which can in turn reduce the risk of litigation.[129] The CQC's role in prosecuting breaches of this provision will thus be crucial in the improvement of healthcare practice.

Support and reparation

Ensuring reparation and providing adequate support to victims of healthcare accidents is another significant issue which needs to be addressed. As discussed throughout this book, research demonstrates that victims of healthcare failings and their families often feel quite removed from the legal proceedings and are unable to obtain answers which could provide them with some closure. Furthermore, victims of healthcare negligence, or failings, may sometimes find it difficult to access compensation in England and Wales, whether it be following civil or criminal proceedings. This was, for instance, demonstrated in the tainted blood scandal in England and Wales.

In France, on the other hand, victims may get civil compensation in either civil or criminal proceedings, but they may also access compensation through a compensation scheme called ONIAM. This scheme aims to provide victims with both rapid compensation for harm resulting from medical accidents and also direct access to their medical records and a free expert report.[130] To receive compensation from ONIAM, the patient or the family of a deceased patient must prove that the patient was harmed as a result of medical treatment on or after 5 September 2001 and that the harm caused the patient to suffer permanent incapacity of over 24%.[131] Compensation may be obtained when the patient has suffered either negligent or non-negligent medical treatment, diagnosis or prevention, and this also includes hospital-acquired infections.[132] If treatment was negligent, compensation is paid by liability insurers, and where there is no fault, compensation is provided by the state fund managed by ONIAM, limiting the 'financial burden on the state' whilst ensuring 'accountability for fault of medical services providers'.[133] This may also have an effect on deterrence and healthcare safety, as there is evidence that 'the introduction of the scheme has led to an overall increase in

127 Ibid.
128 S Taylor, *Medical Accident Liability and Redress in English and French Law* (Cambridge: Cambridge University Press 2015), 141–142.
129 L Lopez et al., 'Disclosure of Hospital Adverse Events and Its Association with Patients' Ratings of the Quality of Care', (2009) 169(20) *Quality of Care Arch Intern Med* 1894.
130 Article L1111-7 Public Health Code. S Taylor, above n128, 86.
131 Article L 1142-1 Public Health Code; S Taylor, above n128 at 54–55.
132 S Taylor, above n128 at 55.
133 Ibid at 56–57.

the number of claims for compensation made in France'.[134] However, 'the lack of openness remains a problem despite the introduction' of the scheme in France.[135]

Taylor further found that 'individual blame retains a substantial role in the law', which has had adverse effects on reporting and openness.[136] Similar compensation schemes were introduced in other countries, including Denmark, Sweden and New Zealand.[137] Although 'it remains an open question whether introducing no-fault in place of liability in private law has had a positive or negative effect on patient safety, or no effect at all',[138] no-fault schemes have been found to effectively provide easy and quick access to compensation for injured patients.[139] In particular, it was found that the adoption of a French-style compensation scheme in England and Wales could 'contribute to improving the cost-efficiency of compensation'. Since its introduction, the French scheme seems to 'have had a calming effect on litigation rates' with criminal prosecutions also appearing to be declining.[140] In England and Wales, the NHS Redress Act 2006 sought to create a Government scheme for compensation for medical injury, but it is 'rather limited in scope and amounts in effect to little more than a formalised settlement procedure for relatively low-value (up to £20,000) tort claims against the public healthcare system',[141] and the scheme has not yet been implemented in England.[142]

No-fault schemes have the potential to 'improve learning from claims and safety, improve candour and improve the experience of those injured'[143] and 'to create an environment that is more conducive to transparency and safety improvement'.[144] The introduction of a compensation scheme in England and Wales does have the potential to improve the doctor-patient relationship, to provide more explanations and closure to harmed patients and to encourage openness as opposed to punitive mechanisms, and should therefore be strongly considered as a reform in England.

134 Ibid at 167.

135 Ibid.

136 Ibid at 168.

137 K Oliphant, 'Beyond Misadventure: Compensation for Medical Injuries in New Zealand', (2007) 15(3) *Medical Law Review* 357; ss. 20–21 Injury, Prevention, Rehabilitation and Compensation Act 2001; V Ulfbeck, M Hartley, M Schultz, 'Malpractice in Scandinavia', (2012) 87(1) *Chicago-Kent Law Review* 111–129.

138 K Oliphant, 'Compensation, Ideology and Patient Safety in New Zealand's No-Fault System', (2009) 3 *Opinio Juris in Comparatione*, 19.

139 V Ulfbeck, M Hartley, M Schultz, above n137 at 129.

140 S Taylor, above n128 at 85–86.

141 K Oliphant, above n138 at 19.

142 AM Farrell, S Devaney, 'Making Amends or Making Things Worse?' (2007) 27(4) *Legal Studies* 630; C Dyer, 'Resolving Clinical Negligence Claims', (2013) 347(f4996) *British Medical Journal* 14.

143 T Draycott et al., 'The Role of Insurers in Maternity Safety: Best Practice and Research', (2015) 29(8) *Clinical Obstetrics and Gynaecology* 1129.

144 M Mello, A Kachalia, D Studdert, *Administrative Compensation for Medical Injuries: Lessons from Three Foreign Systems* (New York, NY: The Commonwealth Fund 2011), 8.

Conclusion

So far, in England and Wales, corporate criminal liability has been unable to provide effective accountability of health institutions, whereas in France, corporate offences have often been used in healthcare cases to hold health institutions to account. There is a concerning lack of accountability of health institutions in England and Wales. Following on from my analysis of the criminalisation of corporate wrongdoing in French law, I argued in this chapter that the criminal law should be used to punish wrongful conduct which amounts to a disregard for the health and safety of patients committed by a health institution. I have shown that in several well-known healthcare scandals, the required level of culpability was met, and this should have justified a criminal law response.

This research has further shown that the difficulty in holding institutions to account for healthcare failings, even if those reflect culpability, calls for the use of offences which do not require proof of a causal link between negligence and harm, such as offences under the HSWA 1974 and offences at s. 21 of the CJCA 2015, which penalise wilful neglect and ill-treatment of patients by care providers. I have pointed out that corporate manslaughter is difficult to use in healthcare systemic cases, but some of the CMCHA 2007 remedial orders could act as deterrents and contribute to prevention of harm in health institutions, such as publicity orders or disqualification orders.

Financial penalties are unlikely to have any deterrent effect on publicly funded healthcare institutions and may even have a harmful effect on safety. However, they may have a deterrent effect on privately funded institutions. Compliance measures taken by the CQC when a health institution does not meet essential standards of safety have the potential to contribute to preserving healthcare safety, but improvements are needed to address issues related to the effectiveness of those measures, including the effectiveness of CQC inspections on safety. Overall, regulatory proceedings, including CQC regulatory processes and GMC proceedings, must be improved to ensure fairness, transparency and effectiveness in safeguarding patient safety.

Finally, victim support and reparation must be strongly reconsidered by English policy-makers, and I have suggested that a French-style compensation scheme for medical accidents, where victims have quick access to both compensation and their medical records, be contemplated in England and Wales.

7 Conclusion

This book has sought to contribute to a better understanding of both why the French criminal process more readily addresses cases of healthcare malpractice than is the case in England and Wales and how far a study of the different ways in which the criminal process relates to medicine in those two countries assists evaluations of the role that the criminal process should play in relation to injury and death in a healthcare setting. Should England and Wales adopt any part of the model offered by French law and procedure in relation to holding health professionals, managers and institutions to account for healthcare malpractice? In asking that question, we have seen both what might be characterised as the usual cases of healthcare negligence and breach of duty by doctors and hospitals, and catastrophic failures in the delivery of national health services, as illustrated by the contaminated blood episode and other healthcare disasters.

This book has advanced recent debates about the role of the criminal process in regulating and responding to healthcare malpractice. Central to the debate is the question of whether the criminal process is designed to punish morally wrongful conduct. This book focused very specifically on the role of the criminal process in healthcare malpractice cases which differ from many other cases of negligence in their complexity, difficulty in establishing causation, and potential impact on patient safety. The gross negligence manslaughter test in England and Wales makes proving negligence difficult and the reliance on experts even more significant. The findings from this study make several contributions to the current literature by focusing on a comparative analysis of the role of the criminal process in France, a civil law jurisdiction, and in England and Wales, a common law jurisdiction, and by analysing the usefulness of the criminal response to cases of healthcare negligence and failure, including the tainted blood episode. Unlike previous studies, this book argued that the criminal law can have an important expressive and retributive function when it is used to punish conduct which has shown disregard for the health and safety of another. The French experience has shown that a more victim-friendly approach is needed to address healthcare malpractice episodes, both within and outside the criminal process.

DOI: 10.4324/9781315099170-7

Explaining differences

This research has argued that features of criminal procedure play a more considerable role than substantive criminal law in the criminalisation of healthcare malpractice. Differences in substantive laws do nonetheless have a role to play. Coming from two different legal traditions, France and England and Wales have different perspectives on criminalising healthcare negligence (Chapter 2). French criminal law provides for a more wide-ranging criminalisation of negligence, which includes a larger range of negligent conduct, from simple negligence to recklessness, as well as conduct resulting in injury short of death and the failure to rescue someone in danger. Conduct offences have a significant role in the criminalisation of healthcare negligence in France. There is greater scope to prosecute for harms caused by negligence on the part of medical professionals and officials. On the other hand, only gross negligence resulting in death has so far been the subject of criminal charges in the context of non-intentional wrongdoing in the healthcare setting in England and Wales. Since April 2015, non-fatal offences which penalise wilful neglect and ill-treatment have been incorporated into criminal law to prosecute cases of healthcare malpractice which result in harm short of death, or no harm at all. But these offences have not yet been used to prosecute medical professionals.

Procedural differences have an even more significant impact than substantive law on the use of the criminal process in healthcare malpractice cases (Chapter 3). Two main procedural factors are responsible for the greater use of the criminal process in the healthcare malpractice context in France. Firstly, the right of victims to become *parties civiles* and launch criminal proceedings against medical professionals, in France, explains why many cases of healthcare malpractice are prosecuted, while many similar cases in England and Wales are not. Secondly, the French inquisitorial system of procedure provides for in-depth pre-trial investigations conducted by a single *juge d'instruction*, which is often in favour of responding to victims' demands for prosecuting medical professionals or decision-makers. *Juges d'instruction* have a significant role in pushing the *Ministère Public* (public prosecution service) to prosecute medical professionals for negligence. On this side of the Channel, victims cannot as easily launch criminal proceedings against healthcare practitioners, and the Crown Prosecution Service in England and Wales has so far shown more reluctance to prosecute healthcare professionals. The involvement of juries in trials for 'medical manslaughter' in England and Wales was shown to explain why few prosecutions actually result in convictions because juries are reluctant to convict healthcare professionals. In France, juries are not present at trials for offences which penalise negligence, and French magistrates have been shown to be more ready to convict defendant healthcare professionals. These factors have been argued to explain the more limited role of the criminal process in healthcare malpractice in England and Wales.

The examination of the use of the criminal law in the HIV-contaminated blood episode in France and England and Wales revealed that substantive and, more importantly, procedural factors were determinant in the use of the criminal process (Chapter 4). The impact of *juges d'instruction* and *parties civiles* on the use of the criminal process explains why so many criminal proceedings were launched in France and none in England and Wales following a similar healthcare disaster. Unlike most other cases of healthcare malpractice, the media and the public had a major impact on the willingness of prosecutors to use the criminal process during this episode. The use of the criminal process did not respond to the episode as well as victims or the public would have hoped, yet it also created outrage amongst the medical profession, who saw the defendants being used as scapegoats.

Findings on the scandals show that similar failings occurred in both countries in the relevant period, and some failings do warrant the use of the criminal law. Health institutions were found to have recklessly continued to provide contaminated blood to patients, even when the risk of contamination was well known and when measures to stop the contamination were available. The health authorities' resistance to allocate the necessary funds to implement such measures demonstrated a disregard for the health, safety and life of patients, which should justify a criminal response.

This book has argued that criminal offences could be used in England and Wales to hold decision-makers and institutions to account for failing to stop the contamination which caused thousands of patients to become infected with HIV and hepatitis C. Proving a causal link between negligence and harm was an obstacle to the success of many French prosecutions following the scandal. The most appropriate offences which have been found to allow potentially successful prosecutions and/or convictions of health institutions and/or health officials following failings in the contaminated blood episode are offences under the Health and Safety at Work Act 1974 (HSWA 1974). Contrary to offences against the person (gross negligence manslaughter or offences penalising the act of causing harm), these offences do not require proof of causation and would enable the courts to secure convictions more easily than when using offences against the person which require proof of causation.

This book has argued that English victims have so far been unable to obtain adequate support or compensation for the harm caused, by comparison to French victims. Payments which they received through various funds did not adequately represent the harm which they had suffered and did not appropriately recognise the responsibility of English health authorities in contributing to that harm. Providing reparation, moral support, explanation and transparency about what happened to victims of the episode will need to be reconsidered by the UK Government, as a first step in ensuring closure and justice for victims of the episode and their families. It is hoped that the Infected Blood Inquiry, chaired by Sir Brian Langstaff, will be able to offer victims the support and justice which they have sought for so long.

Lessons from France

The present study demonstrated that the French model of criminalisation of simple negligence should not be followed in England and Wales, as this would lead to over-criminalisation, which would be more harmful than not to healthcare safety. However, the study of French criminal law, in the healthcare malpractice context, indicates that certain reforms and improvements of English criminal law and/or prosecution policy are needed.

There is at present too great a scope for moral luck in criminal proceedings against healthcare professionals, and reckless conduct resulting in non-fatal injury should be criminalised to allow prosecutions of medical professionals whose disregard for their welfare has caused injury to patients. The gross negligence manslaughter offence should be replaced by a reckless manslaughter offence which requires subjective fault. Prosecution policy should focus on conduct which shows reckless behaviour or a disregard for the life and health of patients, which a prosecution for reckless manslaughter can achieve. For conduct which has not resulted in the death of the patient, the CPS should turn to offences which criminalise wilful neglect or ill-treatment of patients at s. 20 of the Criminal Justice and Courts Act 2015 (CJCA 2015). More clarity is, however, needed in defining the level of *mens rea* needed for these offences, and the scope of liability these offences should provide for.

Rather than blaming only front-line staff, the criminal process should try to include in the scope of liability key decision-makers who have recklessly failed in their obligations, endangering patients and the whole system for the delivery of healthcare. The book has argued that practices within health institutions can only be changed if people who have the power to change those practices are held to account for wrongful acts or omissions. These individuals' conduct is generally quite removed from the harm caused. Conduct offences can help to penalise conduct which is causally remote from the harm. In particular, I have suggested that offences at s. 21 of the CJCA 2015 should be used to permit the criminalisation of decision-makers if there is proof of at least reckless conduct.

This research has found that in England and Wales, there is a concerning lack of accountability of heath institutions. Contrary to what previous studies have argued, corporate liability should not be used as an alternative to individual liability in the healthcare context. Rather, corporate liability should be used in addition to individual liability if there is enough evidence that there has been a disregard for the health and safety of patients at both the individual and the corporate level.

Corporate offences should be used more often to prosecute healthcare institutions which have failed to deliver safe care to patients, when the institution has shown disregard for the health and safety of patients. The use of the criminal law is justified when the institution encourages a culture of conscious risk-taking, with awareness that serious harm may be caused to patients and staff members. Prioritising profit-making and covering up wrongful conduct are examples of disregard for the safety of patients, as we have seen in several healthcare scandals, such as the Mid-Staffordshire (Mid-Staffs) scandal, the Gosport War Memorial Hospital scandal and the contaminated blood scandal.

Following on from the French experience, an appropriate test to prosecute a health institution for causing harm to patients should be close to the French test of *faute caractérisée*: 'exposing another person to a particularly serious risk of which the defendant ought to have been aware'. This research has also shown that holding institutions to account for poor practice is difficult because of the need to prove a causal link between the institution's breaches and the patients' harm or death. Offences under the HSWA 1974 and the CJCA 2015 would allow the criminalisation of serious institutional conduct without the need to prove a causal link between breach and harm to the patient(s).

This book has also considered the effect of criminal sanctions on health institutions, including National Health Service institutions, which are publicly funded. Criminal sanctions can have a constructive effect on health institutions but only if they help to improve safety. In this regard, I have found that financial penalties would impose too great a burden on publicly funded institutions, but remedial, publicity or disqualification orders can contribute to a safer healthcare system because they will allow the removal of particular individuals who may have contributed to creating risks to safety within the institutions.

Improving responses to healthcare failings

The criminal process *alone* is not an appropriate way to learn from our mistakes and ensure safety. There is a need to improve preventive mechanisms and ensure that healthcare failure does not recur in the future. Preventive and regulatory mechanisms have proved insufficient in the past, as demonstrated by the Mid-Staffs scandal, for instance. In an era where healthcare accidents are more frequently coming to light, and more patients are affected, effective solutions need to be found.

Chapter 6 has discussed the need to improve openness and transparency within healthcare institutions and within regulatory processes. Whistleblowing and the duty of candour must be more strongly encouraged and enforced. The General Medical Council and Care Quality Commission regulatory processes which aim to raise standards and promote healthcare safety should be improved as they have been found to be ineffective at times.

The findings of the present study also suggest a role for selective features of the French ONIAM compensation scheme in promoting healthcare safety and in providing reparation and support to harmed patients and their families. The ONIAM scheme allows victims of medical accidents and their relatives to obtain quick compensation for both negligent and non-negligent medical treatment which have caused them harm. There is at present no such compensation scheme in England, and victims of medical negligence must have recourse to court proceedings, which can be expensive, long and draining. The ONIAM scheme in France can also allow patients to access useful information about their medical treatment, thus alleviating criticisms about transparency in the healthcare context. Further work needs to be done to inquire whether this would be feasible in England and Wales, and to what extent the French model could be used, but it was argued that the scheme has the potential to reduce civil claims against medical professionals and, in turn, to alleviate concerns relating to defensive practice which have had a negative impact on the healthcare system and the doctor-patient relationship.

Bibliography

Books and articles

'Acquired Immunodeficiency in Haemophilia', (1983) 321(8327) *The Lancet* 745

'Acquired Immunodeficiency Syndrome', (1983) 321(8317) *The Lancet* 162

'Blood Transfusion, Haemophilia and AIDS', (1984) 324(8417–8418), *The Lancet* 1433

'Surveillance of the Acquired Immune Deficiency Syndrome in the United Kingdom, January 1982-July 1983', (1983) 287(6389) *British Medical Journal* 407

Allen N, 'Medical or Managerial Manslaughter', in Erin C, Ost S (eds), *The Criminal Justice System and Health Care* (Oxford: Oxford University Press 2007)

———, 'Psychiatric Care and Criminal Prosecution', in Griffiths D, Sanders A (eds), *Medicine, Crime and Society* (Cambridge: Cambridge University Press 2013)

Ashworth A, 'Is the Criminal Law a Lost Cause?' (2000) 116 *Law Quarterly Review* 14

Ashworth A, Horder J, *Principles of Criminal Law* (7th edn, Oxford: Oxford University Press 2013)

Ausness RC, 'Retribution and Deterrence: The Role of Punitive Damages in Products Liability Litigation', (1985) 74(1) *Kentucky Law Journal* 40

Ayres I, Braithwaite J, *Responsive Regulation: Transcending the Deregulation Debate* (Oxford: Oxford University Press 1992)

Beaud O, *Le sang contaminé* (Paris: Presses Universitaires de France 1999)

Beaussier AL, Demeritt D, Griffiths A, Rothstein H, 'Accounting for Failure: Risk-based Regulation and the Problem of Ensuring Healthcare Quality in the NHS', (2016) 18(3–4) *Health, Risk & Society* 206

Beckfield J, Olafsdottir S, Sosnaud B, 'Healthcare Systems in Comparative Perspective: Classification, Convergence, Institutions, Inequalities and Five Missed Turns', (2013) 29 *Annual Review of Sociology* 127

Bell J, *French Legal Cultures* (Cambridge: Cambridge University Press 2008)

Bernard-Requin M, 'SIDA et transfusion sanguine ou l'affaire du sang contaminé. Les difficiles qualifications pénales', (1998) 28(1) *Médecine et Maladies Infectieuses* 20

Bernstein S, *Les cultures politiques en France* (Paris: Seuil 1999)

Bertella Geffroy M-O, 'L'évolution des rapport justice-santé', (2004) 4(5) *Les Tribunes de la santé* 21

———, 'Justice Pénale, Santé Individuelle et Santé Publique', (2008) (2) *Droit de la Santé*, Nos 282 à 283

Berridge V, *AIDS in the UK: The Making of Policy. 1981–1994* (Oxford: Oxford University Press 1996)

Bettati C, *Responsables et coupables, Une affaire de sang* (Paris: Seuil 1993)

Beziz-Ayache A, *Dictionnaire de Droit pénal général et procédure pénale* (6th edn, Paris: Ellipses 2016)

Bibby J, Tomkins C, 'Would Criminalising Healthcare Professionals for Wilful Neglect Improve Patient Care?' (2014) 348 *British Medical Journal* 1

Black J, 'What Is Regulatory Innovation?' in Black J, Lodge M, Thatcher M (eds), *Regulatory Innovation* (Cheltenham: Edward Elgar 2005)

Blair P, Germain M, 'Corporate Criminal Intention in the Enforcement of Environmental Law', (2012) 24(1) *Environment Law and Management* 20

Bloom AL, Forbes CD, Rizza CR, 'HTLV-III, Haemophilia and Blood Transfusion', (1985) 290(6485) *British Medical Journal* 1901

Bouloc B, *Procédure Pénale* (27e edn, Paris: Dalloz 2019)

Bouloc B, Matsopoulou H, *Droit pénal général et procédure pénale* (21e edn, Paris: Sirey 2018)

Bradley CM, 'Overview', in Bradley CM, Calamaras JL (eds), *Criminal Procedure, A Worldwide Study* (2nd edn, Durham, NC: Carolina Academic Press 2007)

Brazier M, Alghrani A, 'Fatal Medical Malpractice and Criminal Liability', (2009) 25(2) *Journal of Professional Negligence* 51

Brazier M, Allen N, 'Criminalizing Medical Malpractice', in Erin C, Ost S (eds), *The Criminal Justice System and Health Care* (Oxford: Oxford University Press 2007)

Brazier M, Cave E, *Medicine, Patients and the Law* (6th edn, Manchester: Manchester University Press 2016)

Brazier M et al., 'Improving Healthcare Through the Use of 'Medical Manslaughter'? Facts, Fears and the Future', (2016) 22(5–6) *Clinical Risk* 88

Brearey-Horne P, 'The Corporate Manslaughter and Corporate Homicide Act 2007 and Maternal Death: An Opportunity to Address Systemic Deficiencies in Maternity Services?' in Griffiths D, Sanders A (eds), *Medicine, Crime and Society* (Cambridge: Cambridge University Press 2013)

Brownsword R, *Rights, Regulation and the Technological Revolution* (Oxford: Oxford University Press 2008)

Burgelin JF, 'La médecine saisie par le principe de précaution', (2000) 184(5) *Bulletin de l'Académie Nationale de Médecine* 873

Carrère N, 'Le juge pénal et les professionnels de santé', (2008) 283 *Gazette du Palais* 23

Cartron D, 'Quelle place pour la victime d'un accident médical devant le juge pénal?' (2013) 5(27) *Responsabilité civile et assurance* 1

Cash J, 'The Blood Transfusion Service and the National Health Service', (1987) 295(6599) *British Medical Journal* 617

Casteret AM, *L'affaire du sang* (Paris: La Découverte 1992)

Chalmers J, Leverick F, 'Tracking the Creation of Criminal Offences', (2013) 7 *Criminal Law Review* 543

Chambaud L, 'How Healthy Is the French Health System?' *The Conversation*, 21 September 2017

Chamberlain JM, 'Risk-based Regulation and Reforms to Fitness to Practice Tribunals in the United Kingdom: Serving the Public Interest?' (2016) 18(5–6) *Health, Risk & Society* 323

Childs M, 'Medical Manslaughter and Corporate Liability', (1999) 19(3) *Legal studies* 316

Clarkson CMV, 'Kicking Corporate Bodies and Damning Their Souls', (1996) 59(4) *The Modern Law Review* 557

———, 'General Endangerment Offences: The Way Forward?' (2005) 32 *University of Western Australian Law Review* 131

Clarkson CMV, Keating HM, Cunningham SR, *Criminal Law* (7th edn, London: Thompson Sweet and Maxwell 2010)

Coffee JC, 'No Soul to Damn: No Body to Kick': An Unscandalized Inquiry into the Problem of Corporate Punishment', (1981) 79(3) *Michigan Law Review* 386

Commaret VD, *La Loi Fauchon, 5 ans après* (2006) Chron. N7, spec. N18 *Droit Pénal*

Cotte B, Guihal D, *La Loi Fauchon, 5 ans de mise en oeuvre jurisprudentielle* (2006) chron. N6, et spéc. N44 *Droit Pénal*

Cusson M, *La criminologie* (7e edn, Paris: Hachette 2017)

Dannemann G, 'Chapter 11: Comparative Law: Study of Similarities of Differences?' in Reimann M, Zimmermann R (eds), *The Oxford Handbook of Comparative Law* (Oxford: Oxford University Press 2006)

Daury-Fauveau M, *La responsabilité pénale du médecin* (Bordeaux: Les études hospitalières 2003)

Davis KC et al., 'Acquired Immunodeficiency Syndrome in a Patient with Hemophilia', (1983) 98(3) *Annals of Internal Medicine* 284

De Cruz P, *Comparative Law in a Changing World* (3rd edn, New York, NY: Routledge-Cavendish 2007)

Dervieux V, 'The French System', in Delmas-Marty M, Spencer JR (eds), *European Criminal Procedures* (Cambridge: Cambridge University Press 2002)

Devaney S, Holm S, 'The Transmutation of Deference in Medicine: An Ethico-Legal Perspective', (2018) 26(2) *Medical Law Review* 202

Draycott T et al., 'The Role of Insurers in Maternity Safety. Best Practice and Research', (2015) 29(8) *Clinical Obstetrics and Gynaecology* 1126

Duff A, *Answering for Crime: Responsibility and Liability in the Criminal Law* (Oxford: Hart Publishing 2009)

Dyer C, 'Bristol Inquiry Condemns Hospital's Club Culture', (2001) 323(7306) *British Medical Journal* 181

———, 'Half of Doctors Investigated Over Mid Staffs Have Faced No Action, Says GMC', (2013) 346 *British Medical Journal* 872

———, 'Resolving Clinical Negligence Claims', (2013) 347: f4996 *British Medical Journal* 14

———, 'Senior Surgeon's Conviction for Manslaughter Is Quashed', (2016) *British Medical Journal* 355

———, 'Sellu Is Cleared of Medical Misconduct', (2018) *British Medical Journal* 360

———, 'Society, Anger, Bewilderment: The Fallout from the Bawa-Garba Case', (2018) *British Medical Journal* 360

Elliott C, *French Criminal Law* (Cullompton: Willan 2001)

Engineer R, 'Punishing Corporate Negligence, Industrial Disasters and Criminal Law', (1989) 24(14) *Economic and Political Weekly* 711

Erin C, Ost S (eds), *The Criminal Justice System and Heath Care* (Oxford: Oxford University Press 2007)

Farrell AM, 'Contaminated Blood, a Comparative Study of Policy-Making Arising Out of HIV Contamination of the Blood Supply in France, the United Kingdom and Ireland' (PhD thesis, University of Manchester 2004)

———, *The Politics of Blood* (Cambridge: Cambridge University Press 2012)

Farrell AM, Devaney S, 'Making Amends or Making Things Worse?' (2007) 27(4) *Legal Studies* 630

Farrell AM, Kazarian M, 'The Role of the Criminal Law in Healthcare Malpractice in France: Examining the HIV Blood Contamination Episode', in Griffiths D, Sanders A (eds), *Medicine, Crime and Society* (Cambridge: Cambridge University Press 2013)

Feinberg J, 'The Expressive Function of Punishment', in Feinberg J (ed), *Doing and Deserving* (Princeton: Princeton University Press 1970)

———, *Harm to Others* (Oxford: Oxford University Press 1984)

Ferner RE, 'Medication Errors That Have Led to Manslaughter Charges', (2000) 321(7270) *British Medical Journal* 1212

Ferner RE, McDowell SE, 'Doctors Charged with Manslaughter in the Course of Medical Practice, 1795–2005: A Literature Review', (2006) 99 *Journal of the Royal Society of Medicine* 309

Field S, 'Ten Years On: The Corporate Manslaughter and Corporate Homicide Act 2007: Plus ca Change?' (2018) *International Company and Commercial Law Review* 512

Gand P, 'Les pôles de santé publique, une organisation adaptée aux contentieux en matière de securité sanitaire', (2013) *RDSS* 813

———, 'Le Pôle de Santé Publique face à un contentieux technique et des délits "seriels"', (2014) 198(4–5) *Bulletin de l'Académie Nationale de Médecine* 715

Garfield S, *The End of Innocence: Britain in the Time of AIDS* (London: Faber and Faber 1995)

Gobert J, 'Corporate Criminality: Four Model of Fault', (1994) 14(3) *Legal Studies* 393

Gooderham P, 'No-one Fully Responsible': A 'Collusion of Anonymity' Protecting Health Care Bodies from Manslaughter Charges?' (2011) *Clinical Ethics* 68

Gooderham P, Toft B, 'Involuntary Automaticity: A Potential Legal Defence to an Allegation of Clinical Negligence?' (2009) 18(1) *Quality and Safety in Health Care* 69

———, 'Involuntary Automaticity and Medical Manslaughter', in Griffiths D, Sanders A (eds), *Medicine, Crime and Society* (Cambridge: Cambridge University Press 2013)

Greilsamer L, *Le procès du sang contaminé* (Paris: Le Monde Editions 1992)

Gremy F, 'Contaminated Blood: The State's Renunciation and Incompetence in the Public Health Domain, a Long Tradition', (2002) 2(14) *Santé Publique* 179

Griffiths A, Beaussier AL, Demeritt D, Rothstein H, 'Intelligent Monitoring? Assessing the Ability of the Care Quality Commission's Statistical Surveillance Tool to Predict Quality and Prioritise NHS Hospital Inspections', (2017) 26 *BMJ Quality and Safety* 120

Griffiths D, Quick O, 'Managing Medical Manslaughter Cases: Improving Efficiency and Transparency?' Law Research Paper Series, May 2019, Paper No 007 2019, University of Bristol

Griffiths D, Sanders A (eds), *Medicine, Crime and Society* (Cambridge: Cambridge University Press 2013)

———, 'The Road to the Dock: Prosecution Decision-making in Medical Manslaughter Cases', in Griffiths D, Sanders A (eds), *Medicine, Crime and Society* (Cambridge: Cambridge University Press 2013)

Guigue J, 'Les inconvénients de la pénalisation du droit de la santé', (2008) *Revue de droit sanitaire et social* 36

Hall J, 'Negligence and the General Problem of Criminal Responsibility', (1972) 81 *Yale Law Journal* 949

———, *General Principles of Criminal Law* (Clark, NJ: The Lawbook Exchange 2010)

Hart HLA, 'Negligence, Mens Rea, and Criminal Responsibility', in Hart HLA (ed), *Punishment and Responsibility: Essays in the philosophy of law* (Oxford: Oxford University Press 1968)

Hennion-Jacquet P, 'Quelques aspects de l'ambivalence des responsabilités pénale et civile du praticien', (2004) 14 *Revue générale de droit médicale* 286

Heraud J-A, Kerr F, Burger-Helmchen T, *Management créatif des systèmes complexes* (London: ISTE Editions 2019)

Hermitte MA, *Le sang et le droit. Essai sur la transfusion sanguine* (Paris: Seuil 1996)

Herring J, *Criminal Law: Text, Cases and Materials* (8th edn, Oxford: Oxford University Press 2018)

Hodgson J, 'The Police, the Prosecutor and the Juge d'Instruction', (2001) 41(2) *The British Journal of Criminology* 344

———, 'Hierarchy, Bureaucracy, and Ideology in French Criminal Justice: Some Empirical Observations', (2002) 29(2) *Journal of Law and Society* 227

Horder J, *Ashworth's Principles of Criminal Law* (9th edn, Oxford: Oxford University Press 2019)

Husak D, 'The Criminal Law as Last Resort', (2004) 24(2) *Oxford Journal of Legal Studies* 217

Jamin I, 'La responsabilité pénale en milieu de soin: une préoccupation réelle, une menace relative?' (2009) *Actualité Juridique Pénal* 340

Jorg N, Field S, Brants C, 'Are Inquisitorial and Adversarial Systems Converging?' in Harding C et al. (eds), *Criminal Justice in Europe: A Comparative Study* (Oxford: Oxford University Press 1995)

Kazarian M, *The Role of the Criminal Law and the Criminal Process in Healthcare Malpractice in France and England* (PhD thesis, University of Manchester 2013)

———, 'Who Should We Blame for Healthcare Failings? Lessons from the French Tainted Blood Scandal', (2019) 27(3) *Medical Law Review* 390

Kazarian M, Griffiths D, Brazier M, 'Criminal Responsibility for Medical Malpractice in France', (2011) 27(4) *Journal of Professional Negligence* 188

King G, Keohane RO, Verba S, *Designing Social Inquiry* (Princeton: Princeton University Press 1994)

Kohn L, Corrigan J, Donaldson M (eds), *To Err Is Human: Building a Safer Health System* (Washington, DC: National Academy Press 1999)

Kyd SR, Elliott T, Walters MA, *Clarkson and Keating: Criminal law* (9th edn, London: Sweet and Maxwell 2017)

Lacey N, 'Responsibility Without Consciousness', (2016) 36(2) *Oxford Journal of Legal Studies* 219

Lacey N, Wells C, Quick O, *Reconstructing Criminal Law* (Cambridge: Cambridge University Press 2010)

Lacobucci G, 'CQC-style Inspections Don't Raise Standards or Improve Patient Safety, Say RCGP Members', (2018) 363 *British Medical Journal* 4216

Laird K, 'Filling a Lacuna: The Care Worker and Care Provider Offences in The Criminal Justice and Courts Act 2015', (2016) 37(1) *Statute Law Review* 1

———, 'Manslaughter: R v Rose (Honey Maria) Court of Appeal (Criminal Division), Sir Brian Leveson PQBD, Haddon-Cave J and HH Judge Inman QC: 31 July 2017; [2017] EWCA Crim 1168', (2018) 1 *Criminal Law Review* 76

Lanham D, Bartal BF, Evans RG, 'The Purposes of Criminal Law', in Lanham D, Bartal BF, Evans RG, Wood D (eds), *Criminal Laws in Australia* (Alexandria: The Federation Press 2006)

Laude A, Mathieu B, Tabuteau D, *Droit de la santé* (3e edn, Paris: Presses Universitaires de France 2012)

Leape L, Berwick D, 'Five Years After to Err Is Human: What Have We Learned? (2005) 293(19) *Journal of the American Medical Association* 2384

Leape L, Berwick D et al., 'Transforming Healthcare: A Safety Imperative', (2009) 18 *Quality and Safety Health Care* 425

Leveton LB, Sox Jr HC, Stoto MA, *HIV and the Blood Supply* (Institute of Medicine 1995)

Lijphart A, 'Comparative Politics and the Comparative Method', (1971) 65(3) *American Political Science Review* 682

Lindholm DD, 'Freeze-dried Factor VIII Concentrates and the NHS', (1978) 2(6150) *British Medical Journal* 1450

Lopez L et al., 'Disclosure of Hospital Adverse Events and Its Association with Patients' Ratings of the Quality of Care', (2009) 169(20) *Quality of Care Arch intern Med* 1888

Lord Woolf, 'Are the Courts Excessively Deferential to the Medical Profession?' (2001) 9 *Medical Law Review* 1

Machin H, 'Retooling the State Machine', in Guyomarch A, Machin H, Hall PA, Hayward J (eds), *Developments in French Politics 2* (Basingstoke: Palgrave 2001)

Mannucci PM, 'AIDS, Hepatitis and Hemophilia in the 1980s: Memoirs from an Insider', (2003) 1(10) *Journal of Thrombosis and Haemostasis* 2065

Marchetti M, 'La genèse médiatique du "scandale du sang contaminé",' in *Ethique, sida et société*. Rapport d'activité du Conseil national du sida (Paris: La Documentation Française, Janvier 1993)

Mayaud Y, *Violences involontaires et responsabilité pénale* (Paris: Dalloz Référence 2003)

McCall Smith A, 'Clinical Negligence and the Incompetent Doctor', (1993) 1(3) *Medical Law Review* 336

McGivern G, Fischer M, 'Medical Regulation, Spectacular Transparency and the Blame Business', (2010) 24 *Journal of Health Organisation and Management* 597

Mello M, Kachalia A, Studdert D, *Administrative Compensation for Medical Injuries: Lessons from Three Foreign Systems* (New York, NY: The Commonwealth Fund 2011)

Memeteau G, *Traité de la responsabilité médicale* (Bordeaux: Les études hospitalières 1996)

Merry A, 'When Are Errors a Crime? – Lessons from New Zealand', in Erin C, Ost S (eds), *The Criminal Justice System and Heath Care* (Oxford: Oxford University Press 2007)

Merry A, Brookbanks W, *Merry and McCall Smith's Errors, Medicine and the Law* (2nd edn, Cambridge: Cambridge University Press 2017)

Merry A, McCall Smith, *Errors, Medicine and the Law* (Cambridge: Cambridge University Press 2013)

Mistretta P, Cass.crim.7 mars 2017, No 16–80.754: omission de porter secours: le medecin urgentiste, le malade en fin de vie et les querelles de famille

Mistretta P (ed), *French Law: From a Comparative Law Perspective: For an Overhaul of Medical Criminal Law?* (Institut Universitaire Varenne, Colloques et Essais 2017)

Montagnier L, *Des virus et des hommes* (Paris: Odile-Jacob 1994)

Moore MS, Hurd HM, 'Punishing the Awkward, the Stupid, the Weak, and the Selfish: The Culpability of Negligence', (2011) 5(2) *Criminal Law and Philosophy* 147

Mullock A, 'Gross Negligence (Medical) Manslaughter and the Puzzling Implications of Negligent Ignorance, *Rose v R* [2017] EWCA Crim 1168', (2018) 26(2) *Medical Law Review* 350

Nicholas B, *The French Law of Contract* (2nd edn, Oxford: Oxford University Press 1992)

Obadia M, 'L'expérience d'un pôle de santé publique', (2008) *Revue de droit sanitaire et social* 44

Oliphant K, 'Beyond Misadventure: Compensation for Medical Injuries in New Zealand', (2007) 15(3) *Medical Law Review* 357

———, 'Compensation, Ideology and Patient Safety in New Zealand's No-fault System', (2009) 3 *Opinio Juris in Comparatione* 1

Ost S, Erin C, 'An Ill-Suited and Inappropriate Union? Exploring the Relationship Between the Criminal Justice System and Health Care', in Erin C, Ost S (eds), *The Criminal Justice System and Health Care* (Oxford: Oxford University Press 2007)

Padfield N, Bild J, *Text and Materials on the Criminal Justice Process* (5th edn, London: Routledge 2015)

Pakes F, *Comparative Criminal Justice* (4th edn, London: Routledge 2019)

Papanikolaou D, 'La responsabilité pénale des membres d'une équipe médicale', (2004) 14 *Revue générale de droit medical* 80

Parsons S, 'The Doctrine of Identification, Causation and Corporate Liability for Manslaughter', (2003) 67 *Journal of Criminal Law* 69

Poncela P, *Droit de la peine* (2e edn, Paris: Presses Universitaires de France 2001)

Quick O, 'Prosecuting "Gross" Medical Negligence: Manslaughter, Discretion and the Crown Prosecution Service', (2006) 33 *Journal of Law and Society* 421

———, 'Medical Manslaughter: The Rise (And Replacement) of a Contested Crime?' in Erin C, Ost S (eds), *The Criminal Justice System and Health Care* (Oxford: Oxford University Press 2007)

———, 'Medical Killing: Need for a Specific Offence?' in Clarkson CMV, Cunningham S, (eds), *Criminal Liability for Non-Aggressive Death* (Aldershot: Ashgate 2008)

———, 'Medicines, Mistakes and Manslaughter: A Criminal Combination?' (2010) 69(1) *Cambridge Law Journal* 186

———, 'Expert Evidence and Medical Manslaughter: Vagueness in Action', (2011) 38 *Journal of Law and Society* 496

———, 'Patient Safety and the Problem and Potential of Law', (2012) *Journal of Professional Negligence* 97

———, 'Medical Manslaughter and Expert Evidence: The Role of Context and Character', in Griffiths D, Sanders A (eds), *Medicine, Crime and Society* (Cambridge: Cambridge University Press 2013)

———, *Regulating Patient Safety: The End of Professional Dominance* (Cambridge: Cambridge University Press 2017)

Quirk H, 'Sentencing White Coat Crime: The Need for Guidance in Medical Manslaughter Cases', (2013) 11 *Criminal Law Review* 871

Ragni MV et al., 'Acquired-Immunodeficiency-like-syndrome in Two Haemophiliacs', (1983) 321(8318) *The Lancet* 213

Rimbault P, 'La responsabilité pénale des décideurs et des personnes morales', XXXIVe Congrès Français de criminologie, 14 septembre 2005

Robson RA, 'Crime and Punishment: Rehabilitating Retribution as a Justification for Organizational Criminal Liability', (2010) 47(1) *American Business Law Journal* 124

Rolewicz L, Palmer B, 'The NHS Workforce in Numbers', *The Nuffield Trust*, 8 May 2019

Ruffié J, Sournia JC, *La transfusion sanguine* (Paris: Fayard 1996)

Runciman W et al., 'Towards an International Classification for Patient Safety: Key Concepts and Terms', (2009) 21 *International Journal for Quality in Health Care* 18

Samanta A, Samanta A, 'Gross Negligence Manslaughter and Doctors: Ethical Concerns Following the Case of Dr Bawa-Garba', (2018) 45(1) *Journal of Medical Ethics* 10

Sanders A, 'Victims' Voices, Victims' Interests and Criminal Justice in the Healthcare Setting', in Griffiths D, Sanders A (eds), *Medicine, Crime and Society* (Cambridge: Cambridge University Press 2013)

———, 'The CPS-30 Years On', (2016) 2 *Criminal Law Review* 82

Setbon M, *Pouvoirs contre sida* (Paris: Seuil 1993)

Sourdille J, Huriet C, *La crise du système transfusionnel français*, Rapport de la commission d'enquête du Sénat (Paris: Economica 1992)

Spencer JR, 'The Victims and the Prosecutor', in Bottoms A, Roberts J (eds), *Hearing the Victims: Adversarial Justice, Crime Victims and the State* (Cullompton: Willan Publishing 2010)

Spencer JR, Brajeux MA, 'Criminal Liability for Negligence-a Lesson from Across the Channel?' (2010) 59 *International and Comparative Law Quarterly* 18

Stark F, 'Reckless Manslaughter', (2017) 10 *Criminal Law Review* 771

Starr D, *Blood: An Epic History of Medicine and Commerce* (New York, NY: Harper Collins 1998)

Sureau C, 'L'erreur, la faute, l'aléa, sanction ou prévention?' in Sureau C, Lecourt D, David G, *L'erreur médicale* (Sem.) (Paris: Presses Universitaires de France 2006)

Tadros V, 'Recklessness and the Duty to Take Care', in Shute S, Simester AP (Eds.), *Criminal Law Theory: Doctrines of the General Part* (Oxford: Oxford University Press 2002)

———, 'The Limits of Manslaughter', in Clarkson CMV, Cunningham S (eds), *Criminal Liability for Non-Aggressive Death* (Aldershot: Ashgate 2008)

Tapia M, 'Décadence et fin éventuelle du principe d'identité des fautes pénales et civiles' (2003) 67 *Gazette du Palais* 2

Taylor S, 'Providing Redress for Medical Accidents in France: Conflicting Aims, Effective Solutions?' (2011) 2(1) *Journal of European Tort Law* 61

———, *Medical Accident Liability and Redress in English and French Law* (Cambridge: Cambridge University Press 2015)

Thornton P (Chief Coroner), 'The Coroner System in the 21st Century', The Howard League for Penal Reform–Parmoor Lecture 2012, October 2012

Thouvenin D, *La responsabilité médicale, Analyse des données statistiques disponibles et des arrêts rendus par la cour de cassation et le conseil d'état de 1984 à 1992* (Paris: Médecine-Sciences Flammarion 1999)

Tombs S, 'The UK's Corporate Killing Law: Un/fit for Purpose?' (2018) 18(4) *Criminology and Criminal Justice* 488

Tombs S, Whyte D, *The Corporate Criminal, Why Corporations Should Be Abolished* (London: Routledge 2015)

Trubek LG et al., 'Health Care and New Governance: The Quest for Effective Regulation', (2008) 2 *Regulation and Governance* 1

Turcey V, 'Le point de vue du magistrat', in Dreyfuss D, Lemaire F, Outin H (eds), *La judiciarisation de la médecine* (Paris: Médecine-Sciences Flammarion 2004)

Ulfbeck V, Hartley M, Schultz M, 'Malpractice in Scandinavia', (2012) 87(1) *Chicago-Kent Law Review* 111

Van Den Wyngaert C, *Criminal Procedure Systems in the European Community* (London: Butterworths1993)

Van Ruymbeke R, *Le juge d'instruction* (Paris: Presses Universitaires de France 2016)

Vaughan J, Quick O, Griffiths D, 'Medical Manslaughter: Where Next?' (2018) 100(6) *The Royal College of Surgeon bulletin* 251

Verrest P, 'The French Public Prosecution Service', (2000) 8(3) *European Journal of Crime, Criminal Law and Criminal Justice* 210

Vidmar N, Lempert R, Seidman Diamond S, Hans V, Landman S et al., 'Amicus Brief: *Kumho Tire v Carmichael*', (2000) 24 *Law and Human Behaviour* 387

Vignaud F, 'La judiciarisation de la médecine, comparaison entre droit français et droit américain', in Dreyfuss D, Lemaire F, Outin H (eds), *La judiciarisation de la médecine* (Paris: Médecine-Sciences Flammarion 2004)

Walshe K, *Regulating Healthcare: A Prescription for Improvement* (Maidenhead: Open University Press 2003)

Waterson AP, 'Acquired Immune Deficiency Syndrome', (1983) 286 *British Medical Journal* 743

Watson A, *Legal Transplants. An Approach to Comparative Law* (2nd edn, Athens, GA: The University of Georgia Press 1993)

Wells C, 'Medical Manslaughter: Organisational Liability', in Griffiths D, Sanders A (eds), *Medicine, Crime and Society* (Cambridge: Cambridge University Press 2013)

Wester-Ouisse V, 'Dépénalisation du droit médical', (2008) Hors Série juillet *Revue générale de droit medical* 245

Williams G, *Criminal Law: The General Part* (2nd edn, London: Stevens and Sons Ltd 1964)

Yeung K, Horder J, 'How Can the Criminal Law Support the Provision of Quality in Healthcare?' (2014) 23 *BMJ Quality and Safety* 519

Yin RK, 'The Case Study Crisis: Some Answers', (1981) 26(1) *Administrative Science Quarterly* 58

———, *Case Study Research: Design and Methods* (5th edn, Thousand Oaks, CA: Sage 2014)

Zweigert Z, Kotz H, *An Introduction to Comparative Law* (3rd edn, Oxford: Oxford University Press 1998)

Reports, guidance, policy and consultation documents

Gosport War Memorial Hospital: The report of the Gosport Independent Panel, 20 June 2018

Haemophilia Society React to Government Response to the Archer Report, date unknown

Infected Blood Inquiry, Terms of Reference, July 2018

Infected Blood Inquiry, First Witness Statement of Graham Manning, WITN1367001, 7 June 2019

Infected Blood Inquiry, Written Statement of Annette Hill-Stewart, WITN1001001, 12 July 2019

Infected Blood Inquiry, Written Statement of Barry Fitzgerald, WITN2819001, 12 August 2019

Infected Blood Inquiry, Written Statement of Gaynor Lewis, WITN2368001, 15 February 2019

Infected Blood Inquiry, Written Statement of Louise Marsden, WITN1371001, April 2019

Infected Blood Inquiry, Written Statement of Maria Fletcher, WITN1876001, 14 February 2019

Infected Blood Inquiry, Written Statement of Mr L, WITN0148001, 16 October 2018

Infected Blood Inquiry, Written Statement of Susan Threakall, WITN1564001, December 2018

Assemblée Nationale, *Rapport de la commission d'enquête sur l'état des connaissances scientifiques et les actions menées à l'égard de la transmission du sida* (Union générale d'édition 1993)

Assemblée Nationale, *Rapport n° 2266 fait au nom de la commission des lois constitutionnelles, de la législation et de l'administration générale de la République sur la proposition de loi, adoptée par le Sénat, tendant à préciser la définition des délits non intentionnels*, par M René Dosière, 22 mars 2000

Berwick D, *Improving the Safety of Patients in England, a Promise to Learn-A Commitment to Act*, National Advisory Group on the Safety of Patients in England, August 2013

British Medical Association, *Doctors' Titles: Explained*, 2017

Care Quality Commission, *Annual Report and Accounts 2018/19*, July 2019

Care Quality Commission, *Registration Under the Health and Social Care Act 2008, Warning Notices, Guidance for Registered Providers and Managers*, October 2015

Commission Justice pénale et Droits de l'homme, *La mise en état des affaires pénales*, Rapport final, Paris: La Documentation française 1991E

Department of Health, *An Organisation with a Memory: Report of an Expert Group on Learning from Adverse Events in the NHS Chaired by the Chief Medical Officer*, London: HMSO 2000

Department of Health, *Self-Sufficiency in Blood Products in England and Wales, a Chronology from 1973 to 1991*, 2006

Department of Health, Written Ministerial Statement, Support to Those Affected by Contaminated Blood, 14 October 2010

Department of Health, *Criminal Offence of Ill-treatment or Wilful Neglect, Impact Assessment*, June 2014

Department of Health, *New Offence of Ill-treatment or Wilful Neglect, Government Response to Consultation*, June 2014

Department of Health, *Gross Negligence Manslaughter in Healthcare, The Report of a Rapid Policy Review*, June 2018

Eleanor Grey QC, Professor Sir Ian Kennedy, *The Report of the Independent Review of Children's Cardiac Services in Bristol*, June 2016

Francis R, *Independent Inquiry into Care Provided by Mid Staffordshire NHS Foundation Trust January 2005–March 2009*, Vol I and II (2010)

General Medical Council, *Fair to refer? Reducing disproportionality in fitness to practise concerns reported to the GMC*, June 2019
General Medical Council, *HIV Infection and Aids: The Ethical Considerations*, 1988, PEN0161165
General Medical Council, *Independent Review of Gross Negligence Manslaughter and Culpable Homicide*, June 2019
Health and Safety Executive, *Work-related Deaths, a Protocol for Liaison (England and Wales)*, February 2016
Health and Safety Executive, *Health and Safety at Work, Summary Statistics for Great Britain 2019*, October 2019
House of Commons Debates, Contaminated Blood and Blood Products, HC Deb, 14 October 2010, vol 516, cols 521–571
James G (Chair), *Report of the Independent Inquiry into the Issues Raised by Paterson*, February 2020
Lucas M, *Transfusion Sanguine et SIDA en 1985, Chronologie des faits et des décisions pour ce qui concerne les hémophiles*, Inspection Générale des Affaires Sociales, Septembre 1991 Annexe 5: Ministère des affaires sociales et de la solidarité nationale, Secrétariat d'Etat chargé de la santé, Direction générale de la santé, *Circulaire relative à la prévention de l'éventuelle transmission du syndrôme d'immunodépression acquise (SIDA) par la transfusion sanguine*, DGS/3B n° 569, 20 juin 1983
MACSF, Rapport Annuel 2016 Sur La Sinistralité, Synthèse Des Chiffres Clés
MACSF, Rapport Annuel 2018 Sur La Sinistralité, Synthèse Des Chiffres Clés
MPTS, GMC, Sanctions guidance for members of medical practitioners tribunals and for the General Medical Council's decision makers, April 2017
Mr Justice Horace Krever, *Commission of Inquiry on the Blood System in Canada*, Final Report Vol. 3, 1997
Oxford Haemophilia Centre, *Trials of 'Hepatitis Reduced' Factor VIII-an Update*, 29 March 1984
Professional Standards Authority for Health and Social Care, *Right-touch Regulation*, October 2015
Research and Development Department, BPL, Annual Report to December 1984
Rt Hon Lord Archer et al., *Independent Public Inquiry Report on NHS-Supplied Contaminated Blood and Blood Products*, February 2009
Rt Hon Lord Penrose, *The Penrose Inquiry Final Report*, March 2015
Sénat, Session ordinaire de 1995–1996, Annexe au procès-verbal de la séance du 18 octobre 1995, N° 32, Proposition de loi relative à la responsabilité pénale des élus locaux pour des faits d'imprudence ou de négligence commis dans l'exercice des fonctions, Rapport
Sénat, *Les délits non intentionnels-La Loi Fauchon: 5 ans après*, Actes du colloque, 1er mars 2006, Palais du Luxembourg
Supraregional Haemophilia Reference Centre, Royal Free Hospital, London, *Blood Products and their Problems*, March 1984
Toft B, *External Inquiry into the Adverse Incident That Occurred at Queen's Medical Centre, Nottingham*, Department of Health, 4 January 2001
The All-Party Parliamentary Group on Haemophilia and Contaminated Blood, *Inquiry into the Current Support for Those Affected by the Contaminated Blood Scandal in the UK*, January 2015

The Law Commission, *Legislating the Criminal Code: Involuntary Manslaughter* (Law Com No 237) Item 11 of the Sixth Programme of Law Reform: Criminal Law, 4 March 1996

The Sentencing Council, *Health and Safety Offences, Corporate Manslaughter and Food Safety and Hygiene Offences, Definitive Guideline*, 2015

UK Government, *Government Response to Lord Archer's Independent Inquiry Report on NHS-supplied Contaminated Blood and Blood Products*, 20 May 2009

Newspaper articles

'Affaire de l'hormone de croissance: relaxe des deux derniers prévenus en vie', *Le Monde* (25 January 2016)

'Anger as Fatal Jab Doctor Freed', *BBC News* (23 September 2003)

'Blood Scandal That Cannot Go Unpunished', *Mail on Sunday* (9 July 1995)

'Breast Implants: PIP's Jean-Claude Mas Gets Jail Sentence', *BBC News* (10 December 2013)

'Contaminated Blood: Victims Can Launch Court Damages Action', *BBC News* (26 September 2017)

'David Sellu Trial: Doctor's Conviction Over Patient's Death Quashed', *BBC News* (15 November 2016)

'Doctor and Nurse Given Suspended Jail Terms Over Boy's Negligence Death', *The Guardian* (14 December 2015)

'Haemophiliac HIV Tragedy "Needless"', *BBC News* (3 August 2001)

'Hépatite B: Deux grands laboratoires mis en examen pour "tromperie aggravée"', *Libération* (1 February 2008)

'Hospital Trust Fined for Knee op Death', *The Guardian* (11 April 2006)

'Ian Paterson: "Sheer Volume" of Victims Delays Breast Surgeon Report', *BBC News* (5 April 2019)

'"Liver Branding" Surgeon Simon Bramhall Fined £100,000', *BBC News* (12 January 2018)

'PIP: Les Trois Clés d'une Enquête Complexe', *Le Figaro* (27 January 2012)

'"No One to Be Prosecuted" Over Mid-Staffs Scandal', *The Telegraph* (1 March 2016)

'Scandale de l'amiante: 705 nouveaux dossiers de victimes', *Le Point* (4 April 2012)

'Shipman Jailed for 15 Murders', *BBC News* (31 January 2000)

'Struck Off Dr Hadiza Bawa-Garba Wins Appeal to Work Again', *BBC News* (13 August 2018)

'Tetraplegic Man's Life-support Turned Off by Mistake', *BBC News* (25 October 2010)

'Vincent Barker Death: Optometrist Honey Rose Conviction Quashed', *BBC News* (31 July 2017)

Agelholm H, 'Dr Bawa-Garba: Doctors Threaten to Boycott Their Appraisals Over Treatment of Trainee Paediatrician', *The Independent* (1 February 2018)

Alleyne R, 'Surgeons Who Removed the Wrong Kidney Are Cleared', *The Telegraph* (26 June 2002)

Black D, 'Police Drop 'Bad Blood' Scandal', *The Journal* (7 July 2003)

Boseley S, 'Doctors Sign Letter Expressing Worry Over Criminalisation of Surgeon', *The Guardian* (6 August 2015)

———, 'Gosport Hospital: More Than 450 Patients Died Due to Opioid Drugs Policy', *The Guardian* (20 June 2018)

Boseley S, Topping A, '"A Horrific Human Tragedy": Report Criticises Response to Blood Scandal', *The Guardian* (24 February 2009)
Bowcott O, 'Ministers Reject Calls for Immediate Compensation for Infected Blood Victims', *The Guardian* (28 January 2020)
Carvel J, 'The Day in Politics: Old Lobbying Virtues Win Victory for AIDS Case', *The Guardian* (17 November 1987)
Cazi E, 'Le scandale du Mediator en procès', *Le Monde* (21 September 2019)
Favereau E, 'Le procès du sang contaminé. Les trois accusés et l'avenir. Georgina Dufoix non coupable. Son action a été jugée positive', *Libération* (10 March 1999)
———, 'Laboratoires Servier: anatomie d'un système', *Libération* (20 September 2019)
Gaetner G, 'Le procès d'un scandale', *L'express* (6 February 2008)
———, 'Les juges d'instruction sont les mal aimés du système pénal français', *L'Express* (8 January 2009)
Gorman S, 'Those Left Behind by the Contaminated Blood Scandal Shouldn't Have to Fight for Support', *The Guardian* (16 April 2019)
Jouan A, Lombard MA, 'La Chronologie de l'Affaire', *Le Nouvel Observateur* (15 January 2009)
Katz G, 'No Individual Blame in UK's Tainted Blood Scandal', *ABC News International* (23 February 2009)
Keller A, 'We Just Wanted the Law to Recognise Our Mum Had Been Killed', *Lichfield Mercury* (12 February 2009)
Metthews-King A, 'Bawa-Garba Latest: Jeremy Hunt Orders Review into Manslaughter by Gross Negligence Rulings in the NHS', *The Independent* (6 February 2018)
Sawer P, Donnelly L, 'Stafford Hospital Trust Admits 'Significant' Health and Safety Breaches Related do Deaths of Four Patients', *The Telegraph* (4 November 2015)
Smyth C, 'New NHS Scandal Is Inevitable, Mid Staffs Inquiry Chief Warns', *The Times* (10 February 2017)
Topping A, 'Breast Surgeon Ian Paterson Jailed for 15 Years for Carrying Out Needless Operations', *The Guardian* (31 May 2017)
Walker P, Topping A, 'Theresa May Orders Contaminated Blood Scandal Inquiry', *The Guardian* (11 July 2017)

Cases

UK cases

A and other v National Blood Authority and Another [2001] 3 All ER 289
AB v Leeds Teaching Hospital Trust [2014] EWHC 644
Bawa-Garba v GMC [2018] EWCA Civ 1879
DPP v Kent and Sussex Contractors [1944] KB 146, DC
HIV Haemophiliac Litigation [1990] 41 BMLR 171
Lennards Carrying Co. Ltd v Asiatic Petroleum Ltd [1915] AC 705, HL
Montgomery v Lanarkshire Health Board [2015] UKSC 11
Pearce v United Bristol Healthcare NHS Trust [1999] PIQR 53
R v Adomako [1994] 3 WLR 288
R v Bawa-Garba [2016] EWCA Crim 1841
R v Caldwell [1982] AC 341 (HL)

R v Cato (1976) 62 Cr App R 41
R v Cunningham [1957] 2 QB 396
R v Dica [2004] 3 All ER 593
R v Errol Cornish and Maidstone and Tunbridge Wells NHS Trust [2015] EWHC 2967 (QB)
R v Garg (Sudhanshu) [2012] EWCA Crim 2520
R v Honey Maria Rose [2017] EWCA Crim 1168
R v ICR Haulage Ltd [1944] KB 551, CCA
R v Kennedy (No 2) [2008] UKHL 1 AC 269
R v Mellor [1996] 2 Cr App R 245
R v Mid Staffordshire NHS Foundation Trust, Sentencing Remarks of the Hon Mr Justice Haddon-Cave, 28 April 2014
R v Misra; R v Srivastava [2004] EWCA Crim 2375
R v Mowatt [1968] 1 QB 421
R v Prentice and another; R v Adomako; R v Holloway [1993] 4 All ER 935
R v Rudling [2016] 151 BMLR 79
R v Savage, R v Parmenter [1992] 1 AC 699 (HL)
R v Southampton University Hospital NHS Trust [2006] EWCA Crim 2971
R v Wilson, R v Jenkins [1984] AC 242
Sidaway v Board of Governors of the Bethlem Royal and the Maudsley Hospital [1985] 1 All ER 643
Tesco Supermarket Ltd v Nattrass [1972] AC 153

French cases

CA Grenoble, 12/06/1998, affaire du Drac
CA Nancy 29/03/2001
Cass Crim 22/06/1994 in Pradel J (Dir) *Sang et droit pénal: A propos du sang contaminé*, Travaux de l'Institut de Sciences Criminelles, vol XIV (Editions Cujas 1994)
Cass Crim 2/07/1998 Bull Crim no 211, JCP 1998 II 10132
Cass Crim 11/09/2001 Bull No 176
Cass Crim 26/03/2002 no 01–83.416
Cass Crim 18/06/2002 Bull Crim no 138
Cass Crim 24/09/2003 no 02–81.820
Cass Crim 17/12/2003 no 00–87.872
Cass Crim 10/01/2006 no 04–86.428
Cass Crim 13/02/2007 no 06–82.202 Bull Crim 2007 no 44, 261
Cass Crim 10/02/2009 no 08–80.679 Bull Crim 2009, no 33
Cass Crim 13/04/2010 no 09–86.429
Cass Crim 11/09/2012 no 11–88.269
Cass Crim 16/10/2013 no 12–81.532
Cass Crim 19/04/2017 no 16–83640
Cass Crim 11/07/2017 n°16–86.092
Cass Crim 15/01/2019 no 17–86461
Commission d'instruction de la Cour de Justice de la République, Arrêt portant renvoi devant la Cour de Justice de la République, 17 juillet 1998, D6137
Cour de justice de la République, arrêt 9/03/1999, affaire no 99–001

Réquisitions de Joseph Perfetti, Avocat général près la chambre criminelle de la cour de cassation in Pradel J (Dir.), *Sang et droit pénal: A propos du sang contaminé*, Travaux de l'Institut de Sciences Criminelles, vol XIV (Editions Cujas 1994)

TGI de Paris, 16e Chambre, jugement du 3/09/2003 affaire n° 9926423046

TGI de Paris, Ordonnance de transmission du dossier et des pièces à conviction au procureur général et de non lieu partiel, D20917

Legislation

UK legislation

Children and Young Persons Act 1933
Company Directors Disqualification Act 1986
Consumer Protection Act 1987
Coroners and Justice Act 2009
Corporate Manslaughter and Corporate Homicide Act 2007
Criminal Justice and Courts Act 2015
Criminal Justice and Courts Act 2015 Explanatory Notes
Director of Public Prosecution, Code for Crown Prosecutors, 26 October 2018
Health Act 1999
Health and Safety at Work Act 1974
Health and Social Care Act 2008
Health and Social Care Act 2008 (Regulated Activities) Regulations 2014
Legal Aid, Sentencing and Punishment of Offenders Act 2012
Mental Capacity Act 2005
Mental Health Act 1983
NHS Reform and Health Care Professions Act 2002
Offences Against the Person Act 1861
Police and Criminal Evidence Act 1984

French legislation

Circulaire DGS/PS3/DH/PH1 N° 9631 du 19 janvier 1996 relative au rôle et aux missions des aides-soignants et des auxiliaires de puériculture dans les établissements hospitaliers

Code Civil

Code Pénal

Code de la consommation

Code de la santé publique

Code de procédure pénale

Décret n° 93–345 du 15 mars 1993 relatif aux actes professionnels et à l'exercice de la profession d'infirmier, JORF n° 63 du 15 mars 1993, 4098

Loi du 1er août 1905 sur les fraudes et falsifications en matière de produits ou de services

Loi n° 2000–516 du 15 juin 2000 renforçant la protection de la présomption d'innocence et les droits des victims

Loi n° 2002–303 du 4 mars 2002 relative aux droits des malades et à la qualité du système de santé

Loi no 2018–703 du 3 août 2018 renforçant la lutte contre les violences sexuelles et sexistes

Other

Injury, Prevention, Rehabilitation and Compensation Act 2001 (New Zealand)

Interviews

Interview with A (Cambridge, UK, 3 February 2011)
Interview with B (Paris, France, 17 January 2011)

Index

Note: Page numbers in **bold** indicate a table on the corresponding page.

For Product Safety Concerns and Information please contact our EU representative GPSR@taylorandfrancis.com
Taylor & Francis Verlag GmbH, Kaufingerstraße 24, 80331 München, Germany

www.ingramcontent.com/pod-product-compliance
Ingram Content Group UK Ltd.
Pitfield, Milton Keynes, MK11 3LW, UK
UKHW011015180926
475701UK00004B/765

9780367506681